Well-Bound Words

Words

A Rhetoric

Well-Bound Words

A Rhetoric

John J. Ruszkiewicz

University of Texas at Austin

Scott, Foresman and Company

Glenview, Illinois

Dallas, Tex.   Oakland, N.J.   Palo Alto, Cal.   Tucker, Ga.   London

An *Instructor's Manual* is available. It may be obtained through a local Scott, Foresman representative or by writing the English Editor, College Division, Scott, Foresman and Company, 1900 East Lake Avenue, Glenview, Illinois 60025.

Library of Congress Cataloging in Publication Data

Ruszkiewicz, John J   1950-
    Well-bound words.

    Includes index.
1. English language--Rhetoric.   I.   Title.
PE1408.R87   808′.042   80-27209
ISBN 0-673-15355-X

123456 - RRC - 858483828180

Acknowledgements

Chapter 2 American Heritage Dictionary—© 1980 by Houghton Mifflin Company. Reprinted by permission from *The American Heritage Dictionary of the English Language.* Crooks—Donald M. Crooks and Dayton L. Kingman. "Poison Ivy, Poison Oak, and Poison Sumac." Farmers' Bulletin No. 1972, U.S. Department of Agriculture. Dodge—From "Assist Starting Procedures if Battery is Low," *Dodge Diplomat Operator's Instructions & Product Information,* pp. 58-59. Reprinted by permission of Chrysler Corporation. Kinneavy—From Kinneavy et al: *Writing—Basic Modes of Organization.* Copyright © 1976 by James L. Kinneavy, John Q. Cope, Jr., and John W. Campbell. Kendall/Hunt Publishing Company, Dubuque, Iowa. Reprinted by permission of James L. Kinneavy. New Columbia Encyclopedia—From *The New Columbia Encyclopedia.* Copyright © Columbia University Press 1975. Reprinted by permission. O'Sullivan Industries—"Instructions for Building a Home Entertainment Center." Reprinted by permission of O'Sullivan Industries, Inc. Texas Monthly—Texas Monthly Staff. "The Ten Best and, Sigh, the Ten Worst Legislators." *Texas Monthly,* July, 1975.

Chapter 3 Kinneavy—From Kinneavy, James L: *Theory of Discourse.* Copyright © 1971 by James L. Kinneavy. Prentice-Hall, Inc., Englewood Cliffs, N.J. Reprinted by permission of James L. Kinneavy.

Chapter 4 Jordan—From "I Wants to Go to the Prose" by Suzanne Britt Jordan in *My Turn, Newsweek,* November 14, 1977. Copyright 1977 by Newsweek, Inc. All Rights Reserved. Reprinted by permission. Sidney—From "Astrophel & Stella," *The Poems of Sir Philip Sidney,* edited by William A. Ringler Jr.; © Oxford University Press 1962. Reprinted by permission of Oxford University Press.

Chapter 5 Baldwin—Copyright © 1962 by James Baldwin. Reprinted from *Creative America* (Ridge Press) by permission of the author. Daily Texan—From "Yanks say 'Moon' Tale Twisted," *The Daily Texan,* 8/14/79. Reprinted by permission of United Press International. Darwin—Adapted from *The Descent of Man* by Charles Darwin from the Norton Critical Edition, edited by Philip Applebaum. Copyright © 1979, 1970 by W. W. Norton & Company, Inc. Reprinted by permission. Didion—From "Why I Write" by Joan Didion. Copyright © 1976 by Joan Didion. First appeared in *The New York Times Book Review.* Reprinted by permission of Wallace & Sheil Agency, Inc. Einstein—From "Science and Religion" by Albert Einstein, *Out of My Later Years.* Published by the Philosophical Library, Inc., 1950. Reprinted by permission of the Estate of Albert Einstein. Krutch—From "Some Unsentimental Confessions of a Nature Writer" by Joseph Wood Krutch, *The New York Herald Tribune Book Review,* June 15, 1952. Reprinted by permission of The Trustees of Columbia University in the City of New York. Lewis—From "Supreme Court Confidential", review of *The Brethren* by Anthony Lewis, from *The New York Review of Books* (February 7, 1980). © 1980 by The New York Times Company. Reprinted by permission. New York Times—From "Banished Sakharov untarnished" from *The New York Times* (January 23, 1980). © 1980 by The New York Times Company. Reprinted by permission. Oxford English Dictionary—From *Oxford English Dictionary* Compact Edition. © Oxford University Press 1971. Reprinted by permission of Oxford University Press. Runner's World—Adaptation of the Table of Contents, reprinted with permission from *Runner's World Magazine,* 1400 Stierlin Road, Mountain View CA 94043. Copyright © 1979 by Runner's World Magazine Company, Inc.

. . . word ober fand

soðe gebunden . . .

—Beowulf

(he found new words,
truly bound)

The congurent and harmonious fitting
of parts in a sentence hath almost the
fastening and force of knitting and
connexion.

—*Ben Jonson,* Timber

For my father and my brother

Preface

Well-Bound Words: A Rhetoric is designed to teach students both how to write and how to think about writing. Because it works from a comprehensive framework, students using the text will encounter principles of analysis and composition that apply not only in introductory and more advanced writing courses, but also in most "real-world" situations that require writing. Students who learn the distinguishing features of self-expressive, informative, demonstrative, exploratory, and persuasive discourse will not have to unlearn anything if they take subsequent instruction in literary analysis, journalism, advertising, technical writing, legal writing, or business writing. Similarly, if they can describe, narrate, classify, and evaluate, they have the basic tools they will need to handle most subjects intelligently. No textbook—however lengthy or comprehensive—can prepare students for all the particular problems they will face as writers. What *Well-Bound Words* does is present general principles that will enable students to make intelligent choices on their own when they encounter situations their textbook never mentioned.

The structure of this text is based upon the comprehensive view of discourse advanced by James Kinneavy in *A Theory of Discourse* (Prentice-Hall, 1971; Norton, 1980). While Kinneavy's analysis of written language is rigorous, innovative, and often abstract, his categories of aims and modes are drawn from classical and contemporary traditions that will be familiar to most teachers of writing.

The first part of *Well-Bound Words* explains the modes of writing and then the reasons for writing. Logically, the reasons for writing (what Kinneavy calls the aims of discourse) might precede the means of achieving those aims, but I believe most instructors will find the arrangement of the first part of the book more workable because the short, relatively simple assignments in the various modes lead naturally into discussions about the purposes of writing. The second part of the text deals with the particular components and processes that make up an essay (sentences, paragraphs, transitions, revision). After treating the modes, a teacher can delve into this second part of the text to present the sentence, paragraph, and essay structures students will need as they proceed through the chapters on the aims of writing.

The two parts of *Well-Bound Words* are carefully related. Sentences, for example, are explored in terms of the strategies of modification a writer can employ in achieving a given purpose. The same is true of paragraphs. The full chapters on transitions and revision can be introduced when teachers feel their students will benefit from them most. In addition, there are sections on employing induction and deduction, eliminating wordiness, using the library, assessing sources, introducing quotations, cutting-and-pasting, taking essay exams—even an exploration of why all-nighters sometimes produce effective essays. As the comprehensive table of contents suggests, *Well-Bound Words* can be adapted to a variety of approaches.

The design of the text requires certain kinds of repetition. Rather than pretend that a single form of thesis statement will serve all purposes, *Well-Bound Words* offers a separate treatment of the thesis for each kind of essay that requires one. Rather than present a single chapter on invention, *Well-Bound Words* suggests separate heuristic techniques for each of the major reasons for writing, and a comprehensive scheme for modal invention. Rather than isolate investigative writing, like some academic pariah, in a section of its own, I have made the research paper the concluding part of the chapter on informative, demonstrative, and exploratory writing. Different research assignments are suggested for each of these types of referential writing so that teachers can choose the kind of investigation they want their students to pursue. I have also been repetitive in treating aspects of composition where such repetition suggests a unity in the writing process: in the handling of sentence, paragraph, and essay structures; in describing the uses of parallel constructions; and in explaining devices of transition and cohesion. Thus at the same time that students are learning to tailor their prose to specific aims, they are discovering some of the ways words and ideas cohere.

I intended *Well-Bound Words* to be candid, engaging, and clear. To that end, the manuscript was critiqued by student reviewers who diligently circled unclear explanations, inappropriate vocabulary items, and unappealing exercises. I'm certain that their efforts have helped produce a readable, even enjoyable, book. I've culled examples from many different areas for illustrative materials, but I have also emphasized certain subjects in order to give *Well-Bound Words* an internal coherence that goes beyond its subject matter. The Glossary of Grammar and Usage that concludes the text is complete enough for most situations.

But some instructors may prefer to use this text along with a complete handbook. A rhetorically organized reader will supplement many of the discussions.

Many thanks to all who contributed, directly or indirectly, to *Well-Bound Words*. My greatest debts are to my colleagues, James Kinneavy and Maxine Hairston. I am grateful to my reviewers, Cleo McNelly, Marilyn Cooper, Tori Haring-Smith, Frank Hubbard, Wilma Ebbitt, Constance J. Gefvert, Carol T. Williams, David Skwire, Richard Harp, and Tillie Eggers, and to my indefatigable and genial editors, Harriett Prentiss and Kathleen Kleinheksel. Special thanks to Cynthia Selfe for suggesting that the manuscript be read by students, and to those student reviewers, Kirsten Jansson, Katherine Bohn, Mark Strozewski, Anthony Beach, and Stephen Murphy. I've benefited from the work of many scholars and teachers in the field of rhetoric and composition, among them Frank D'Angelo, the late Francis Christensen, Chaim Perelman, Donald Murray, Edward Corbett, Richard Young, Susan Miller, Donald Good, and Nancy Sommers. In a variety of ways, I've been assisted or encouraged by John Walter, Steve Witte, Lester Faigley, James Wimsatt, John Trimble, Lynda Boose, John Velz, Michael Mewshaw, Jana Wainright, Tom Halliburton, Ann Graybiel, Greg Smith, Keith Stinnett, Julie Richter, Lon Cargill, Ray Cook, Adelina Oxford, Kevin Krist, Karen Lunos, and my racquetball partner, Chris Dillard.

John J. Ruszkiewicz

Overview

Contents

PART *Whole to Part*   *7*

PART

2 Part to Whole   *181*

Well-Bound Words

A Rhetoric

1

Introduction

You are a tough audience. While writing this book, I have tried to imagine what you are like by calling to mind my students, past and present. But you outnumber them and resist this simple characterization. Many of you are young, just out of high school, enjoying the liberties and opportunities college offers. Early versions of my manuscript were addressed almost exclusively to you in repeated allusions to dormitory life, food fights, and campus issues. Some of these references remain. But I have deleted others because a college writing course may have little to do with college life for those of you holding full-time jobs, supporting spouses and families, or returning from military service. Your concerns and interests may have grown beyond the classroom and the campus.

Perhaps you are skeptical about attempts to improve your writing. Although a long chapter in this text explores persuasion, I do not want to spend time here arguing that your abilities as a writer will secure life, liberty, and prosperity. Consciously or unconsciously, you may have al-

A course in composition

ready decided how important writing will be to your future. You have considered the arguments of teachers who make writing the cornerstone of a liberal education. You may appreciate the skill it takes to put thoughts into words; you may value writing as a way of learning, of making connections, of making sense of things. You are probably familiar with all the practical reasons for honing writing skills to a fine edge: the need to prepare reports, résumés, memos, letters of complaint, position papers, research articles. And yet, knowing all these arguments and reasons, you still may not respond enthusiastically to any of them. As a teacher of writing, I'd prefer that you enjoy a course in composition. But as a writer, I share with you the fears and reservations that are an inseparable part of filling blank pages with words. You can value writing without demonstrating enthusiasm for composing. That's your prerogative, and I respect it.

An audience　　　　In writing this text, I deliberately invited one character to join my imagined audience. He is the good-natured student who sits near the back of the classroom, gazing out the windows, thinking of a dozen other places he would rather be. His mental skills are considerable, but he doesn't care much for writing. In fact, he finds English teachers trivial and silly, excessively concerned with commas and compositions. To him, learning to write is a waste of time, an attitude he conveys to his instructor by timely yawns, mild sneers, and colossal bouts of stretching. I have created this figure to keep this text down to earth, to silently edit discussions that tend to ramble, to delete assignments that seem like busywork, to enliven examples that droop and drowse. I have not written this book to please my imaginary reader; in fact, portions are apt to set him yawning with a vengeance. But I have found his cynicism and impatience potent checks on unexamined assumptions and long-winded orations.

I have tried to weave a diverse pattern of interests and enthusiasms into the fabric of discussions and examples that make up the text. You will find Aristotle and skydiving, inflation and Xerxes' invasion of Greece, baseball standings and Shakespeare posed side by side to demonstrate points about writing. I have used literary examples when I thought them memorable and appropriate. But I have not assumed that you are destined to be English majors or that writing about literature will be even a minor concern for most of you. A capable writer must know how to handle many situations; hence this text must draw from a variety of fields and interests. I have tended to strike allusions and passages that seemed unconnected to the experiences of most members of the audience. Yet some eccentric examples and enthusiasms linger: I don't want this book to seem like the work of an automaton. I wrote it. You will find me in it.

I have imagined you as an audience both male and female—and struggled to express that diversity. Pronouns are a major problem here.

In the past, masculine pronouns *(he, his, him)* conventionally implied the presence of both genders in a general statement:

> *He* who laughs last laughs best.
>
> After discovering *his* subject, the *writer* begins to develop it.
>
> Every*one* needs a place to call *his* own.

Sexist language

But many readers, editors, publishers, teachers, and students now argue that the masculine expression does not contain the feminine. Instead, it implies an exclusion of women from the language and from the world controlled by language. *He* is understood as a man; *man*kind implies men; a chair*man* isn't a madam. These arguments, backed by formidable evidence, deserve attention and action. But I have found that addressing you simultaneously—male and female—is not always easy.

I tried, for example, to be thoroughly consistent about alternating the masculine and feminine pronouns. At first I used a card with *he* on one side and *she* on the other, turning it over with every pronoun to remind me of the gender to employ the next time. But that way madness lies. After a while I lost the card in the shuffle of papers that inevitably clutter a writer's desktop. So I decided to rely on my memory to vary the pronoun genders. The tactic worked well enough. But when I reviewed my sentences for revision and rethinking, I began tinkering with referents, sometimes for consistency, sometimes to repair damage done earlier by the flip of the card:

> The mayor denied that ~~she~~ *he* had taken the bribe offered by the utility monopoly.

I found myself manipulating pronoun references to seem liberal, to avoid putting women in a bad light. What I was actually doing, though, was acting with condescension toward women and being unfair to men. I have since compromised as best I can, resorting to more plural pronouns than in my first drafts (he + she ⟶ they) and varying the shifts of gender less mechanically. I am afraid more *he*s may appear in the text than *she*s, but intend no slight to the women in my audience if that is the case. I think that the best solution to this problem may be for men to use the masculine pronouns and for women to use the feminine versions when they write, but few of my professional colleagues would agree. What matters here, I think, is that you understand the problem. You will face it, and others like it, when you compose.

What is good writing?

An assumption I began this book with many months ago was that most of you approach a writing course asking one question: what is good writing? And the answer is: it depends. James Thurber, in a memorable comic essay entitled "The Macbeth Murder Mystery," narrates the dilemma of a woman who buys a copy of Shakespeare's *Macbeth,* thinking it is a detective story. But as she soon discovers, it lacks something as a murder mystery:

> "Did you like it?" I asked. "No, I did not," she said, decisively. "In the first place, I don't think for a moment that Macbeth did it."

Judged by the woman's expectations, Shakespeare's play lacks suspense, plausibility, and intrigue. But most readers recognize that Shakespeare intended to write a tragedy, not a murder mystery. *Macbeth* is a classic because it fulfills the expectations an author and his audience have for tragedy; its characters, situations, settings, and language are appropriate to the notions they share of what a tragedy should do and be.

Similarly, when evaluative terms, such as *good, classic, effective,* and *successful,* are applied to other kinds of writing (reports, essays, novels, editorials, sermons, etc.), the terms have meaning only when they consider what a writer's purpose is and how an audience is helped to understand it. For example, the qualities of a good biology lab report are not the same as the qualities of an effective newspaper editorial. In some situations, the language of a piece is appropriately stark, direct, and impersonal. A doctor writing a memo to explain the condition of a patient does not pause to consider how her language might be made more lively or friendly. In other situations, lively and personal prose is expected. A letter to a friend written to the standards of a lab report would almost surely be unsuccessful.

Put simply, no absolute standards define the goodness and effectiveness of what you write. Discussing style, Aristotle makes exactly this point in the first significant textbook of rhetoric:

> We must not fail to notice that each kind of rhetoric has its own appropriate style.
>
> —*Rhetoric,* trans. Lane Cooper

Modes and purposes of writing

You must consider what type of writing you are doing and what sort of audience you are addressing. Those considerations shape every aspect of your prose, from the placement of a thesis statement (when a thesis is appropriate) to the length and rhythms of your sentences. For that reason, this text begins with chapters on the modes and purposes of discourse, and then proceeds to matters of sentence, paragraph, and essay development. The answer to what constitutes good writing lies in understanding what you are trying to accomplish by writing and in sharing that understanding with your readers.

A Theory of Discourse

In defining the modes and purposes of writing in the first part of this text, I follow a design set down by James Kinneavy in a formidable work called *A Theory of Discourse.* I have tried to present aspects of his theory clearly and accurately, but more than a few times, I have varied from Kinneavy in the terms I use and in the shape I give to the modes and purposes of writing. I have simplified a great deal. Whatever weaknesses or inconsistencies this text may have in conception and design are much more likely attributable to me than to *A Theory of Discourse*.

The second part of the book examines sentences, paragraphs, revision, and editing in light of the purposes of writing, but not strictly so. You can read these chapters before or in tandem with the earlier part of the text, for writing differs from skills that can be learned step by step. In acquiring mathematical skills, you probably moved progressively from addition, subtraction, multiplication, and division, to these same operations with fractions and decimals, and then on to algebra, trigonometry, and perhaps even to calculus. Within each general field, you moved from the easier operation to the more difficult, from simple equations in algebra to the quadratic.

But when you are asked to write a report or an argument, you need all a writer's skills and operations at once. You must be able to define aim, audience, structure, length, and tone. You must be able to manipulate sentences, construct paragraphs, and invent transitions. You must know how to revise and how to edit. And the classic dilemma in writing courses is what to teach first—the parts which make up a whole or the whole which defines the shape of the parts. By dividing the text into two sections, I have tried to open the possibility of considering the whole and the parts together. But by placing the aims and modes of writing first, I am indicating where I place my allegiance.

The writer's dilemma

For Discussion

1. Review this chapter, marking those parts that address you directly, noting those that exclude you. What effect does being addressed as *you* have on your reading? Could the information in this chapter be conveyed without this form of address? What are the advantages of this strategy? The disadvantages? In what situations might you want to employ *you?*

2. Parts of this chapter allude to the process of revision. In what ways has the author altered his text? For what purposes? When do you think those changes occurred—very near the completion of the manuscript? Throughout the process of writing? How does knowing what your readers are like make revising easier?

3. What type of readers do the following publications try to reach?

> *The National Enquirer*   *Sports Illustrated*
> *Cosmopolitan*   *Playboy*
> *Consumer Reports*   *The New Yorker*
> *The Montgomery Ward Catalogue*

How do these publications appeal to their distinct audiences? Consider content, size, layout, prose style, and advertising. What do the contents suggest about the age and education of readers? What do the ads suggest about their incomes? Can you detect political emphases?

4. Describe some specific audience you have addressed in writing. How have you shaped and reshaped what you have written to fit the abilities and expectations of that audience? Can an audience consist of one person? Can you be your own audience? (Consider all the types of writing you do, from a formal research paper to a memo or marginal note.)

Writing Assignments

5. Do you agree with the author's suggestion that female writers should use feminine pronoun forms and males the masculine? Write a short letter of support or dissent to the author. In what ways would you have to alter your letter if you decided to present your arguments in a paper to be read to your classmates?

6. Examine three or four different types of writing that share the common characteristic of brevity: editorials, advertisements, instructions, warranties, dictionary entries, recipes, letters to the editor, etc. For each type of writing, construct a list of the criteria which distinguish it from the other kinds you are considering. For example:

> *Characteristics of most recipes*
> 1. They explain how to cook something.
> 2. They are impersonal.
> 3. They give orders: stir this, boil that.
> 4. They include a list of ingredients.
> 5. They include measurements and timings.
> 6. They employ a special vocabulary: pare, chop, mince, scald, fold, etc.
> 7. They often appear on cards designed for filing.

The criteria you have listed ought to enable a writer to produce an editorial, recipe, TV listing, or letter to the editor. But instead of writing an appropriate example of one of these short writing forms, compose an inappropriate one, violating several (but not all) of the criteria you have set down.

7. Have you ever been confused by a novel, film, short story, or play the way that the woman in Thurber's story was confused by *Macbeth*? Write a short essay explaining your difficulty. Give particular attention to how you discovered what the purpose of what you were reading or seeing really was.

Whole to Part

Modes

Description   Narration

Classification   Evaluation

Reasons

Persuasion

Self-Expression   Information

2

Modes of Writing

Description, Narration, Classification, Evaluation

Modes are ways of doing things. Writing has four basic modes: description, narration, classification, and evaluation. We can illustrate these familiar modes through examples:

Description:

1975 Datsun B–210—new battery, new brakes, ugly but runs well. $1,400. Call after 4 p.m. S. Tebo.

Narration:

When Geoffrey's father, John Chaucer, was not yet fourteen, he was kidnapped by his Aunt Agnes.

—Marchette Chute, *Geoffrey Chaucer of England*

Classification:

The aluminum alloys, like those of other commercial metals, can be divided into two broad classes: (1) wrought alloys and (2) casting alloys.

—*Little and Ives Complete Book of Science*

Evaluation:

Nikita Khrushchev, a crude bear of a man who had risen from the ranks, was the leader of the Communist party. Khrushchev's rough manners, bad grammar, and heavy drinking caused many Western journalists and diplomats to underestimate him. But despite his rough edges, he had a keen mind and a ruthless grasp of power politics.

—Richard Nixon, *RN, The Memoirs of Richard Nixon*

We can illustrate these four modes more formally by describing what happens to an idea or an object when a particular mode operates on it.

Description
Description takes a person, place, event, or idea and sketches it in words as if it were frozen in time. The thing being described may, of course, be moving, but the concern of description is to examine what the motion is, not what it does. When you depict the whir of a propeller, you are describing. When you describe the character and features of your Uncle Joe, you are describing. But when that propeller tangles your uncle's fishing line and he responds with a modest obscenity, your report of the event is likely to move into the narrative mode.

Narration
Narration considers an object—perhaps a person, a group, an institution, an idea—as it moves in time or acts. Narration is concerned with what a thing does, with events, processes, happenings, causes, and effects. Description and narration are closely related. Both modes can operate within a single sentence:

Adam,

    a towheaded boy with | ———— description
    freckles and a cowlick |

slid into second base. |———— narration

The first part of the sentence contains a descriptive pause—a freeze frame—that shows us what Adam looks like just before his moment of glory in the second part of the sentence. Both description and narration provide details, but of different kinds.

Classification
Classification, like description, is static, but this mode focuses on the relationships between groups of things. Classification surveys a range of objects to discover the similarities and differences that define them. Anything can be classified according to an almost infinite number of principles and a variety of purposes. Astronomers, for example, have found it useful to classify visible stars according to magnitudes of brightness:

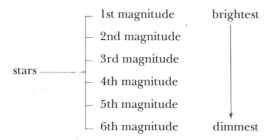

But scientists also classify stars according to temperature, mass, motion, and color, depending upon what features or properties of the astral bodies they are seeking to examine or explain. Astrologers, on the other hand, classify stars and planets according to their relationships to each other in the zodiac and their supposed influences on human behavior, not according to any properties of the bodies themselves. Classifications can thus serve to examine systematically the general properties of things (definition) or plot the relationships between objects and ideas (comparison/contrast).

Evaluation

The fourth mode, evaluation, is comparative and active or dynamic. This mode begins with a group of things, defines standards by which the group can be judged, and then applies these standards to individual objects or members of the group. For example, a teacher may take a piece of prose belonging to the class of writing called research papers and establish these criteria for a good one:

1. interesting topic,
2. adequate use of sources,
3. logical organization, and
4. clear style.

Then he would judge individual representatives of the class, research papers, by these general standards. Papers meeting all four standards might be given an *A,* those that meet none an *F,* and so on.

Interrelationship of modes

You can see from this overview that the four modes are closely related. In practice, they are usually inseparable. It is often difficult to say precisely where classification ends and evaluation begins, where description ceases and narration takes over. Sometimes the modes operate simultaneously. Examine, for a moment, a structure familiar to any sports fan, the baseball standings. In this statistical rendering, baseball teams are ranked according to their win/loss records, expressed in a percentage. This classificatory arrangement also provides a way for a reader to evaluate the teams, since the "best" teams (those with the most victories) end up on top and the less successful ones fall into the basement.

AMERICAN LEAGUE

East

	Won	Lost	Pct.	Games behind
Cleveland	87	46	.654	—
Milwaukee	81	56	.591	8
Boston	78	54	.591	8½
New York	72	60	.545	14½
Detroit	73	63	.537	15½
Baltimore	69	67	.507	19½
Toronto	43	92	.319	45

As a writer, you will rarely have to distinguish between the modes, but you will have to describe, narrate, classify, and evaluate. So that while separating the modes may seem artificial (you will probably detect overlap in the sections that follow), examining them one by one is probably the best way of learning how to use them.

Exercise Examine an essay in a serious periodical or from an anthology to determine the dominant mode employed in the first ten or fifteen paragraphs. How often do the modes overlap?

Description

The descriptive mode uses language to depict the features and qualities of an idea or thing. Perhaps you associate this mode with an assignment traditional in elementary and secondary schools in many parts of the country: the required essay on "The Beauties of Autumn." Every September or October, thousands of students are required to paint the leaves of fall in colors and combinations wilder than any nature fashioned. In these essays, stately oaks dance and sway like frenzied ballerinas, the air is choked by burning foliage, and dew is rising (inevitably) from patches of swollen pumpkins.

"That's what the teacher wanted," you sigh, remembering the five or six times you splashed a streak of vermillion on a trembling sycamore bough. Perhaps you recall a variant of this task on "The Glories of Spring" or "Snowflakes." Or maybe you recall a less specific assignment, simply: "Describe some familiar object." You responded with a paragraph sufficiently clear and detailed to distinguish one particular object from all others of its kind, but undirected by any real purpose:

My grandfather's car is an ancient Plymouth Belvedere two-door hardtop. It has a white roof, a yellow body, and a yellow interior. Two chrome fins stand above the taillights, and on the hood is a replica of the Mayflower. On the driver's side, there's a dent where I ran into it with my bicycle. The back bumper is also dented from when Dad rolled into Aunt Mildred. The license number of the car is AE-341.

But a *C* or *D* suggested that your paragraph was not what the teacher wanted: "Not descriptive enough." Because of such experiences, many people associate the descriptive mode with strings of stuffed adjectives and hyperactive verbs, and with vague, impractical assignments.

The associations are sometimes fair but are not accurate for all **What description does** uses of description. Description for its own sake can be tedious. But accurate portrayals of facts, situations, ideas, settings, or human characters are essential to writing that informs, persuades, or entertains. The aim of a particular essay determines what kind of description is appropriate. The depiction of the old car given above would be descriptive enough for certain types of informative writing. What the teacher who downgraded the essay may have wanted was a picture that entertained:

> Like a big, yellow gourd, the old Plymouth Belvedere squats in the driveway, a bulging mass of chrome and glitter. On the hood sits a plastic replica of the Mayflower cutting its way through rough seas, followed by the rest of the bulbous hardtop. At the back, tiny fins cap the taillights, metallic pennants signalling "the end." A single minor abrasion mars the proud flanks where an out-of-control bicycle challenged the Plymouth's right of way—and lost. There's a dent in the back bumper too, a monument to Aunt Mildred's near-fatal confrontation with the same vehicle. Hopeless, all such challenges. The fat, little Plymouth rests secure in its garish, yellow glory.

But not all descriptions serve to amuse. A want ad, a diagram of a corporate structure, a damage report to an insurance company, a builder's brochure, a pharmaceutical catalogue, an FBI most-wanted poster, and a set of instructions all use description without any intention of enlivening their subject matters with glittering adjectives and adverbs:

> You can figure out which panel is which by looking at these pictures and the number of drilled holes. Panel (C) has 5 holes on one side only. Panel (D) has 7 holes on one side and 5 holes on the other side, and panel (E) has seven holes on one side only. The edge with the woodgrain finish is the front of the unit.
>
> —Instructions for building a home entertainment center, O'Sullivan Industries, Inc.

Such description, designed to inform, is completely adequate and appropriate in many situations.

Whatever its aim, description should be accurate, systematic, se- **Accurate description** lective, and (sometimes) comparative. The accuracy of any description relies on an agreement between a writer and reader on the meaning of terms. But such agreement is not always sure. An inch may be an inch and a meter a meter, but exactly what shade of red is vermillion, how big is huge, what degree of poverty is wretched? Because words and meanings don't always share a one-to-one correspondence, attempts to describe images and ideas sometimes fail. But authors and audiences can be brought closer together by nouns, verbs, modifiers, details, and qualifications accurate enough to satisfy the careful writer, yet clear enough to serve the impatient reader.

Details: the extremes

At one extreme, lawyers preparing legal documents may attempt to describe something—a contract, a parcel of land—with absolute, all-loopholes-closed precision. But the prose that results is often so specific and carefully qualified that it becomes virtually unintelligible to most readers:

> Borrower, in consideration of the indebtedness herein recited and the trust herein created, irrevocably grants and conveys to Trustee, in trust, with power of sale, the following property . . . together with all the improvements now or hereafter erected on the property, and all easements, rights, appurtenances, rents . . . royalties, mineral, oil and gas rights and profits, water, water rights, and water stock, and all the fixtures now or hereafter attached to the property. . . .

In legal situations, accuracy is usually more important than readability.

On the other hand, a writer may be so ambiguous, abstract, and undetailed in a descriptive passage that readers may be unable to make an appropriate judgment:

> Leaves of poison sumac consist of several elongated leaflets. In spring the leaves are orange. Later they turn green with scarlet midribs. In fall they turn red.

A more useful description of poison sumac adds the distinguishing characteristics that make it possible to identify and avoid the plant:

> Leaves of poison sumac consist of 7 to 13 leaflets, arranged in pairs with a single leaflet at the end of the midrib. . . .
> The leaflets are elongated oval without marginal teeth or serrations. They are 3 to 4 inches long, 1 to 2 inches wide, and have a smooth velvetlike texture. In early spring, their color is bright orange. Later, they become dark green and glossy on the upper surface, and pale green on the lower, and have scarlet midribs. In the early fall, leaves turn to a brilliant red-orange or russet shade.
>
> —Donald M. Crooks and Dayton L. Kingman, "Poison Ivy, Poison Oak, and Poison Sumac"

In many situations that require description, a writer must steer a **A middle course** middle course between the need for accurate description and the need for clarity. The two aren't incompatible:

> During the decades when factories went unregulated, men, women, and children worked at monotonous tasks, the forerunner of the twentieth century's production line, for as many as fourteen or even sixteen hours a day, six days a week. They were deafened by the noise of the steam engines and the clattering machinery and stifled in air that not only was laden with dust but, in the absence of ventilation, was heated to as high as eighty-five degrees. The workers were driven to maximum output by strict overseers, fined for spoiling goods, dozing off, looking out the window, and other derelictions, and forever imperiled by unguarded shafts, belts, and flywheels. Industrial diseases and those caused simply by the proximity of many unwashed, chronically ill human bodies conspired with accidents to disable and kill them.
>
> —Richard Altick, *Victorian People and Ideas*

What helps any description achieve accuracy and clarity is a sys- **Ordering details** tematic approach to the material. If you are describing something physical—a landscape, a building—the reader ought to be able to detect an order in the arrangement of details. Perhaps your description follows the movement of an eye from left to right, top to bottom, far to near. Or perhaps you trace some other pattern. The reader ought to be told—or should be able to infer—in what direction the descriptive eye is moving. The description of poison sumac cited earlier, for example, first outlines the shape of the full sumac leaf, then describes the individual leaflets, and finally tells what colors the leaflets bear in spring, summer, and fall. The description is clear and simple.

But not all descriptions are physical. In describing characters, for example, you can't move from left to right. In such cases, your description needs some other appropriate order. You can, for example, focus on a general feature and add details:

> The French have the most ridiculous fondness for their hair, and this I believe they inherit from their remote ancestors. . . .
>
> —Tobias Smollett, *Travels Through France and Italy*

Or you can contrast a series of related characteristics:

> He was very fearless in his person, but not enterprising; and had excellent understanding, but was not confident enough of it. . . .
>
> —Edward Hyde, "The Character of Charles I"

Or you can note and comment on some idiosyncratic behavior:

He kept bottles of wine at his lodgings, and many times he would drink liberally by himself to refresh his spirits and exalt his muse. . . .

—John Aubrey, *Brief Lives*

Any arrangement that readers can follow easily will work. In general, the longer the description, the greater the need for careful organization and explicit transitions.

Selecting details

No description can be absolutely thorough; every description involves selection. In describing a human face or figure, a writer could dwell at length on each feature, measuring the nose, coloring the iris, contouring the cheeks and chin. Readers may yawn in reply. Or the writer can ignore the commonplace features to explore the special ones—the shock of golden hair or the ears wide enough to serve as sails:

Old Singleton, the oldest able seaman in the ship, sat apart on the deck right under the lamps, stripped to the waist, tattooed like a cannibal chief all over his powerful chest and enormous biceps. Between the blue and red patterns his white skin gleamed like satin; his bare back was propped against the heel of the bow-sprit, and he held a book at arm's length before his big, sunburnt face.

—Joseph Conrad, *The Nigger of the "Narcissus"*

Good description thrives on sharp, particular, and unusual detail. When the details are fetching, the reader's imagination works overtime to fill in gaps. In selecting details, feel free to explore your own reactions to objects or situations. Intuition can be trusted to ferret out what is striking or intriguing. And then the personal reaction can be shaped into words that depict the intriguing details. Successful description can be almost magical:

. . . the roar of the multitude grows deep. Paris wholly has got to the acme of its frenzy; whirled, all ways, by panic madness. At every street-barricade, there whirls simmering a minor whirlpool,—strengthening the barricade, since God knows what is coming; and all minor whirlpools play distractedly into that grand Fire-Maelstrom which is lashing round the Bastille.
    And so it lashes and it roars. . . .

—Thomas Carlyle, *The French Revolution*

In this passage, Carlyle evokes a powerful sense of tumult and chaos by employing a minimum of details: a roaring crowd, a barricade, a great fire. These details and the language that surrounds them create an image greater than the sum of its parts. The mind of the reader, drawn into the fire storm, fills in the gaps.

Another way of increasing the dimensions of descriptions is through comparisons. The human mind freely and naturally reaches out to what is familiar to understand what is not:

> The *heart* is a *pump* pushing blood through the body.

> The new *committee* will function like a *traffic cop,* intercepting proposals that belong in other jurisdictions.

> But to folks who think of automobiles in the same way they think of toaster-ovens—as appliances—it probably won't matter much that the lowball *Volaré* is automotive *hamburger* and not *veal Marsala.* (italics added)

> —Rich Ceppos, "Plymouth Volaré," *Car and Driver*

Such comparisons expand our understanding of ideas and, at the same time, add interest.

Effective comparisons are both surprising and unforced. The most familiar are often down-to-earth, a bit shopworn, but enduringly charming:

> At his news conference, the President seemed as nervous as a long-tailed cat in a room full of rocking chairs.

Some folks have a gift for inventing colorful and accurate comparisons. But illustrative metaphors and similes can be the product of conscious invention, of asking the right questions. How tall is the fellow who sits in front of you? List some tall things: a grandfather clock, a street sign, a barber pole, the corn at harvest. Which comparison fits the young man best? Use it. Faced with describing an irritating problem? List some things that irritate you: ants at a picnic, in-laws coming to visit, zippers that stick. Then choose.

You may find that a striking comparison can be extended beyond a single phrase. For example, you may choose to describe the high incidence of arson in inner-city neighborhoods as a lingering infection—in itself not a very interesting comparison. But then you realize that, like an infection, the problem of arson has a tendency to spread. You know that certain conditions feed infections. What conditions encourage arson? You know that certain medicines cure infections. What's the remedy for arson? Gradually you extend a single comparison into a full *analogy,* a systematic description of the correspondences between things that are basically dissimilar. In an analogy, the descriptive mode merges with classification to become a way of creating and exploring new ideas.

Infections:

1. destroy,
2. spread,
3. thrive under certain conditions,
4. cause pain and suffering,
5. can be cured.

Arson:

1. destroys,
2. spreads,
3. thrives under certain conditions,
4. causes pain and suffering,
5. can be cured.

For Discussion

1. How do shifts in perspective and point of view alter what you see?

a. Take the time to observe the colors in a garden under different qualities of light: in the early morning, at noon, during and after storms, at sunset.

b. Consider how the quality of light in a museum might alter the appearance of a work of art painted or sculpted in a different setting.

c. Examine a classroom from the point of view of students sitting in different rows. Then step behind the podium or desk. How does a teacher's perspective differ from a student's?

d. Compare the feeling for a town or city you can acquire from a map with the experience of the actual roadways. What does a map fail to suggest about distances and terrain? What does a map suggest that the actual streets cannot?

e. Examine the way several books of different size, quality, and price are constructed. Examine the spine, the stitching (if any), the endpapers, the quality of the paper, etc.

f. Examine the inside of a camera.

Exercises

2. Transform a classified ad from the newspaper's "personals" section into a character sketch. Use hints in the original ad to suggest details you may have to invent.

Can you run 6 miles in 40 minutes? Can you jog all afternoon in the hot Texas sun? I can. I'm a 32-year-old jock with ambition who's looking for a female athletic partner. If you love sports and the great outdoors, call Joe at . . .

By the time most men reach their thirties, they are growing fat and bald. But not Joe Johnson. On a sizzling Austin afternoon, when most normal, middle-aged folks are lolling under a live oak, Joe is wearing his Nikes thin trodding the jogging paths around Town Lake . . .

3. Examine descriptive passages in textbooks from several different fields (physics, anthropology, history, philosophy). Can you detect differences between the passages that might be attributed to the different subject matters? Which texts seem to have the most detailed descriptions? Which the clearest? Can you understand all the descriptions? If a descriptive passage fails to convey an image or idea to you, try to point out where and why it fails.

4. Call to mind some familiar and accessible scene or object (the lobby of an art museum, the dome of a local cathedral, the view from a bridge) and list the features you consider most distinctive. Then, with your list in hand, go and observe the actual scene. How well do the features you listed capture the actual scene? Modify your list if necessary and then write two short descriptive paragraphs. Let the first paragraph record the scene as an uninspired photographer might. In the second paragraph, attempt to express the feeling the scene conveys.

5. Without telling a story or stating an argument, describe some static scene or situation that would move a reader to take action. You might describe a scene of grinding poverty or horrendous waste. You might strategically list the weapon systems in some national arsenal. Or you might describe the conditions in some restaurant's kitchen. Control your language carefully. Allow the details you select and their arrangement to subtly persuade the reader. Do not address your readers directly. Do not exaggerate. 400 words.

6. Describe someone you know well in two ways:

a. Write a short, informative sketch, plain and impersonal, that lists physical traits, background information (date/place of birth, education, marital status, occupation), and personal accomplishments. Order the sketch carefully. Imagine that your description might be used to assess your acquaintance's fitness for a key government position. Limit your essay to 200 words or less.

b. Describe the same person in a way that captures his or her personality through vivid details and comparisons. The aim of this piece is to entertain your reader by your portrait. Physical details are essential, but try to connect them—when possible—to habits of behavior. Avoid narration; don't tell a story about your subject. Remember that description freezes an object in time. Keep this description short too: 250–400 words.

7. Write an essay on "The Beauties of Autumn" from the point of view of someone who has read one too many such essays. Mock the

traditional subject and the customary details. Exaggerate whenever possible. Use lurid colors. Strain to invent ludicrous comparisons. Leave your audience—your fellow students—begging for more. 300 words.

8. For several weeks, keep a daily journal in which you record physical details of the world around you. Whether you live in town, in the suburbs, or in the country, take particular note of the changes in nature, weather, and everyday routines. Here's a passage from Dorothy Wordsworth's *Alfoxden Journal* you may want to use as a model:

> Feb. 10. Walked to Woodlands, and to the waterfall. The adder's tongue and the ferns green in the low damp dell. These plants now in perpetual motion from the current of the air; in summer only moved by the drippings of the rocks. A cloudy day.

9. Take a significant social problem or issue (defense spending, genetic engineering, women as priests) and describe it through the use of an analogy. Be sure that the analogy reveals your attitude toward the problem. For example, in the nineteenth century, the French author, Emile Zola, expressed his outrage against conditions in coal mines by writing a novel, *Germinal*. In *Germinal*, one of the mines, Le Voreux, is portrayed as a fierce, devouring animal. Here are two short passages that develop the analogy:

> With its squat brick buildings huddled in a valley, and the chimney sticking up like a menacing horn, the pit was evil-looking, a voracious beast crouching ready to devour the world.
>
> ....
>
> And, huddled in its lair like some evil beast, Le Voreux crouched ever lower and its breath came in longer and deeper gasps, as though it were struggling to digest its meal of human flesh.
>
> —trans. L. W. Tancock

In the latter passage, Zola is describing the mine just after a shift of miners has descended into it. The comparison works perfectly.

Try to find an analogy to describe the problem you have chosen to depict that has the emotional appeal of Zola's devouring beast.

Narration

What narration does

The narrative mode develops a subject or idea by explaining what happened, how it happened, or why it happened. We turn to narration when we deal with history. We rely on narratives to provide the background information needed for understanding significant people and events and for tracing the growth, development, and dissemination of ideas:

> It is understandable that philosophy scarcely flourished during the turbulent years of the fall of the Roman Empire and the successive invasions. Even though the Goths were by no means entirely barbaric, what learning existed was to be found chiefly in the monasteries. St. Benedict lived from 480 until 543; and the monasteries which owed their inspiration to his Rule became the channel whereby some of the old Latin culture was transmitted to the "barbarian" peoples.
>
> —F. C. Copleston, *Medieval Philosophy*

Narration shows us how things work and examines familiar processes:

> The writer is now deeply within the process of writing. He is changing and shaping and developing what he has to say. He is a craftsman who has choices to make. This point can be moved down here, that one built up over there. The writer is always forming, always changing, until he has composed a piece of writing which is not too long, not too short, which has a tone. . . .
>
> —Donald M. Murray, *A Writer Teaches Writing*

Narratives can document moral truths or document assertions:

> But when thou art bidden, go and sit down in the lowest room; that when he that bade thee cometh, he may say unto thee, Friend, go up higher: then shalt thou have worship in the presence of them that sit at meat with thee.
>   For whosoever exalteth himself shall be abased; and he that humbleth himself shall be exalted.
>
> —Luke 14:10–11

And, of course, narratives can simply amuse readers. That's reason enough to tell a joke or write a novel.

A narrative is shaped by its purpose. Both a detective story and a police officer's homicide report may tell a tale of murder. But the mystery story probably arranges its details and incidents to heighten suspense and baffle readers until, breathless, they reach the final chapter. The police report will be simpler in structure and shorter. "Just the facts, ma'am."

Time and order are the first concerns of a writer developing an idea by narration. The simplest events follow an order from beginning to end:

Time

I unbuckled my shoulder harness, opened the door, and stepped out of the car.

Tampering with this order may raise immediate questions:

I opened the door, stepped out of the car, and unbuckled my shoulder harness.

How was that possible? An additional clause is required:

I opened the door, stepped out of the car, and unbuckled the faulty shoulder harness that trailed after me like a noose.

Process

More complicated narrations require explicit signals that key a reader in to the sequence of events. Those signals are, usually, words that indicate some progression of time: *and then; thereafter; next; subsequently; later; earlier; first, second, third.* When a process is narrated, numbers may provide the organizing signals:

Assist Starting Procedures If Battery Is Low

Proceed with the following steps:
1. Turn off the lights, heater and other electrical loads.
2. Remove the vent caps from the booster and discharge battery. Lay a cloth over the vent wells of each battery.
3. Make sure electrolyte is at proper level. If electrolyte is not visible, or appears frozen, Do Not Attempt Assist Starting! A battery might rupture or explode if the temperature is below the freezing point or it is not filled to the proper level.
4. Connect one end of a jumper cable to the positive terminal of the booster battery. Connect the other end to the positive terminal of the discharged battery.
5. Connect the other cable to the negative terminal of the booster battery and then to the alternator mounting bracket of your car. Make sure you have a good ground contact on the bracket!
6. Start the car.
7. Reverse the above sequence exactly when moving the jumper cables.

—*Dodge Operator's Instructions & Product Information,* 1977

Notice how plain and purposeful the language of this process narrative is. Yet the same subject may be treated and the same order followed in a narrative with a different purpose:

Ellen and Hilary

No doubt about it. *The battery was dead.* Snow falling, wind howling, Ellen muttering, and I'm stuck in the A & P parking lot. I had already called Hilary for assistance.

Step 1

"Turn off the light switch and the radio," I told Ellen. She did so   Step 2
with a groan.

I removed the vent caps from the battery to check the electrolyte. It   Step 3
looked healthy and unfrozen. Ellen pointed to a familiar car
approaching. It was Hilary's. His car was fourteen years old,
mine four months.

Silently, *he pulled a tangle of wires* from his trunk and strung   Step 4
them from battery to battery. I watched, Ellen standing close
behind me now to protect herself from the wind. She had gotten
out of the car when Hilary arrived.

As Hilary attached the last cable to the alternator bracket, a   Step 5
sizable spark crackled across the cold metal. Startled, I jumped
backward, falling into Ellen. Ellen fell with a thud onto the soft
snow, and I crashed on top of her. She kicked and cursed and
called me a fool. Snow clung to her hair and filled her purse.
Getting up, I crushed her foot.

In the meantime, *Hilary had started my car* and removed the   Step 6
cables.

Ellen went home with him.

Here the writer is interested in telling a story for its own sake. How to
jump-start a battery fades as a concern. Yet that procedure still provides
the narrative structure.

In the process of telling a tale, you control the movement of time.
In "Ellen and Hilary," notice how a series of narrative details ("She
kicked and cursed and called me a fool") prolongs the struggle between
Ellen and the narrator. Such an extension of time can be achieved easily.
For example, the action in the following sentence occurs without inter-
ruption:

An arrow arched over the shield wall and ripped into King Harold's
eye.

Freezing time

To slow events, you might freeze the arrow in flight for a moment while
you narrate a part of the action occurring simultaneously. You can do
this by simply adding clauses of detail:

An arrow, *crudely carved but keen,* arched over the shield wall and, *as
hundreds of Saxon warriors watched helplessly,* it ripped into King Harold's
eye.

Time can even be thrown backwards by a clause that operates like a
flashback in a film, recalling action that has already taken place:

Hamlet, *remembering the murder of his father, the death of Polonius, the
suicide of Ophelia,* forced the poisoned drink down Claudius' throat.

What works on a small scale in narrative sentences can also work in full essays. In organizing a narrative, you have to choose which events to include and in what order. When details are added between major events, you change the character and pace of the story. For example, you may want to provide a straightforward account of what happened when you went tobogganing:

> Finally we tried another slope. We started off without any problem, but one-quarter of the way down the hill, the toboggan rocked. Then it slid sideways, turning through an arc of 180°. Soon we were heading backwards down the slope. When we reached the bottom, we were relieved.

The passage serves your original informative purpose. But say that you want to amuse your readers with an exciting report of your adventures. How might you build suspense and increase the action? One way would be to add details emphasizing the danger of the plunge and delaying the final assurance that all is well:

> Before long only one slope remained untried, the biggest, meanest, steepest hill in the whole area. No trees complicated the excitement; it just went straight down to a narrow drainage ditch filled with slush, ice, and mud.
>
> "What's 'a matter? Are we chicken?" someone asked.
>
> Frank, the strategist, was more reasonable. "We'll make it OK if we don't tip over, and if we get up enough momentum to carry us over the ditch. It's your turn to lead, Mark."
>
> "The hell it is," said Mark.
>
> We were by this time blue and shivering, but one more venture was inevitable. Frank, again our leader, planted his feet up front as we piled on. Mark insinuated his way to the back again. This time we had no problems getting started. Frank barely had time to jam his feet into the toboggan before it took off like a shot down the perilous run. We picked up speed alarmingly.
>
> The stinging spray bit worse than it had on any other decline as we zipped down in a tunnel of snow. Suddenly, not halfway down the slope, we lurched and the toboggan spun, then righted itself, and— Lord, have mercy—we were plunging down the hill backwards.
>
> Mark, now our lead man, his back splitting the air as we rushed toward oblivion, moaned, but our laughter silenced him. We couldn't believe it. Not even the danger that our rear slats would now plow directly into the drainage ditch, flipping us and our expensive sled into the slush and mud, probably breaking us and it into pieces, could sober us. We were moving too fast to care. All we could see through the thick spray was the distant hilltop fading rapidly away. In a moment there was a jolt and we bounced into the air, five peas sprung from a pod. We landed hard, but for a second our toboggan was still under us. Then it was gone and we spun apart in an explosion of arms, legs, and snow.
>
> Silence, and then a cheer. We had made it.

This longer passage also provides details of setting and characterization missing in the original version. Out of place in the factual account, they provide the delays that allow suspense to build in the entertaining one.

But details of setting and characterization can do more than alter time sequences. When appropriate, they add texture to a narrative, allowing a reader to understand the relationships between a sequence of events. Factually, this information may suffice:

> Frank, Mark, Jim, Mario, and I bought a toboggan and took to the hills one December evening after a heavy snow.

But if the value of the toboggan is to worry us as it hurtles toward destruction, then this sequence may convey more pertinent information:

> The snow had finally fallen that would allow us to try our new toboggan. We had saved all autumn for it, depriving ourselves of a painful number of lunches, nights out, and beers. The snow lay thick on the hills around campus, and the moon shone so brightly it carved shadows. With a whoop, Frank, Mark, and Jim sped out of the dormitory and across the soccer field to where the first shallow hills pushed up ridges of snow. Mario and I trudged more sedately, the toboggan cradled under our arms.

Similarly we may not need to know any more about Frank than what a single modifying phrase tells us:

> Frank, *our leader,* gave directions.

But if understanding Frank's character will heighten our appreciation of later developments, then his leadership might be asserted through a bit of dialogue:

> "Now look, when I yell *right,* we all lean right; and when I yell *left,* we all lean left," he thundered.

Even narratives that do not involve characters or settings may use descriptive devices to clarify the sequences they are explaining. A process narrative may pause to define or portray an object or term many readers might not recognize:

> After $1^{1}/_{2}$–2 hours in the initial sleep stage, an individual enters a deeper stage called REM sleep *(named after the rapid eye movements observed during this period).* Following REM sleep . . .

> To control the nuclear reaction, adjustable control rods are lowered into the reactor core. *These rods, made of cadmium or other metals that capture neutrons, slow down or stop the nuclear chain reaction.*

The narrative may even be interrupted by a figure that clarifies the discussion:

> At the height of the compression stroke, the valves are closed and the spark plug fires, igniting the compressed fuel-air mixture and forcing the piston downward (see Figure 4).

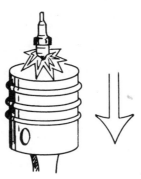

Figure 4. Powerstroke

Whether telling a story or explaining a process, it is your job to select the incidents, details, and information that purposefully serve your readers' needs.

Causality

An important function of the narrative mode is to trace *causality*, the relationships between causes and effects. An inquiry into why something (an accident, a social upheaval, a fad) happened may begin with an exploration of how things happen or under what conditions things can occur. Historians, for example, interpret the sweep of events according to their perceptions of causality:

> The rise and fall of nations and of classes can no longer be regarded as anomalous phenomena, to be explained only by the spontaneous efflorescence of individual genius and of national will, or to be left unexplained as the result of chance or of inscrutable destiny: *All political changes are the results, or, rather, the superficial indications, of the interplay of deeper social, economic, and intellectual changes.* All these, in turn, may be referred to scientific or technical inventions by which that intelligent animal, man, adjusts himself to his environment so as to secure the maximum chance of survival for his species and his group. (italics added)
>
> Preserved Smith, *The Enlightenment 1687–1776*

Sometimes the writer must determine whether the direct (proximate) cause of an event is as significant as a more distant (remote) cause. A rise in housing costs, for example, may be the proximate cause for an increase in the monthly inflation index, but the more significant factor in an analysis of the rise may be a remote cause: the growing exportation of wood products, which drives up the price of domestic building materials. Thus a building boom in Japan may be the "real" cause for increased inflation in North America. **Proximate and remote causes**

Very often, a writer finds that several events or conditions may be responsible for a phenomenon. It may be impossible then to plot a single causal sequence:

> Who can say which was more responsible for the heightened appreciation of murder in Victorian times: an early cluster of sensational ones, or the accident that they occurred during a brief passage in English history—between 1823 and 1837, the year the Queen came to the throne—when journalism was ready and eager to exploit crime, even ordinary crime, as it had never been exploited before?
>
> —Richard D. Altick, *Victorian Studies in Scarlet*

Causality must be given special attention whenever facts and figures are involved. Many writers and readers play fast and loose with numbers, giving the quickest and most sensational explanation of how one set of facts ties in with others. Let us examine what might be done with the budget figures and test scores of an imaginary high school: **Facts and figures**

	Total operating expenditures	Average ECT score of graduating seniors
1965	$ 600,000	510
1970	820,000	485
1975	1,400,000	460
1980	2,050,000	450

An angry citizen might argue that the figures prove "that the more we spend on education, the less we get. We're spending more than three times as much for our high school as we did fifteen years ago, and yet college entry scores have dropped sixty points in the same period of time!"

Did the increased funding for the high school cause the decline in test scores? Probably not. Dozens of other potential factors—and the relationships between them—would have to be examined before it would be possible to state why test scores in the particular school declined while revenues to support it rose. Did the population of the school change in some significant way? Did state or federal agencies require spending increases in nonacademic areas? Did academic policies change in a way that might alter curriculum and test scores? Were programs added to the nonacademic curriculum, attracting students away from more traditional subjects? Was there a high rate of faculty turnover? Was there an increase in vandalism? Truancy? Other discipline problems? Did a larger proportion of the student body take the ECT test in 1980 than in 1965? And so on. A thorough analysis of the situation at the high school would probably produce a conclusion far less stirring than the irate citizen's:

> The decline in test scores at _____ High School during the last fifteen years may have been caused by an increase in the student/faculty ratio from 22/1 to 30/1 as the school underwent rapid growth due to an increasing suburban population. Additionally, the federal and state governments required substantial increases in extracurricular and special education projects without providing additional funding for them. Finally, a reduction in the number of required English courses from 4 to 2 since 1974 may have weakened some students' basic skills. This combination of factors . . .

A thorough (if somewhat jargon-plagued) conclusion like this one does more than set the facts in order; it raises serious questions about the legitimacy of correlating rising costs with declining test scores. Complex problems rarely have simple stories to tell.

For Discussion

1. What devices do moviemakers use to suggest the passage of time? What equivalent devices are available to writers?

2. Have you ever witnessed an event later reported in the newspapers or on television? How did your perception of events differ from the news account? What events did the news report include? Which details were excluded? How did the selection of events and details shape the report?

3. Do you agree with Preserved Smith's ideas (quoted earlier in this chapter) about what causes changes in societies?

Exercises

4. Carefully examine an article dealing with a significant social or political problem. (The article may be a chapter from a book or a selection from a serious periodical or anthology.) Note those passages that deal with causality. Whenever you can, summarize the causal relations in single sentences:

The arms race must lead to war.

The Soviets are responsible for the renewed nuclear arms race.

Arms sales around the world reduce the economic growth of developing nations.

Then discuss the sentences. Has the author addressed proximate or remote causes? Do you agree with the author's analysis of the problem? Where might you criticize the causal sequence the author employs?

5. In a paragraph or so, explain how one of the following works:

a Foucault pendulum   a wing
a kidney   a flying buttress
a concordance   a Rorschach test
a Galilean telescope

Assume that your reader has no special knowledge of any of the fields pertinent to the devices. You may use a simple diagram to supplement your explanation.

6. Use an almanac to tabulate the population figures of Cleveland, Detroit, Houston, and Los Angeles in 1950, 1960, 1970, and 1980:

	Cleveland	Detroit	Houston	Los Angeles
1950				
1960				
1970				
1980				

When you have gathered the numbers, examine them closely to spot any population trends. Then, in a short essay, explore some of the factors that might explain why some cities have grown in population while others have shrunk.

7. Compile a table listing the federal budgets and deficits in the presidential election years since 1956:

	Budget	Deficit
1956		
1960		
1964		
1968		
1972		
1976		
1980		

What conclusions might a Democrat want to draw from the figures? A Republican? An irate citizen? What has caused the increase in federal spending?

Writing Assignments

8. Choose a significant historical event and write a concise narrative detailing the circumstances leading up to it (500+ words). Pay particular attention to social, economic, political, or military considerations that may help to explain the occurrence. Provide as much detail about individuals involved in the event as is necessary to understand it and them.

Try to trace causal sequences. Why did this happen? What or who was responsible?

Keep your focus on the background of the event, not on its consequences or the event itself. Do as much reading and research as is necessary to report the facts accurately. List your sources at the end of the essay. Assume that your readers are familiar with the event itself but not with its causes. Some suggested events:

> the Battle of Hastings
> the first marathon run
> the founding of the Abbey of Monte Cassino
> the 1929 stock market crash
> the imprisonment of Jomo Kenyatta
> the Saint Bartholomew's Day massacre
> the Aroostook War
> the storming of the Alamo
> the creation of Pakistan
> the storming of the Bastille

9. In an essay, narrate the events surrounding the publication of one of the following books. In your narrative, try to answer some of these questions:

> a. Did the author expect the work to cause a controversy?
> b. Was the author urged not to publish?
> c. What compelled the author to publish?
> d. What were the immediate consequences of publication? A trial?
> Fame for the author? Revolution?

You should be able to find information about many of these books in encyclopedias. Some of the more recent works may require research in periodicals.

> *Dialogue on the Two Chief Systems of the World,* Galileo
> *Madame Bovary,* Gustave Flaubert

Origin of Species, Charles Darwin
Das Kapital, Karl Marx
Apologia Pro Vita Sua, John Henry Newman
Ulysses, James Joyce
Lady Chatterley's Lover, D. H. Lawrence
The Awakening, Kate Chopin
Jane Eyre, Charlotte Brontë
The Female Eunuch, Germaine Greer
Future Shock, Alvin Toffler

10. Write a pair of narratives, the first informative and stark—like an insurance report or brief news account—the second amusing and personal.

What are possible topics for your narratives? Perhaps some incident in your life that amused, frightened, or embarrassed you or, better yet, a relatively simple incident that changed you in some important way.

Keep the first narrative short (200–300 words). The second version of the tale may be as long as necessary. The audience for the informative narrative should be some figure of authority who might be interested in your story: a parent, a principal, a police officer, a judge. Write the second version for the benefit of your friends who aren't involved.

Classification

When we classify, we examine groups of things to discover the similarities and differences that order and define them:

> The world may be divided into people that read, people that write, people that think, and fox-hunters.
>
> —William Shenstone, *On Writing and Books*

We classify constantly, often unaware that we are employing the mode. Seeing a barstool, a rocker, and a recliner, we think of the more general category, chair. Swatting flies, mosquitoes, and roaches, we complain to the apartment manager about bugs. Unsure whether Rover is more poodle, dachsund, or schnauzer, we call him a mutt.

When we classify objects or ideas more systematically, we follow certain guidelines. First of all, classifications should be *exhaustive;* that is, every member of a larger class should find a place in one of the smaller ones. A mineralogist begins to give order to the different kinds of rocks by identifying three categories that include them all:

Classifications should be exhaustive

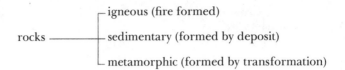

rocks
- igneous (fire formed)
- sedimentary (formed by deposit)
- metamorphic (formed by transformation)

A writer planning an article on sports cars may organize his piece by classifying them according to body style:

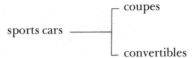

sports cars
- coupes
- convertibles

If there were such a vehicle as a sports station wagon, then the writer would have to add a third subclass to make the classification exhaustive.

Sometimes, though, a general class may be so large that a writer may be unable or unwilling to name every one of its subclasses. A student preparing an essay on the subfields of psychology may find her subject growing too large to handle adequately:

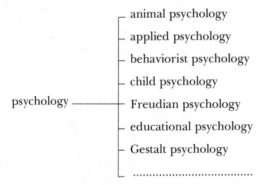

psychology
- animal psychology
- applied psychology
- behaviorist psychology
- child psychology
- Freudian psychology
- educational psychology
- Gestalt psychology
- ....

In such a case, the unnamed subclasses and those the writer chooses to exclude can be consolidated under the category of *"other"*:

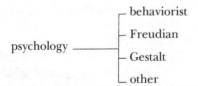

psychology
- behaviorist
- Freudian
- Gestalt
- other

"Other" is a useful subclass when a general class is dominated by several major subclasses and a host of minor ones:

Modes of Writing

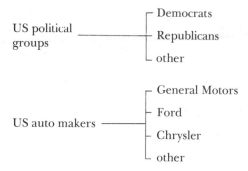

US political groups
- Democrats
- Republicans
- other

US auto makers
- General Motors
- Ford
- Chrysler
- other

Principles of division

A second guideline requires that formal classifications operate according to a single *principle of division* at each subclass level. The purpose a classification is to serve determines the principle of division. Botanists, for example, have attempted to construct systems that organize the entire vast plant kingdom. Some have classified plants according to evolutionary structures, others according to reproductive structures. Under either of these principles, an attempt is made to find a way of ordering the entire plant kingdom.

But most principles of classification have the effect of narrowing our perspective on a larger group. A literary critic interested in the poetry of a given century may find it useful to divide the era's poems by subject matter, by verse form, by authorship, or by influences. Each of these would be a different principle of division. A student considering elective classes in a course schedule may divide them up, first, according to subject matter or department, and then according to instructor, location, and time. Eventually, all these principles of division will have a bearing on the choice of a class, but the student probably begins his selection process with the most important and manageable category.

Problems can occur in formal systems of classification when more than one principle of division operates at the same level. An example of faulty classification is the best instructor here:

sports cars
- coupes
- convertibles
- British

In this example, all three of the subclasses define a type of sports car, but while coupes and convertibles describe body styles, British designates the place of manufacture. The example attempts to divide up the general class of sports cars by two different principles simultaneously. To correct this problem, we can either apply those principles separately (a.) or have them operate at different levels of division within the same system of classification (b.):

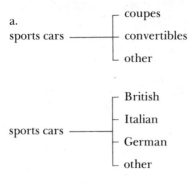

a.

sports cars
- coupes
- convertibles
- other

sports cars
- British
- Italian
- German
- other

b.

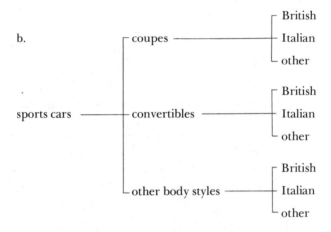

sports cars
- coupes
  - British
  - Italian
  - other
- convertibles
  - British
  - Italian
  - other
- other body styles
  - British
  - Italian
  - other

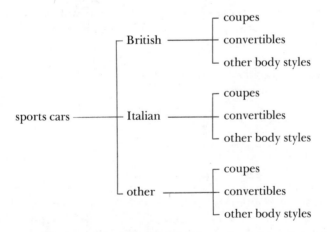

sports cars
- British
  - coupes
  - convertibles
  - other body styles
- Italian
  - coupes
  - convertibles
  - other body styles
- other
  - coupes
  - convertibles
  - other body styles

A writer at this point might drop the category of "other" to develop an article on British and Italian sports cars using the outline the system of classification provides. The article could now go on to list and describe the various automobiles, or it could systematically compare and contrast them. In either case, the analysis should be well organized and thorough because of the careful classification that undergirds it.

A third principle of classification requires that every subcategory be *smaller than the class preceding it.* If a classification is operating properly, subclasses will be smaller than classes by definition. For example, we can divide up US political groups according to three principles: (1) major political parties (ignoring "other"), (2) philosophical leanings, (3) gender:

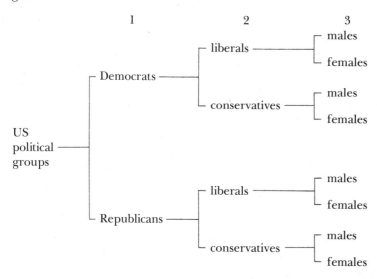

Gender may seem like the most inclusive of the three principles. But because that principle is applied after two others, the subclasses that result from the third subdivision do not include individually all males and all females. Instead, the eight subclasses are defined by reading them from right to left:

Members of US Political Groups
1. male liberal Democrats
2. female liberal Democrats
3. male conservative Democrats
4. female conservative Democrats
5. male liberal Republicans
6. female liberal Republicans
7. male conservative Republicans
8. female conservative Republicans

Some of these subclasses may be considerably larger than others. There may be more female liberal Democrats, for example, than female conservative Republicans. But none of these eight groups is larger than the classes that precede them on the diagram.

Finally, *subclasses* in a formal system of classification *should not overlap*. Members of one subclass should not be members of any other:

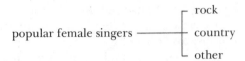

A writer using this system of classification to structure an essay on women in popular music might find it difficult to place Linda Ronstadt or Dolly Parton, who sing both country and rock tunes. When subclasses overlap, it may be because two principles of division are operating at the same time (as discussed in the preceding section) or because the subclasses are not properly identified. More precise categories might solve this writer's problem:

```
                                  ┌─ rock only
popular female singers ───────────┼─ country only
                                  └─ country/rock
```

But even accurate systems of classification can run into problems:

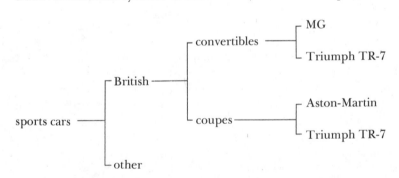

How is it possible for the TR-7 to fit into two categories? Is something wrong with the principle of division? No. The vehicles in the two categories are different. The first TR-7s manufactured were coupes; later the coupe was replaced by a convertible. Hence, the brand name of the product is capable of division:

```
          ┌─ convertibles
TR-7s ────┤
          └─ coupes
```

And the division could go on until we are at the point of naming individual vehicles: the 1981 yellow TR-7 coupe owned by Betsy Brown.

Almost all researchers who attempt to describe large disciplines or areas (the plant kingdom, human behavior, history, literature) discover some objects or phenomena that can't be pigeon-holed neatly. The platypus lays eggs when most other mammals do not. The single-celled euglena has the characteristics of both plant and animal. Light itself behaves like particles and waves. And literary critics still debate whether Shakespeare's *Troilus and Cressida* ia a tragedy, comedy, or satire. But even in these and countless other cases where systems of classification break down, those systems help us understand and appreciate the complexities and limitations on our ways of perceiving things.

Division and Analysis

Formal classification helps us to place objects into carefully related categories. But sometimes a writer needs to examine the various parts and components of an object or idea. This *division* into parts usually involves a preliminary act of classification. But the division itself may be less systematic and single-minded. When Aristotle, in his *Rhetoric*, assigns all speeches to one of three general categories according to the purpose they serve, he is classifying:

Division

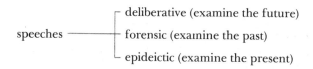

But when he says that speeches generally have three parts,

1. a beginning,
2. a middle, and
3. an end,

he is dividing.

As Aristotle's example shows, division can be relatively uncomplicated, being the means by which a writer breaks a larger topic into more manageable divisions. A simple naming of parts or characteristics can be a useful principle of division and organization for a writer:

An atom is composed of neutrons, protons, and electrons.

The great apes include the gorilla, the orangutan, the chimpanzee, and the gibbon.

Minerals are examined according to their color, lustre, hardness, cleavage, fracture, and heft.

In these three examples, the body of an informative essay might subsequently be structured by a consideration of each component:

The Atom	The Great Apes	Minerals (characteristics)
neutrons	gorillas	color
protons	orangutans	lustre
electrons	chimpanzees	hardness
	gibbons	cleavage
		fracture
		heft

Sometimes a simple list requires some classification and rearrangement before it becomes a practical outline:

> The typical internal combustion engine has a carburetor, air-cleaner, intake manifold, spark plugs, valves, crankshaft, fan, oil filter, exhaust manifolds, radiator, water pump, fuel pump, distributor . . .

An essay developed from this initial, random division is headed for trouble. A better order is needed. Perhaps the individual parts can be better understood if they are first classified by function:

> The typical internal combustion engine has a fuel system, an exhaust system, a lubrication system, a cooling system, and an ignition system.

Then the individual parts can be discussed as components of particular subsystems. The narrative/process mode might then be used in discussing how each subsystem operates.

Analysis   Not all divisions are quite as automatic as the naming of parts and characteristics. Many divisions result from the *analysis* of a phenomenon or problem. In the following example, the significance of the Olympic movement in Soviet Russia is detailed:

> In terms of Communist goals, it has aided in the military preparedness of the nation, has helped to raise labor productivity, has increased Soviet international prestige, and has served as a means of social control in attracting and directing individuals in Party-sponsored activities.
>
> —Henry W. Morton, "Sport and Society: USSR vs. US"

The four considerations raised in the sentence (military preparedness, productivity, prestige, social control) are aspects of the Soviet sports system. There may be others, but the author has chosen to focus on these in particular.

Similarly, in the following example, a writer confronts the problem of technological failure by dividing it into parts:

Since technology cannot be abandoned, the next logical step is to see what can be done to avoid repetition of technological mistakes that have been made in the past. Toward that end, let us consider the types of mistakes that engineers have made, and the reasons for them.

First, there are the mistakes that have been made by carelessness or error. . . .

—Samuel C. Florman, "Engineering Mistakes"

In both cases, division provides a way of studying a complex subject, analyzing it, and organizing an essay that deals with it.

Comparison and Contrast

When objects are classified, we begin almost automatically to consider their likenesses and differences, how they compare and how they contrast. Comparisons often begin, then, with objects already in some significant relationship. If you were a consumer advocate, for example, you might compare a Jaguar XJ sedan to a Rabbit in matters of comfort, luxury, style, room, handling, and economy because, as automobiles, both would possess these qualities to some extent. But the study would be pointless unless you initially factored in the enormous differences in their prices and the markets they attempt to reach. You aren't going to interest or inform anyone with the conclusion that the Rabbit is more economical than the Jaguar or that the Jaguar is more sumptuous than the Rabbit. But if you pit the cars against their real competitors, your study gains in interest and significance:

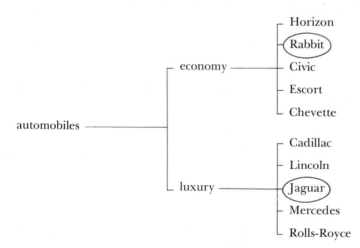

In informative writing, comparisons within a class are more likely to prove significant than those between classes. Thus you might compare and contrast the general concept of luxury cars with the general concept

Effective comparisons

of economy cars and use particular vehicles to demonstrate your points. But you would not want to pit a particular luxury car against a particular economy car because the individual products are already separated by branches of the classification diagram.

There is a cliche that warns against comparing apples and oranges, but you can compare dissimilar objects if you choose to. Sometimes the vast differences between objects being compared suggest relationships never considered before:

My Love's like a red, red rose. . . .

—Robert Burns, "A Red, Red Rose"

Even apples and oranges share many features that define a relationship between them:

$$
\text{fruits} \quad
\begin{cases}
\text{apples} \\
\text{oranges} \\
\text{other}
\end{cases}
$$

Beginning there, it is possible to find common qualities that can be compared and contrasted:

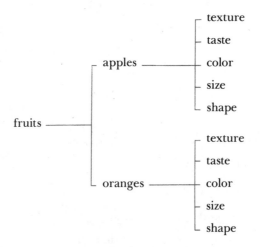

Patterns of comparison/contrast

Comparisons are usually organized according to one of two patterns. An essay considering the advantages and disadvantages of two particular energy sources might begin with an initial classification:

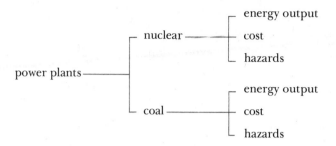

Then the resulting essay might consider the first subject of analysis (nuclear power plants) in its three aspects and follow with an analysis of the second subject in its three aspects. In outline, the essay developed subject-by-subject might look like this:

Nuclear Power VS Coal Power

    I.   Introduction
    II. Nuclear power plants
         A.   Energy output
         B.   Costs
         C.   Hazards
    III. Coal power plants
         A.   Energy output
         B.   Costs
         C.   Hazards
    IV. Conclusions

Such a pattern of development allows you to talk about one subject at a time, developing it fully and in detail. But it puts a burden on your readers to mark the contrasts and likenesses between the subjects. In this pattern, the conclusion can play an important role in summarizing the important relationships the essay has discovered.

A second pattern develops point-by-point. It requires more transitions, more switching back and forth between subjects. A single subject cannot be developed fully. But this pattern focuses more effectively than does the first one on the significant examples and instances of contrast and comparison. The reader does a little less work:

Nuclear Power VS Coal Power

    I.   Introduction
    II. Energy outputs
         A.   Nuclear plants
         B.   Coal plants
    III. Costs
         A.   Nuclear plants
         B.   Coal plants
    IV. Hazards
         A.   Nuclear plants
         B.   Coal plants
    V.   Conclusions

Definition

In defining objects or ideas, we make use of the general principles of classification and, to a lesser extent, of description and narration. Definition is a process of identifying things, of saying what they are. There are many kinds of definitions and many ways of defining.

Reading a classification diagram can be an exercise in definition:

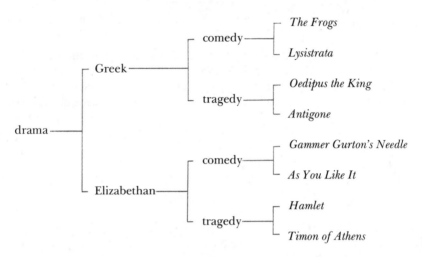

General class and characteristics

By examining this diagram, you could define *Gammer Gurton's Needle* as an Elizabethan comedy and *Antigone* as a Greek tragedy without knowing either play. The works are defined by the classes they fall into. The scientific names of animals are based upon a similar structure. An animal is designated first by its genus and then by the next smaller class to which it belongs, its species: *Musca domestica* (house fly); *Panthera leo* (lion). Many dictionary definitions follow a similar pattern, first identifying the general class to which an object belongs and then narrowing down to more specific features and characteristics:

> *organ grinder* A street musician who plays a hurdy-gurdy.
>
> — *The American Heritage Dictionary*

General category: musician

Details: plays on the street
       plays a hurdy gurdy

> *hurdy-gurdy* . . . A medieval instrument shaped like a lute, played by street musicians with a crank that causes a resin-covered wheel to scrape across the strings.
>
> — *The American Heritage Dictionary*

General category: musical instrument

Details: medieval
      shaped like a lute
      played by street musicians
      has a crank that causes a wheel to scrape across strings

Other methods
of definition

Notice, however, that both of these formal definitions define the objects in part by their general classes and in part by what they do. Describing what a thing does is another method of definition:

> *sports car* An automobile . . . designed for precise control at high speed on curving roads.
>
> — *The American Heritage Dictionary*

An object may also be defined by listing its major components:

> *sports car* A sports car is a small automobile, usually with limited accommodations, having a floor-mounted stickshift, disc brakes, real-leather bucket seats, and a drafty convertible top.

Similarly, an object may be defined by what it does not have or does not do:

> *sports car* A sports car is a small automobile without a back seat, a large trunk, a smooth ride, or four doors. It is not designed for effortless cruising down interstate highways while loaded with luggage and kids.

Or it may be defined by example:

> *sports car* A small, performance-oriented vehicle, such as a Porsche or Corvette.

When it is possible to name all the members of a particular class, then that list can be a definition:

> *American sports cars:* Corvette
>
> *Planets:* Mercury, Venus, Earth, Mars, Jupiter, Saturn, Neptune, Uranus, Pluto

And, of course, an object can be defined by whatever combination of these techniques is appropriate:

> *sports car* A small automobile, usually with bucket seats and a taut suspension, designed to accommodate two persons (rarely, four) and to

demonstrate extraordinary handling, braking, and acceleration. Sports cars are not built for families or heavy haulers, but for people who enjoy driving. They rarely offer power assists or large trunks. Some outstanding sports cars are the Porsche 928, the Triumph TR-series, the Datsun 280-ZX, and the Chevrolet Corvette.

Extended definition

Extended definitions are essay or even book-length attempts to define ideas or concepts. Much informative writing can be viewed as extended definition. This entry from the *New Columbia Encyclopedia* defines *mastiff* using all four modes to present a full picture of its subject:

classification	*mastiff* . . . , breed of very large, powerful working dog developed in England more than 2,000 years ago. It stands from 27 to 33 in.
description	(68.6–83.8 cm) high at the shoulder and weighs from 165 to 185 lb (74.9–83.9 kg). Its coarse, short, close-lying coat may be silver fawn, apricot, or dark fawn brindle in color, with a black muzzle, nose, and ears and black around the eyes. The mastiff was first bred as a fighting
narration	dog and guardian. As a fighter it was cited for its physical prowess and courage by Caesar in his account of the Roman invasion of Britain in 55 B.C. Indeed, it was later imported to Rome to fight in the arena. In its native country the mastiff was a popular antagonist in bullbaiting and bearbaiting contests and in organized dogfights until these blood sports were outlawed in 1835. However, throughout the entire history of the breed in England its greatest popularity has derived from its
evaluation	widespread use as a guardian of home and family. This centuries-old association with man is undoubtedly responsible for the mastiff's unexcelled suitability for the role of family companion and its particular devotion to and gentleness with children.

When you are asked to compose an extended definition, you may want to consider which of the various ways of defining a subject is best suited to yours. In most cases, you will want to begin with a classification that sets your subject in a larger context or class:

Magnanimity is a virtue . . .

Impressionism is a school of painting . . .

Microsurgery is a surgical technique . . .

But then you are free to develop your topic according to any appropriate mode. You may find that *magnanimity* can be defined by providing narrative examples of magnanimous behavior:

Magnanimity

example 1   example 3

example 2   example 4

Or you may prefer to list characteristics:

Magnanimity
characteristic 1
characteristic 2
characteristic 3

You may decide that an effective way of defining impressionism is to describe several impressionist paintings by Monet or Renoir. But you might also want to include some historical background:

Impressionism
historical background
description: Monet
description: Renoir

And for microsurgery, a description of the tools used followed by a narration of the process may be the combination of modes most appropriate to an extended definition:

Microsurgery
description: the tools
narration: the process

For Discussion

1. Here are some systems of classification that operate at colleges and universities:

grades
class levels (freshman, sophomore, junior, senior, graduate)
upper division/lower division courses
administrators, teachers, students
colleges (of business, liberal arts, social science)

Can you name others? Which of these systems are classifications and which are divisions? Is that distinction always easy to make?

2. Can you think of other things like the platypus and Shakespeare's *Troilus and Cressida* that are hard to classify? What makes them difficult to classify? What advantages/disadvantages are there to finding categories for them to fit in? Consider politicians, songs, vehicles, historical figures, entertainers, religions, etc.

Exercises

3. Define *two* general classes that would include most or all of the items in each of the following groups:

a. *Harper's, The New Yorker, Saturday Review, Commentary*
b. dictionary, thesaurus, telephone book, atlas, encyclopedia
c. Lady Macbeth, Cleopatra, Juliet, Ophelia, Desdemona
d. British Columbia, Alberta, Saskatchewan, Manitoba
e. Bordeaux, Epernay, Dijon, Cognac
f. bugle, cornet, trombone, trumpet, tuba

4. Are the following classifications exhaustive? Why or why not?

a. people — male / female

b. presidents of the US — Democrats / Republicans

c. major world powers — communist / capitalist

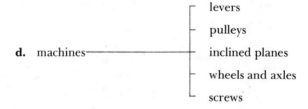

d. machines — levers / pulleys / inclined planes / wheels and axles / screws

e. art — sculpture / painting / mosaic

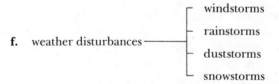

f. weather disturbances — windstorms / rainstorms / duststorms / snowstorms

g. grades — letter (A, B, C, D, etc.) / credit/no credit

5. Two principles of classification are operating within each of the following simple classification diagrams. Revise the diagram so that only one principle operates at a time. Add elements to the diagram if necessary.

Example:

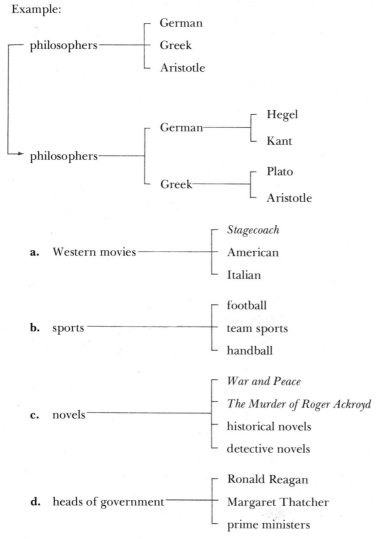

a. Western movies
  ┌ *Stagecoach*
  ├ American
  └ Italian

b. sports
  ┌ football
  ├ team sports
  └ handball

c. novels
  ┌ *War and Peace*
  ├ *The Murder of Roger Ackroyd*
  ├ historical novels
  └ detective novels

d. heads of government
  ┌ Ronald Reagan
  ├ Margaret Thatcher
  └ prime ministers

6. Beginning with some general term, construct a classification diagram with three principles of division. List those principles of division under the diagram.

7. Take a theatrical or sports event and divide it into an appropriate number of parts. Then write a paragraph in which each part is discussed in a sentence or two.

8. Take a mechanical object whose operation you understand and list its major components. If necessary, categorize those components in an appropriate fashion (see the discussion of the internal combustion engine in this section). Then explain how the object works by discussing the function of the components.

Writing Assignments

9. Choose some familiar general class and break it down into a subclass with at least three divisions. Although your general class may be common, choose an intriguing principle of division. For example, if you begin with students, don't divide them up into obvious subclasses:

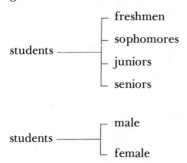

students ── freshmen / sophomores / juniors / seniors

students ── male / female

Instead, choose a principle of division that reflects a more particular way of classifying students:

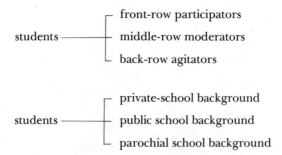

students ── front-row participators / middle-row moderators / back-row agitators

students ── private-school background / public school background / parochial school background

Having established these divisions, define the members of each subclass by using several methods of definition. Develop each paragraph fully. Be sure that your definitions reflect real classes of individual things, ones that you may have observed yourself:

> On the first day of class, front-row participators claim the desks right in front of the teacher and hold on to them the entire term. They dress immaculately, sometimes provocatively, to catch the teacher's eye. That failing, they wave arms frantically at every question whether they know the answers or not. Or they ask, "What page are we on?" or, "Could you

repeat that comment?" Front-row participators are rarely late for class, never unprepared. Pencils sharpened, legal pads stacked, they are ready to go and make sure the teacher knows it.

Some general classes you may want to start with:

political systems	human personality
economic systems	behavior
tests	cities
restaurants	teachers
politicians	summer jobs
relatives	bosses
films	secretaries
mystery novels	alleys
arguments	athletes
drivers	entertainers

Length: 400–600 words.

10. Bring an abstract term to life by composing an extended definition. Use any techniques of definition appropriate to your subject. Some terms you might tackle:

perspicuity	discombobulation
indolence	altruism
quietude	puerility
sagacity	fortitude

Your audience for this essay is a bored group of high-school seniors. Enlighten them.

11. Make a technical term clear by writing an extended definition. You may use a figure or diagram to clarify your discussion when appropriate. Length: 100–300 words. Some suggested terms:

Ptolemaic astronomy	radiation
collective unconscious	kinetic art
oxidation	inflation
pincer movement	horticulture
golden section	defense mechanism

12. In an extended definition, explain one of the following human types. Be sympathetic or critical:

intellectual	liberal
jock	extrovert
conservative	introvert

13. Classify 12–15 magazines according to the interests and audiences they address. These may be popular magazines or, better, journals of significance in your major area. Then, choosing a subclass that contains 3–4 magazines, write an essay that systematically compares or contrasts these magazines. Do not evaluate the periodicals. The aim of this essay is to convey information. Consider at least three significant features common to the magazines you are classifying. The essay you produce should be short. In fact, you may organize your analysis as if it were a catalogue of information that a reader might use in a library to quickly discover the differences between, for example, *Newsweek* and *U.S. News and World Report.* In this case, your "essay" does not need an introduction or conclusion.

14. Classifications play an important role in almost every subject of study or every job. Identify a major system of classification in an area of significant interest to you and write a short essay explaining the principle(s) of classification operating within it.

If you work in an office, you might examine the qualifications by which office staff members are classified and given particular titles. How does an administrative assistant differ from an administrative secretary?

If your major interest is psychology, you might choose some significant division within the field (Freudian, Jungian, Gestalt) as your topic.

If you play or follow sports, you can consider the significant classifications that operate within teams, leagues, or the games themselves.

Your essay should be factual and informative. Assume that your audience is not as familiar with your topic as you are. Keep the report short and functional.

Evaluation

We make evaluations so casually, naturally, and often that we tend to ignore the mechanics of our judgments until they are challenged. Often, such challenges push us into uncomfortable corners:

"What a wonderful movie that was!"
"Oh, did you think so? What do you mean by wonderful?"
"I mean it was great, really super."
"Super in what sense?"
"I dunno. It was good. Can't we just leave it at that?"

In conversation, we sometimes can just leave it at that. But when evaluations are committed to paper, they can become permanent and controversial:

> [September 29, 1662] . . . To the King's Theater, where we saw
> *Midsummer's Night's Dream,* which I had never seen before, nor shall ever
> again, for it is the most insipid, ridiculous play that ever I saw in my life.
>
> —Samuel Pepys, *Diary of Samuel Pepys*

Pepys perhaps never expected his diary to be published; hence, his critique of Shakespeare's play has the vigor and bluntness of self-expressive writing. But his remarks would need more substantiation to fly as informative or even persuasive comment. When you intend to inform or persuade, your reader will want to know not only what your opinion is, but how you reached it. They may want to follow your weighing of evidence and your citing of authorities:

Opinion and evidence

> Akira Kurosawa's Japanese *Macbeth, Throne of Blood* . . . has been called
> "the finest of Shakespeare movies" by Grigori Kozintsev, a
> "masterpiece" by Peter Brook.
>
> —Jack J. Jorgens, *Shakespeare on Film*

They may expect a healthy and vigorous skepticism:

> While there can be little argument with the obvious fact that black
> performances in sports have been and continue to be superior, on the
> whole, to those of whites, there is room for considerable debate over the
> identity and character of the factors that have determined that
> superiority and contributed to its perpetuation.
>
> —Harry Edwards, "The Myth of the Racially Superior Athlete"

They will appreciate frank and concise summary:

> So on paper, at least, it seems that the 510 has all the necessary
> ingredients for happiness in the little-car leagues. But in the harsh light
> of day, the 510 falls behind the first-rank small cars in desirability, and
> not because of any serious flaws in its basic design. Rather, Nissan has
> missed the mark in its execution of some important details.
>
> —Rick Ceppos, "Datsun 510"

Formal evaluation usually begins with a survey of some general class: movies, automobiles, economic systems, baseball teams. Then the general class is broken down into some narrower subclass: adventure films, passenger sedans, contemporary economic systems, professional baseball teams. Finally, an evaluative term is affixed: a *good* historical

Evaluative terms

novel, an *economical* passenger sedan, an *oppressive* contemporary economic system, a *first-rate* professional baseball team. Then the work begins. What is it that makes an historical novel good, a sedan economical, an economic system oppressive, or a pro ball team first-rate? To answer these questions, you must establish criteria of evaluation based upon the values you expect your intended audience to hold:

1. A good historical novel combines lively and realistic action with plausible characters, exotic locales, and solid background research.

2. An economical passenger sedan gets 35 mpg.

3. An oppressive economic system is one that denies individuals the right to generate, accumulate, possess, and distribute wealth as they choose.

4. A first-rate baseball team wins more than 100 games in the regular season.

Before an evaluation can proceed, the writer and reader must agree on criteria such as these. Since criteria are, in fact, arbitrary (you could invent dozens of different criteria for any one of these topics), agreement between writer and reader is essential. When a writer can safely assume that readers will share her values, she may embed the criteria in her essay:

Last night's performance of the Edenborn Ballet left the audience roaring with laughter long after the curtain mercifully fell. The dancers moved like sacks of Gold Medal flour, stumbling over props, their partners, themselves. The scenery shook, the costumes were tasteless and gaudy, and the orchestra noticeably off tempo. The pianist distinguished himself by playing like a chimp wearing mittens. . . .

An analysis like this may abuse the formal standards of evaluation. One suspects the butchering critic of enjoying her work too much. Yet legitimate criteria of evaluation can be extracted from the passage, standards most folks would agree to:

1. Good dancers move gracefully.

2. Good productions require professional-quality scenery and costumes.

3. Good ballet requires a competent orchestra.

When a writer chooses more controversial criteria—standards that may not reflect the values of most of his readers at the outset—then he must be prepared to justify and defend them. Quite often, the more precise a standard is, the more explanation it requires:

Some may argue the 100-victories standard is either an excessively high figure to demand for baseball excellence or a meaningless one. Some

100+ teams have been clobbered in the world series. Teams coming into the series with far fewer victories have been successful because they faced tougher competition all season than did their 100+ rivals. Still, an analysis of statistics supports the 100+ figure as the most reliable if you take into account . . . .

And so on.

Once a criterion is established (or more accurately, once a writer believes that the defense of a criterion is adequate), all that remains is to evaluate an individual member of the general class according to the standard. The structure of evaluations is relatively simple:

1. A _____   _____
             evaluative term   general class

     does/has   a. _____,
                  b. _____,
     and/or   c. _____.

2. _____X_____
   member of general class does-doesn't/

     has/hasn't   a. _____,
                   b. _____,
     and/or   c. _____.

3. Therefore, _____X_____ is/isn't

_____
     evaluative term

1. A first-rate professional baseball team must win 100+ games during the regular season.

2. The 1979 Baltimore Orioles won more than 100 games.

3. Therefore, the 1979 Baltimore Orioles were a first-rate baseball team.

1. An economical passenger sedan gets 35 MPG.

2. The Cadillac Seville does not get 35 MPG.

3. Therefore, the Cadillac Seville is not an economical sedan.

These models of evaluation are simplified; evaluations rarely proceed with such facile logic, nor will criteria always be so narrow or conveniently numerical. In some situations, even strong evidence must be tempered by cautious assessment:

No other general in history faced such adversity or such formidable odds as Hannibal. His inspiring leadership, his consummate tactical and strategic skill, and his accomplishments with inferior material against the most dynamic and militarily efficient nation in the world have prompted many historians and military theorists to rank him as the greatest general of history. Objective assessment makes if impossible to rank him ahead of Alexander, Genghis Khan, or Napoleon; equally, it is impossible to rank them significantly ahead of him.

—R. Ernest Dupuy and Trevor N. Dupuy, *The Encyclopedia of Military History*

Criteria themselves may cause interpretive difficulties when their terms require additional definition and refinement:

A good historical novel combines lively and realistic action with plausible characters, exotic locales, and solid background research.

The writer working with this standard will have to grapple with what he means by *lively* action, *realistic* action, *plausible* characters, *exotic* locales, and *solid* background research. In dealing with ideas like these not subject to easy measurement, a writer must be prepared to explain and defend the critical and controversial terms:

In choosing the best and the worst legislators, we avoided any consideration of their political philosophy. The test of a good member—or a bad one—should be the same whether a person is conservative or liberal. A good legislator is intelligent, hard-working, well prepared, and accessible to reason; because of these qualities he is respected by his colleagues and effective in debate. He uses power skillfully but does not abuse it. . . .

—"The Ten Best and, Sigh, the Ten Worst Legislators," *Texas Monthly*

For Discussion   1. How often do you make evaluations? Think about the snap judgments you offer about food, members of the opposite sex, politics, essays, novels, library services, films, etc., in a single day. Which decisions tend to be the best considered? What makes it possible for you to make evaluations so rapidly in some cases?

2. Consider some of the local, national, and international award programs you are familiar with: the Nobel prizes, the Academy Awards, most valuable player awards, best poem/short story contests, etc. What criteria of evaluation are used in these programs? How legitimate do you think they are?

3. In what professional fields and disciplines do you think evaluations

are crucial? Is a doctor's diagnosis an evaluation? A historian's assessment of facts? A chemist's observations? A law officer's judgments?

4. The familiar movie ratings *(G, PG, R, X)* are standards of evaluation. Discuss their value. Would you modify the system?

Exercises

5. The government regularly establishes product and performance standards for consumer items—everything from lawnmowers to baby toys. Try your hand at establishing standards for some things the government is not likely to try to regulate.

6. A tough exercise: how ought writing to be evaluated in a writing course? What criteria ought to guide the grading of written products? Consider the issue carefully, and then set down your thoughts in a concise paragraph. Be prepared for discussion.

Writing Assignments

7. Consider some major problem—political, social, or economic—and list the criteria which a good solution to the problem would have to satisfy: what conditions would have to be changed or alleviated? What kind of budget limitations would have to be met? What political pressures would have to be anticipated or countered? Having established your criteria, examine some of the solutions currently offered for the problem in light of your standards. Write an essay explaining your findings.

8. Examine some controversial work of art or architecture in your local community. Evaluate it in an essay addressed to an initially neutral audience of out-of-towners. Be sure to make your criteria of evaluation specific and convincing.

9. Examine a copy of *Consumer Reports.* Then gather a number of different brands or types of a familiar item and apply the *Consumer Reports* method to the items. You might study five brands of running shoes, measuring and judging their weight, flexibility, quality of materials and stitching, and more. Or you might gather a half dozen brands of toothpaste, evaluating price, texture, breath-freshening ability, and taste. Or examine several textbooks in the same general field from different publishers, comparing price, thoroughness, clarity, print quality, quality of binding, adequacy of indexing, and so on.

When you have completed your evaluation, write up a report in the analytical style of *Consumer Reports,* keeping the language objective and factual. Use charts and diagrams when necessary. Your audience is the same one *Consumer Reports* aims for.

10. If you own a car, camera, boat, stereo, or some other item regularly reviewed in enthusiasts' periodicals *(Motor Trend, Stereo and Hifi, Popular Photography),* read an appropriate publication, observing how it creates criteria, either explicitly or implicitly. Then review the product you own, modeling your essay after the professional evaluation. The item need not be new. But if you are evaluating an older item, be sure to adjust your criteria to its condition and age. A twenty-year-old VW may be fine for city traffic but a clunker on the interstate. By what traffic situation do you intend to judge it?

Write for the same audience reached by your favorite periodical in the field.

11. Find a book review, copy it, and then read it carefully, underlining every evaluative term or criterion in it. When you have finished, classify the various criteria used in the article. Try to reduce the separate evaluations to several general types.

Then, in an essay, evaluate the criteria. Can they be generally applied or do they fit only this particular type of book? Are they clearly explained? Are they adequately defended? If you find the criteria used in the review to be inadequate, suggest better ones.

Your audience here will be your classmates. Length: 450 words.

Invention: Using the Modes to Generate Ideas

You can use the four modes as a means of discovering what can be said about a topic. Because the modes represent the basic ways of approaching any subject, you will have to employ them, singly or in combination, when you write about an idea. Hence, a run through the modes at the point prior to writing when you are thinking about an idea can be an effective way of exploring a topic and discovering aspects you may want to deal with: what happens to your subject when it is regarded as a sequence of events (narration)? As a system of ideas (classification)? As a thing in itself (description)? As an object with a purpose (evaluation)?

In many cases, you will know from the start what modes will dominate your work. A writing assignment may actually be phrased modally *(describe* conditions in the housing project; *narrate* the events that led up to the recession; *classify* the pesticides used; *evaluate* the State Department's performance). Remembering how each mode typically operates can suggest effective ways to develop your topic. With a given topic, here are some questions you might ask about it from a modal perspective:

Description
1. What are the features or qualities of your subject?
2. What size, shape, structure, quantity, color, texture, weight, aroma does your subject have?

3. What are the distinctive features of your subject?
4. How are the features or qualities of your subject organized or arranged?
5. How does your subject change when you alter your point of view?
6. What limitations are there in your descriptive terms? How can you convey an appreciation of those limits to your audience?
7. With what can you compare your subject? What does it operate, behave, or look like?

Narration

1. What happened? How did it happen? When did it happen? Why did it happen?
2. What were the direct causes of the event? The indirect causes? What were its historical circumstances? What were its effects? Can these be determined accurately?
3. What was the exact sequence of events? What would happen if the sequence were altered?
4. How is the event altered by a shift in perspective?
5. What individual actions had the greatest significance in the chain of events?

Classification

1. How are your subjects alike? What common features do they have?
2. How do your subjects differ? How do those differences help to distinguish them from one another?
3. To what general class(es) do your particular subjects belong?
4. What particular objects belong to your general class? Is your classification exhaustive? Can it be? Does it name all members of a class? If not, why not?
5. What relationships can you establish between the objects in an existing system of classification? Does the system separate them by function, characteristics, locales, belief, degree? Are those relationships significant enough to justify the classificatory system?
6. What characteristics define a member of a class? Which characteristics of the class are essential? Which are incidental?
7. How is the object defined? Formally? Functionally? By components? By example?
8. Where does the system of classification or definition overlap or break down? What causes the failure of the system at that point?

Evaluation

1. How has your subject been evaluated? Favorably? Unfavorably? By whom? For what purpose?

2. To what general class does your subject belong? What other objects belong to that class?
3. What criteria have been established for the general class? How have those criteria been established? By whom? When? From what point of view?
4. Do the criteria of evaluation still apply?
5. Does your subject meet the criteria? In what ways? In what ways does it fail? Why? What do the criteria measure?
6. Are the failures of your subject significant or incidental? Are the deficiencies subject to correction? Is such correction practical?

While these questions may seem abstract, they must be so in order to apply to a variety of practical situations. The answer to any one (or group) could furnish the matter for an entire report or discussion. For example, if in a history course you were asked to assess the effectiveness of a particular economic move made by the federal government (the imposition of wage and price controls by the Nixon administration in 1971, for example), you could transform several of the questions from the evaluative list into more specific inquiries about the 1971 economic controls:

How has your subject been evaluated? Favorably? Unfavorably?

How have economists viewed these particular economic controls? How have economists regarded controls in general?

What criteria have been established for the general class? How have those criteria been established?

What would determine the success of wage/price controls? The rate of inflation? Was it higher or lower at the end of the period of controls?

Do the criteria of evaluation still apply?

By current standards of inflation, would the controls of 1971 be regarded as successful?

In answering these questions, you might employ other modes to describe circumstances, or narrate a sequence of events and consequences:

When mandatory wage and price controls came to a complete end in 1974, the aftermath was far from pleasant. Energy shortages and high food costs contributed to an increase in inflation and to recession, and the pressures that built up after the period of controls led into the destructive double-digit inflation that plagued the early months of the Ford administration. Three years after controls had completely ended, both unemployment and inflation hovered around 7 percent, and there was even nostalgia for the "good old days" in 1971 when we had only 4 percent inflation and 6 percent unemployment.

—Richard Nixon, *RN, The Memoirs of Richard Nixon*

The modes of writing, then, furnish you with one relatively systematic way of thinking about subjects and asking useful questions. Such questions lead toward answers—and sometimes more questions.

Exercises

1. Take an inanimate object and run it through the modes, regarding it first descriptively and then narratively. Classify the object and, finally, evaluate it.

2. Take a person you know well and examine him/her modally.

3. Take an idea or concept (racism, abortion, freedom of the press, idealism, busing) and examine it modally. Which mode(s) would you emphasize in a persuasive essay on that topic? Which in an informative essay? How likely would you be to use all of them?

Writing Assignment

4. Pick a topic from the list below or choose a topic of your own derived from your studies or work experience. Subject it to an interrogation by the appropriate mode(s). Write out the questions that this grilling produces and select those you think offer the greatest promise for additional exploration. Then write an informative essay of approximately 600 words. Some possible topics:

> economic systems
> coed dorms
> the Three Mile Island crisis
> carnivorous plants
> Michelangelo
> the Internal Revenue Service
> *Kramer vs Kramer* (or some more recent film)
> genetic engineering
> the open classroom
> feminism
> word processors
> jogging and running shoes

You may need to do some reading to answer the questions generated by the modal analysis. Credit any sources you use, but don't turn this essay into a full research paper. Rely on personal knowledge whenever you can (a good reason to choose a subject of your own). Audience: compose your essay to serve someone needing concise and reasonably detailed information.

3

Reasons for Writing

An Overview

The previous chapter introduced you to four modes of writing, the basic patterns by which thoughts and language are organized to convey ideas: description, narration, classification, and evaluation. These modes operate in most situations that require language. They may operate singly, as when you recall a favorite story (narration), a cherished scene (description), a slicing bit of name-calling (classification), or a bitter complaint (evaluation). Or you may encounter them in various combinations. That favorite story—a *narrative* about your encounters with a federal or state bureaucracy—might also include a pithy *description* of a fierce secretary ("milky skin, and eyes that cut objections into ribbons of red tape"), a *classification* of the lengths of lines encountered (the all-the-way-down-the-corridor line; the down-the-stairs-and-into-the-street line; the line without end), and an *evaluation* of the efficiency of the clerks (plant-life stupid).

Whatever combination of modes an essay employs, whatever the dominant mode may be, the point of a piece of writing rarely is to produce modes. They are not ordinarily the reason for writing, no more than a batter's reason for walking to the plate during a baseball game is to display his powerful swing. The swing may be an awesome thing, technically perfect in itself. But its purpose or aim is to score runs and win the game. Similarly, the modes of writing—alone or in combination—serve more basic aims.

In theory, we can identify and isolate four basic writing aims. In practice, the aims tend to merge and become almost as hard to separate as flavors in a fruit punch. Even so, in most writing we can identify a dominant aim that answers the question, "Why was this written?" To the writer about to compose, the question becomes, "Why am I writing this?" The answer to that question determines many of the choices to be made in the rest of the composition, from the selection of appropriate modes to the choice of the most apt sentence structures.

Four aims of writing

The four basic aims or reasons for writing are the *self-expressive,* the *literary,* the *informative,* and the *persuasive.* These aims of writing grow out of an examination of the act of communication itself. Written communication involves the interplay of four basic components or elements:

1. the writer,
2. the essay,
3. the subject matter, and
4. the reader.

We can fit other forms of communication within the same framework:

1. the writer (speaker, lecturer, preacher, employee, etc.),
2. the essay (speech, lecture, sermon, memo, etc.),
3. the subject matter (topic, theme, lesson, business, etc.), and
4. the reader (audience, students, congregation, boss, etc.).

If the primary emphasis in a piece of communication or *discourse* is on the writer exploring himself, deciding what he believes, discovering what he wants to say, then the aim of the work is *self-expressive.* The writer writes to himself. The subject matter and style aim to please no other audience. When you sit down with a pen and list your goals, you are writing self-expressively. When you record your private thoughts in a journal or diary, you are composing self-expressively. When you doodle an outrageous comment on the top of your legal pad during an endless lecture, you are writing to satisfy an inner need. The comment explains how you feel. It is self-expression. Sometimes whole groups will declare how they feel and what they believe in declarations or manifestoes. These too are self-expressions. Though much self-expressive discourse is narrative, it is tied to no one mode of organization.

Self-expressive writing

Literature

If the primary emphasis in a piece of writing is on the work itself, on the form it takes, on the craft of its language, on the elegant fitting together of parts, on the relationship of those parts to the whole so that a reader is made to admire the power and beauty of the work and to enjoy the verbal performance, then the aim of the work is *literary*. The writer may employ any mode in achieving a literary aim. Novels are essentially narrative; poems are often descriptive. Satires tend toward classification and evaluation. Most literary works combine the modes and do more than concern themselves with the play of language. Jonathan Swift's well-known satire, "A Modest Proposal," has become a piece of literature because of the brilliance of its wit and form, but no doubt Dr. Swift wrote this attack on British colonialism in Ireland for an originally persuasive purpose. Much romantic poetry seems to be, in part, self-expressive. And though not the fashion any more, poetry can be informative. Alexander Pope's "Essay on Man," for example, is entirely in verse.

The special nature of literature puts it out of the province of most beginning writing courses. Few college assignments have a literary aim; hence, no chapter in this text will deal specifically with literary writing.

Informative writing

When the primary emphasis in a piece of writing falls on the subject matter (rather than on the form that subject matter takes), then the result is *informative writing*. In informative writing, an author seeks to tell her readers new facts about some topic: astronomy, philosophy, history. The writer is not interested in persuading an audience that it ought to act in some particular way. Nor is she concerned with conveying her information in an artful or original way. The aim is to provide information and to uncover knowledge. A lab report, a news account, a textbook, an article in a scholarly journal, a technical analysis, a summary, and the directions on a box of pudding are all examples of informative discourse. Readers go to these sources to gather information they did not have before.

Like literary discourse, informative writing regularly employs all four modes. A news story on a colossal skyscraper fire, for example, might narrate the progress of the blaze from floor to floor, describe the ferocity of the flames lapping the fringes of a night sky, classify the reactions of onlookers, and finally evaluate the efforts of firefighters. Informative discourse can also be a relatively pure aim. A lab report simply describes an experiment without mentioning who performed it and without concern for elegant or emotive style. Facts suffice.

Yet like all the others, the informative aim often works in tandem with a secondary purpose. Much informative writing carries a subtle persuasive motive. The television news with a political slant is informative discourse with a passenger in the sidecar giving directions. So is a classroom lecture that advocates a particular view of history, politics, government, or religion. Personality too can intrude into an informative aim. Sometimes a well-known author, cordial in style and personality, makes a once dull subject interesting. Carl Sagan does this for astronomy, Dr. Spock for pediatrics, Julia Child for French cooking. But even in these cases, the authors aren't so interested in revealing facts about themselves as in explaining their areas of expertise. They inform.

Finally, when the writer's purpose is to change the opinion held by her readers or audience, then the aim is *persuasive*. Some theorists regard most writing as argumentative—as trying to slide readers from one position to another. This view may overstate the importance of persuasive prose. But there is no denying that a great deal of what a writer does is designed to move an audience to react in a certain, preferred way. The distinctions between informative and persuasive prose are often blurred since both aims often work with the same subject matters. Informative discourse is concerned with an audience to the extent that material presented must be clear and coherent:

Persuasive writing

> Two hundred miners were trapped today by the collapse of a shaft in the Thompson #1 mine forty miles southwest of Pittsburgh.

The reader is left to react to the information in her own fashion. Persuasive discourse is concerned with shaping the reader's response in a more particular way:

> Because of inadequate safety precautions on the part of the management of Thompson #1 and shoddy inspection by federal safety authorities, two hundred miners now huddle together somewhere deep under the earth, cut off from families and friends by tons of rock and timber while poisonous gases accumulate, threatening another explosion.

Persuasive writing deals with a subject matter and often involves a strong personal appeal by the author. It often employs devices of language to heighten its appeal: repetition, alliteration, parallelism, allusions. It uses all of the modes. What distinguishes persuasion from the other aims is its determination that the audience come to agree with the opinions of the author. Political speeches, advertisements, sermons, and editorials are familiar examples of persuasion.

The following table summarizes the relationships between the aims and modes of discourse. The table (like most systems of classification) simplifies matters by dividing the aims and modes neatly from each other. It is worth emphasizing one more time that while these distinctions are useful for purposes of study and analysis, they do not carry over so neatly in actual writing.

Writing Component	Aim	Mode
An emphasis on the	produces	using
Writer	**Self-expression**	Description Narration Classification Evaluation
Form	**Literature**	Description Narration Classification Evaluation
Subject matter	**Information**	Description Narration Classification Evaluation
Reader	**Persuasion**	Description Narration Classification Evaluation

For Discussion

1. Some people argue that all writing is persuasive to some degree. What do you think?

2. As with the modes of writing, the aims are viewed separately for the purpose of study. In practice, they merge and interact. Can you think of examples of writing that are purely informative, persuasive, expressive, or literary?

Exercises

3. Indicate the primary aim and any secondary aims of each of the following:

a subpoena	a lab report
an electric bill	a joke
a personal letter	a fix-it manual
a thesis or dissertation	a textbook
an obituary	a greeting card verse
an essay exam	

4. Examine the table of contents of several popular monthly or bimonthly magazines. Classify the articles, features, or sections of the magazine as serving the aim of self-expression, information, persuasion, or literature. Does a single type of writing tend to dominate each of the magazines you have examined? Some magazines you might consider:

Reader's Digest
Cosmopolitan
Ms.
Playboy
Saturday Evening Post
Life
People
Texas Monthly
The New Yorker
Road & Track

5. Look in a college reader for two or three articles on a controversial subject. Are the articles persuasive or informative or both? Are any portions of the essays self-expressive? Can you imagine the articles being regarded as literature?

6. Make a list of the types of writing you have done in the last several weeks. Include all the species of discourse you have employed and can remember—from a term paper in economics to a grocery list. Classify the writing you typically do under the four headings: informative, persuasive, literary, self-expressive. What purpose does most of your writing have? What type of writing do you do least often or not at all?

Reasons for Writing

Self-Expression

Self-expressive writing can record the intensely private moments of a man or woman alone in thought or the dramatic spectacle of a nation defining itself. It can be an exciting fusion of language and living, what the American poet, Walt Whitman, called a "song of myself":

> I celebrate myself, and sing myself
> And what I assume you shall assume,
> For every atom belonging to me as good belongs to you.
>
> I loafe and invite my soul,
> I lean and loafe at my ease observing a spear of summer grass.
>
> —"Song of Myself"

Occasions for self-expression

It can be an autobiography, a journal, a manifesto, a declaration, an angry remark, a confession, a comment in the margin of a notebook, a statement of policy, a letter that brings to mind favorite people and the circumstances they are involved in:

. . . well, I finally got your bird in my grip (he got tired of flying I think) and transported him inside of a towel screaming and cursing back to his cage. In the process (as I later discovered) I put the cage back together the wrong way, which of course, helped create the next escape episode. Instead of getting the metal tray underneath the plastic one, I got it on top of it, which—as I subsequently figured out—means that whenever the bottom drawer is pulled out it creates a big hole out of which bird escapes. Bird escaped. This time, however, dumb bird showed actual signs of learning. He rushed into covert places and inaccessible corners where I couldn't get him with the towel. At one point I almost had him but he wriggled free and I discovered myself with a giant handful of tail feathers. Yup, got every one. . . . So finally (12:30 A.M.) I lured him out of his dark hiding place by putting on the Brandenburg Concertos. He fell for it and I nabbed him.

—Lynda Boose

Self-expressive discourse captures the writer's self as it evolves emotion-ally, intellectually, and intuitively toward an understanding of its pur-poses and goals, toward a definition of its nature and personality.

The author's voice

In self-expressive writing, we hear the voice, feel the pulse, detect the personality of an author at work, churning over the facts the world presents. Even in writing that is not primarily expressive, we are stirred by feeling that we are in the presence of a lively intelligence capable of shaping our feeling and thoughts into sympathy and judgment:

> What Virgil wrote in the vigour of his age, in plenty and at ease, I have undertaken to translate in my declining years; struggling with wants, oppressed with sickness, curbed in my genius, liable to be misconstrued in all I write; and my judges, if they are not very equitable, already prejudiced against me by the lying character which has been given them of my morals. Yet steady to my principles, and not dispirited with my afflictions, I have, by the blessing of God on my endeavours, overcome all difficulties and, in some measure, acquitted myself of the debt which I owed the public when I undertook this work.
>
> —John Dryden, *Postscript to the Reader* (on his translation of the *Aeneid*), 1697

When we share the deepest thoughts and feelings of an author, the dis-tance between writer and reader diminishes. We feel the writer's person-ality holding a string of ideas together. What would be imperfections in other work can be revealing and significant in self-expression. The prose is not a dye-stamped product. It breathes. We understand Whitman when he exclaims:

> Do I contradict myself?
> Very well then I contradict myself,
> (I am large, I contain multitudes.)

By its very nature, self-expressive discourse can free a writer from the concerns and conventions of an audience. Hence, in journals and diaries—probably the most common forms of self-expression—writers don't have to define terms, juggle transitions, manage clauses, or be certain their concluding sentence follows logically from the sentences that precede it:

> [October 13, 1660] I went out to Charing Cross, to see Major-General Harrison hanged, drawn, and quartered; which was done there, he looking as cheerful as any man could do in that condition. He was presently cut down, and his head and heart shown to the people, at which there was great shouts of joy. It is said that he said that he was sure to come shortly at the right hand of Christ to judge them that now had judged him; and that his wife do expect his coming again. Thus it was my chance to see the King beheaded at Whitehall, and to see the first blood shed in revenge for the King at Charing Cross. Setting up shelves in my study.
>
> —Samuel Pepys, *Diary of Samuel Pepys*

But even though (or perhaps because) self-expressive writing addresses general audiences less consciously and considerately than the more informative and persuasive forms of writing, it can still be very good writing, sometimes the best prose a writer can produce. Under no pressure to be clear, lively, or intriguing, a writer unexpectedly discovers a verbal personality that is all those things: a personal style.

In self-expressive writing, you can be lively. Liveliness follows from a writer's claiming a subject and probing it intensely and economically. The writing is right to the point, sharp as sparks crackling off a log. The author knows what he wants to say and says it. Nothing gets in the way of getting down on the page the words that please the writer. For five lines or fifty, the writer declares independence:

> It seems like all your life people are telling you that there will come a time for this or that & you must work hard and strive for that time. BUNK! I wish just once I had the courage & was calloused enough to turn to the wise elder & say that. I'd like to say—hey! this is a time. This is one of my times. Why do I have to downplay this time for another that may not even come? Sorry I got carried away, but I'd just like to say that I'm having a damn good time right now!

There's no waffling, no mask to cover the frown. Even the punctuation conveys energy.

Self-expression is also splendidly particular. A writer dissecting personal feelings may fall back on conventional expressions and clichés, but more often the general quality is discovered in a real thing or real event. The young woman's "boy trouble" is named Gary or Ward or

Gaylon, not "He." And Gaylon has made life rough because he was seen in the library toying with Mary Alice's curls, not because "young men are not dependable in their interpersonal relationships." Self-expressive writing has the guts and audacity to trust memorable details to say what long explications of feelings cannot. Descriptions may be telegraphic, unsystematic, even ungrammatical, but all's well if the portrait breathes. The writer knows what he writes about:

> The church basement. We're kindergartners. We've never been in these dim places before, hiding forms and figures, strange tableau of angels and saints, a banner held aloft, a manger half-covered with a sheet, boxes of candles, and the sweet-sticky smell of wax. A huge furnace, grim and black, metal pipes branching upward far above our heads, wrapped in thick, soft, yellow fabric. A monster.

Self-expressive writing claims a subject, surrounds it, celebrates it, exhausts it. What in formal prose might be dull and pedantic suddenly bristles with life:

> My father-in-law is the head of the history department in the high school Elizabeth and I went to. He and I sometimes sit around & discuss the meaning of life between belches, burps, and coughs. Plato & Socrates never had it better. We usually end up at odds though because he thinks after death there is *nothing!* I think that you at least are living in spirit in a blade of grass or something. Anything! Just not nothing. He calls me an egomaniac for thinking I'll last forever. I call him a turkey. We burp, belch, and laugh.

Self-expressive writing is unpretentious. It calls a spade a spade, a friend a friend, a fool a fool. When it is self-righteous, it still speaks honestly and openly, without the protective devices that parry blunt assertions in other kinds of prose. It avoids the blankness of jargon and employs clichés with delightful appropriateness. Writers can, of course, paint themselves in false colors in self-expressive passages. And sometimes modesty is dishonest in the face of genuine accomplishment. But real importance shies away from language that is empty or grandly premeditated. Speaking to ourselves, we prefer to speak true and speak direct. And that's not a bad formula for most kinds of writing.

Yet not every bit of self-expression you produce will be vigorous, detailed, and compelling. Just the opposite is true sometimes. But at least you are writing, gaining a feel for the way words fit together, practicing the hard job of putting thoughts onto a page. And all the while you are learning to satisfy a tough, hypercritical audience you know like the back of your hand: yourself. Self-expressive writing is satisfying in its own right, a way of escaping the constraints of more formal prose. Yet the virtues of self-expressive discourse (liveliness, specificity, direct-

Self-expression and informative and persuasive writing

ness) belong in persuasive and informative writing too. The strengths you develop in one area will carry over to the others.

Can writing in the other "aims," the informative and the persuasive, be as lively, particular, uninhibited, and unpretentious as self-expressive discourse? In most cases, no. But almost all of us have shared an experience that demonstrates how surprisingly powerful the intuitive qualities of expressive writing can be when applied (even unintentionally) to another kind of writing. In one class or another, we've all turned in a hastily composed paper that ends up getting a higher grade than essays we've labored over for days. The scenario goes something like this:

All-nighters

It's midnight and "The Significance of Marriage Customs in Western African Cultures of the Nineteenth Century," due at 9 A.M., exists only in title, some notes scattered atop the desk, and a clutter of books shoved under the bed. Better get to work. Your roommate snores, the coffee percolates, and you recall your last grade report. Hurried reading is followed by even more headlong writing. You write, rewrite, crumple up pad after pad, chew the pencil. Finally, a paper greets the dawn's early light and you slink off to class, half-dozing, leaving your whistling roommate to calisthenics and discourses on the pleasures of sound sleep. When the teacher demands the assignment, you sheepishly proffer your all-night labor and watch as it rolls toward the front of the room, sandwiched between essays a tablet thick, typed in carbon ribbon on 20-weight paper, bound in folders, and illustrated in gilt. You resign your humble enterprise to a *C*, admit the possibility of a *D,* and sigh. A week later the papers are back and—surprise—an *A!* And the professor's comment: "Your best work all semester. Clear. Detailed handling of the subject. Authoritative tone. Keep up the good work."

What happened? Is there no justice? Or are you simply a genius? Most students in this situation conclude quickly that teachers are incompetent judges of written work or that the assessment of writing is capricious and arbitrary. We'd like to believe that grades are assigned in proportion to work done. How then can an essay produced in the heat of the night under a caffeine overdose be any good?

Sometimes it isn't. But when it is, it's usually because the press of circumstances has forced a writer to rely on his best, most natural language resources. There's no time to fiddle with pompous phrasing, to toy with digressions, to waffle, to pad, to moon over every objection a reader can make. What matters in the night is getting the project done, and that entails writing, writing, writing—and thinking about writing. For three, four, five hours you are engaged totally by a subject and by language. You hear yourself thinking out problems rapidly, finding words to fit ideas. You eliminate excess, keying in on the best examples, the most pertinent figures. You are tough on yourself. You watch the clock and set goals: three pages by 2:00 A.M., another three by 4:30. Every word works. Every thought sets another into motion. The whole experience—sometimes—is exhilarating, spoiled only by your doubts that anything composed in haste cannot be good.

If you find that all-nighters turn out better essays for you than more systematic day labor, that following such a scheme of procrastination and midnight oil consistently produces better work than calmer, more systematic writing, you should not resign yourself to endless, madding nights of Maxwell House and snoring roommates. Or if self-expressive efforts in your journal provoke your teacher to remark that "your best writing is in these pages" or "why can't you write like this in your graded assignments?" you should not conclude that you just weren't born to inform or persuade. In both circumstances, you need to build on the strengths your self-expressive efforts prove you have. If formal writing makes you stiff, pretentious, wordy, or abstract, relax. Allow your essays to display some of the spontaneity of your less-prepared work. Be yourself. Be confident.

In different ways, all-nighters and self-expression remove the fears that often restrict composing to what's safe and dull. But not everyone writes well under pressure. Not everyone writes well in a journal. Hence not everyone can expect to find that his writing improves when a nod or smile conveyed in language stamps a piece of writing "my own." Nor does a writer want to allow the personal voice to interrupt too often in informative or persuasive writing, to intrude too much where, like a noisy child, it doesn't belong. **When the personal voice intrudes**

Where doesn't the personal voice belong? Wherever the intrusion of a human presence adds little to the explanation of a subject. That's a formidable generalization. What it means is that you must evaluate what happens when you begin communicating directly with the reader. Does the reader understand the subject better, is he more forcefully persuaded by the reminder that a real, breathing person has sometime, somewhere held these opinions, discovered these facts, decided upon this language? Or is your appearance in the subject a self-indulgent performance that takes a reader off course?

It is tempting—and easy—to be chatty in prose, to explain every opinion in a parenthetical clause that draws attention to the writer's cleverness. But in writing that is not by its primary aim self-expressive, the human voice, when it is heard, should speak for an intelligent mind examining, evaluating, thinking, cajoling, explaining, criticizing. It may be a mediating presence, the referee who sets down the rules: **The personal voice used effectively**

> I'm aware that I sound like a curmudgeon. But I have accepted what most educators can't seem to face. The function of schools is not to probe tender psyches, not to feed and clothe the homeless, not to be the papa and mama a kid never had. The function is to teach.

And the teacher's job is to know his or her subject, and convey it. Period. Remember Miss Dinwiddie, who could recite 40 lines of the *Aeneid* at a clip? Or Mr. Wassleheimer, who could give a zero to a cheater without pausing in his lecture on frogs? They were the teachers we despised, and later admired.

I want them back, those fearsome, awe-inspiring experts. I want them back because they knew what school was for. They were hard, even at times unjust. But when they were through, we knew those multiplication tables blindfolded.

—Suzanne Britt Jordan, "I Wants to Go to the Prose"

Or it may be a guide, thoughtfully providing directions:

In these pages, however, I have no intention of providing a systematic treatise on the critical examination of evidence; there are several good books on the subject, most of them written by and for professional historians. . . . Instead of a set of rules, I shall simply offer a selection of case histories and instances, small and medium-sized, which will suggest the variety of misinformation that lurks in the data we receive from our predecessors. In the end you will, I think, have a sense of the spirit of vigilance and skepticism that presides over every good scholar's desk.

—Richard D. Altick, *The Art of Literary Research*

Or the frank, humane respondent to a difficult situation:

It may be a humbling experience for the teacher to reveal his writing difficulty to his students. I know. As a professional writer I have gone into the high school classroom and done assignments, and I did not perform as well as some students in the class. The students were disappointed, not elated, when they found this out. Another myth was destroyed.

—Donald M. Murray, *A Writer Teaches Writing*

Toughness

There's toughness in much personal writing. Not brutality, but the toughness signalled by honesty, vigor, economy, wisdom, and authority. Intelligent readers don't like whining, frivolity, banality, or parades of excuses. They like the toughness of real sympathy, the toughness of the truth, the clarity of an unpopular opinion voiced bravely behind a prominent first person: *I, we.*

In its pure state, self-expression can be whining, doubting, outrageous, incoherent. But it tends more often to be bold in the best sorts of ways, in ways that transfer effectively to other kinds of writing. Here, for example, is an informative piece of prose that becomes a song of self, a self-expressive declaration of purpose and independence. The essay has faults: some irritating repetitions (school, travel), a comma splice in the second paragraph. But they seem insignificant when compared against the picture of the carpenter enjoying his labor. We feel good for the person who has made this bold declaration:

> Unlike many of the students going to school here at the University of Texas in Austin, I know exactly what I want to make out of myself in life. I'm going to be one of the world's best carpenters. My school career is coming to an end. I'm giving up all this senseless school work that has been upsetting me for the last few months.
>
> I will find a place next to my old friends in a free and easy life, easy on my nerves, tough in other respects. I will be the strong, dark-skinned carpenter cutting his rafters in the hot sun, my saw screaming, my helpers nailing the wood together, impressing the inspector who watches, trying to find mistakes. I will drive up to the job site, attracting all the carpenters on the street, my new four wheel drive pickup will back up to my frame package, the wheels tall and wide, the paint clean and shining. I'll travel to Mexico just for fun whenever I feel like it. After I save up enough money I'm going to travel all over the states, stopping whenever I find a place I think is beautiful, build a few houses, see the land and the lakes, and move on when I get the urge.

Invention for Self-Expressive Writing

Thus, great with child to speak, and helpless in my throes,
Biting my truant pen, beating myself for spite:
"Fool," said my Muse to me, "look in thy heart, and write!"

—Sir Philip Sidney, "Astrophel and Stella"

For some writers in some situations, the advice of Sir Philip Sidney's muse is enough to get an essay rolling. For other writers, the process of writing itself generates ideas; the formulating of a main idea leads to more specific topics that can be further amplified by details and examples, which in turn suggest qualifications of the main idea, which lead to still other thoughts in need of amplifying and qualifying—and so on to the conclusion of the essay. But writers cannot always count on intuitions or serendipity to uncover subject matter or to suggest lines of argument for them. Sometimes you must be more systematic in approaching, developing, and inventing ideas.

Invention

We are accustomed to seeing the word *invention* used to describe clever implements or devices concocted by ingenious men or women to solve problems. In this sense, Thomas Edison was a master of invention. But the term *invention* has an honorable history that much predates its contemporary technological connotations. In classical rhetoric, invention was the process of discovering the best evidence and arguments available to support a case. In some situations, ideas would be supported by the gathering of what we could call evidence: facts, figures, testimony of witnesses, authorities, and laws. In other cases, arguments would be developed or discovered by examining certain fundamental relationships between things and ideas: substance, quantity, relation, place, time, etc. These relationships were called *topoi* or *topics*. The writer with an idea would study it by applying the various topics to it.

Devices that help a writer to explore an idea are called aids to invention. At first glance, you might think that self-expressive writing would need no outside stimuli. "Look in thy heart and write" would seem the right advice when filling a journal, writing a letter, or stating the goals of a group to which you belong. Yet at times, writing about ourselves can be the most difficult enterprise of all. We are so close to, so aware of our subject that there seems little left to say. The result is a blank page. To write self-expressively, we need to learn how to think about ourselves and the world around us.

But self-expressive discourse is more than writing about the self. Sometimes it links personal insights to the eventual examination of those thoughts in expository and persuasive writing. Archimedes' "Eureka!" was a burst of self-expression at the moment he discovered the principle of displacement. Great ideas may begin with just such random thoughts waiting to be captured and amplified into concepts, theses, and ideas. Much writing that ends up as information or persuasion may have begun as self-expression.

The first aid to self-expressive writing is an amazingly obvious one.

Thinking

Thinking is unpredictable. Sometimes our minds focus on big issues and we try to solve the problems of the world. At other times we're drawn to simple things: a crack in a wall, a spider's motion in weaving its web. When we feel obligated to think seriously about problems, we call what we do then concentrating, or cogitating, or brainstorming. We try to follow some logical or systematic path from point *A* to point *B*. And often, our brainstorms raise only dust. Then, while we are washing the car or chopping firewood, the concept we were seeking arrives unannounced and unexpected. Eureka! We've found it.

When we aren't concentrating, we may do our best thinking flat on a bed or reclining against a tree. Music may provoke images, the images memories, and the memories ideas. Writing then follows. Simple physical activities, especially walking, can stimulate thinking; parts of this text were conceived on a jogging trail and in a weight room. When our bodies are placidly, repetitively, or predictably occupied, our minds are free to play and speculate, to mull over the events and details from which we derive concepts. When daydreaming, you may actually be preparing to write.

Self-expressive thinking and writing often operate associatively. A word, phrase, person, or locale leads us to think about some related word or concept. The connection may be logical and causal, emotional and personal, or unpredictable and irrational. And the free association may form a thought and provide the subject matter for a paragraph or an essay. A writer engaged in self-expression welcomes the thought that seems to come from nowhere.

The Senses

The senses can be gateways to experience and composition. A writer, particularly one interested in narration and description, benefits from attention given to the vibrations of the physical world. The focus on fine detail, the precise reconstruction in language of a taste, a smell, a touch can lead you into discoveries about the likenesses and differences between objects.

Sight:

What do I see? Exactly? How does that perception change with time or point of view? What have I seen that is like this? How much do I value what I see now? How can I recreate this scene in words?

Smell:

What's that smell? With what do I associate it? How does the smell alter with time? What does the smell resemble? Do I like the aroma? Why or why not? Can I recreate this smell in words?

Taste:

How would I describe this taste? What physical images does the taste create in my mind? How does the taste develop or change? To what can I compare the taste? Another taste? A smell? Why do I like this flavor? How can I recreate this sensation?

Hearing:

How would I describe the feeling, the rhythm, the volume, the pitch of this sound, those voices, these instruments? How do the sounds change as my position alters? How does the music I like change as I grow older? What have I heard like this before? What visual images does this sound raise in me? Why do I find this sound pleasant, that one irritating? How can I recreate the sound in words?

Touch:

> What is the impression of touching? What do I feel? How does the feeling change? Develop? What is the source of the touch? Where do I feel it? What does it feel like? Do I like this texture, that feeling? How can I recreate this feeling in words?

Decompartmentalizing

Probably as a means of protecting our sanity, many of us compartmentalize our lives, separating our "job" from our "free time," our professional lives from our families, our thoughts and ideas from our beliefs and activities. But we can become so adept at erecting walls between the various aspects of our lives that we rarely risk seeing things as they might fit together.

Students are notorious compartmentalizers. The very way colleges and courses are organized encourages separations between life and learning. Philosophical ideas belong in one department, literature in another, business-engineering in a third. And in all these separate departments are still more divisions and schisms.

Try, occasionally, to break down the walls in your life. Consciously examine what you are doing in your anthropology course in light of what you just learned in economics. Explore and strengthen whatever connections you can find between your favorite past times and your least favorite endeavors. How does that movie you watched fit into the larger pattern of your intellectual life? What routines do you follow faithfully? What rituals? How do all the things you do fit together? Should they? You may want to make a diagram of your most rigid compartments and then—in journal entries—try to break down some of the walls between them:

Sociology course	Math course	Cycling	Monday night football
Writing to friends	Religious beliefs	Home	Dinner with friends
Planning a career	English class	What's his/her name	Politics
Racquetball	Volunteer work	French class	Sex

Past, Present, and Future

Confronted by the task of writing a letter or a journal entry, we sometimes wonder what we can say about ourselves. Our thoughts may be scattered, unfocused, uninteresting, unsatisfying; our senses dull and unresponding. It is time, perhaps, for some personal assessment. We can ask questions about our past, present, and future to stimulate thought and composing.

Past:

What made me the way I am?
What do I remember about age six? Eight? Ten?
How did I learn to make choices about morals? About people?
  About values?
How did my parents put up with me?
How have my children developed and grown?

Present:

Why do I feel nervous so often?
Why does writing make me feel uncomfortable?
What do I seem like to my friends?
How can I acquire a better appreciation of history?
What can I do to reduce my expenses?

Future:

Why do I want to be a lawyer?
Where do I want to raise a family?
What am I looking for in a spouse? Shall I marry at all?
How will I define *success* in ten years? In twenty?

For Discussion

1. Reconsider this textbook from a self-expressive point of view. Does the first person *(I)* viewpoint in the introductory chapter represent an unwarranted intrusion into an informative discourse (a textbook), or is it a legitimate use of the personal voice? Can you tell anything about the author's interests from his choice of examples throughout the text?

Exercises

2. Have you ever had an experience with an all-nighter similar to the one described in this chapter? What kind of essay did you produce? Was it successful? In what sense? Write a short narrative about the all-nighter and evaluate the writing you produced.

3. Read the journals kept by published authors and famous people: Caesar's *Commentaries,* the diaries of Samuel Sewall, Samuel Pepys, John Evelyn, Dorothy Wordsworth, Anaïs Nin, the journals or notebooks of Emerson, Thoreau, May Sarton, Woody Allen. What are

their typical subjects? How long are their entries? How regular? Why do you think the diary or journal was kept? Was it written to be read by someone other than the author? How can you tell?

4. If you doodle habitually, select some representative examples of your art and analyze them. What do they say about you—or the circumstances that prompted you to produce them? Can you classify the features that characterize your work? Do your doodles reveal a passion for order? Do you tend to sketch familiar objects, or do you create a geometric universe? Keep the analysis short and personal.

5. Immediately after reading a book, seeing a film, watching a play, or attending a concert, record your reactions. Take a notebook with you to the event if that's convenient. Later, turn these immediate reactions into several paragraphs of commentary.

Writing Assignments

6. Try your hand at keeping a journal, filling it daily with the stream of your thoughts, recording in it battles and confrontations, discoveries and pleasures, dreams and speculations. Talk to yourself about your goals, the people you meet, the surroundings you endure, the expectations placed upon you. Dwell on the little things—the shape of your dog's spots, the habit your roommate has of sharpening pencils to needle points, the labor of a spider to rebuild a destroyed lair. Take the whole world for your subject, the large and the small. Speculate on the nature of being or the eccentric character of your landlady. How do turtles make love? Who is your favorite comedian? What would it be like if you weren't male? Female? Black? White? What is your earliest memory? Why do you jog?

After a month or so, review your journal entries. Which please you? Which don't? What subjects did you write on most often? How often are your feelings the subjects of the entries? What language devices do you enjoy using when you aren't under pressure? What sentences strike you as clever or memorable?

Read a paragraph of your journal back to back with a formal, academic assignment. How do they differ? Which sounds more like you?

7. Turn a journal entry into a more formal piece of writing. What kinds of changes must you make? Must you compromise the directness and vigor of your original expression? How do the changes alter the original? For the better or worse?

5

Reasons for Writing

Informing, Demonstrating, Exploring; The Research Paper

When you write with an informative aim, you usually present facts and information, demonstrate assertions, or explore new ideas.

Informing

The class of writing that presents facts and information includes some of the most familiar and practical kinds of language, everything from office memos and census forms to news articles and encyclopedia entries, from the instructions for building a cabinet to a dissertation on economics, from notes and summaries you prepare during a lecture to the essay exam you take after it, from a résumé you send a potential employer to the term paper that completes your degree requirements. It is not easy to generalize about the appropriate content, structure, and style of all these particular ways of conveying information since they will vary according to time, place, and discipline.

Summaries

In preparing a summary, for example, you may choose one of several forms. A simple type of summary extracts a main idea from each major part of the piece being abstracted, moving narratively through it from beginning to end. A summary of this type of Lincoln's Gettysburg Address might look like this:

1st point   Lincoln opens his Gettysburg Address by reminding his audience of the nation's founding eighty-seven years earlier on the principle that "all men are created equal." The civil

2nd point   war yet raging, Lincoln notes the fitness of dedicating a battlefield "as a final resting place" for those that defended

3rd point   the nation and the principle. Yet the battlefield has already been consecrated by the dead. It is for the living, says

4th point   Lincoln, to see "that government of the people, by the people, for the people, shall not perish from the earth."

Or perhaps you need to be more analytical. Rather than retracing the sequential movement of your subject piece, you look for the major points and the significant supporting details. Such summaries tend to be classificatory:

Major point   In the Gettysburg Address, Lincoln champions principles of equality and democracy. He offers these principles as the

Supporting   rationale for dedicating the battlefield at Gettysburg, for
details   justifying the past sacrifices of the Union dead, and for the continuing efforts of the living.

Or perhaps you are taking notes for an exam or gathering material for a paper. In such cases, you will want to highlight important facts, examples, and conclusions. A full chapter or section of a book might be summarized in a paragraph; nine pages of *England in the Nineteenth Century* (*The Pelican History of England:* 8), for example, can be reduced to this single passage by extracting the major ideas from individual paragraphs or pages:

Ch. 1 *Britain in 1815,* "The Social Scene," pp. 11–19.

England's population of *13,000,000* in *1815* would double by *1871* (p. 11). Cities grew dramatically as British industries developed in cotton textiles, wool, iron, coal, and engineering (p. 13). Yet about *half* the population still worked the farms which were fertile, well-tended, and profitable. There was much rural poverty, as social critic *William Cobbett* pointed out (pp. 14–15). Cobbett constantly blamed rural poverty on a new breed of *landed gentry* interested primarily in profit, not in the land or its workers (pp. 14–15). While the *Napoleonic Wars* had driven up corn prices to the benefit of the gentry, the laboring and manufacturing classes were driven to poor relief under the *Speenhamland* system (p. 15). Small farms survived, but their numbers steadily declined after 1832.

The working classes faced a strict legal system and stricter punishments that included transportation for life and capital punishment for 220 offenses (p. 18). But in the century there was a softening of the laws. Social conditions in the city of London varied from the "sweated labour and cellar dwellings" of the poorer classes to the foppish behavior of the *Regency dandies* enjoying their fashions, hobby horses, novels, and prize fights (p. 19).

Which approach you take to summarizing information will be determined by the type of work you are condensing and the use you will make of the summary.

Similarly, an assigned book report may require no more from you than a compilation of material facts about the work: title, author, date of publication, summary of contents. Or it may require a more active analysis: an evaluation. When informative writing follows from rigid or particular conventions, you want to be sure to get the instructions right so that your work will conform to your reader's (or teacher's or boss') expectations in choice of subject, arrangement, and format.

Thesis Statement

When you are asked to provide information on rather general subjects, as frequently happens in academic situations, you may have more leeway in choosing and focusing on a topic than you would, for example, preparing a budget analysis for a corporation. But deciding on a subject and coming up with a *thesis statement* that directs your approach to the subject is no simple matter. You cannot simply decide to write about England in the nineteenth century, American political parties, nuclear reactors, or Gothic architecture. These are all subject areas that hold potential, but they are far from being thesis statements that can guide a short essay.

In informative writing, a thesis statement is a sentence that indicates precisely to the reader what aspects of a subject you intend to treat. The thesis sometimes will explain how you intend to treat the subject, to divide it, or to limit it.

What a thesis statement does

There are a variety of methods of finding a thesis. Some writers like to start with a general idea and gradually add limitations and qualifications until the subject is sufficiently narrow to begin research:

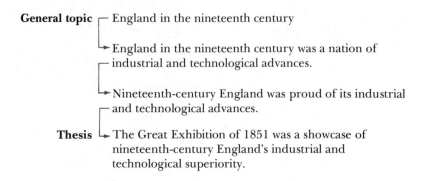

General topic — England in the nineteenth century

England in the nineteenth century was a nation of industrial and technological advances.

Nineteenth-century England was proud of its industrial and technological advances.

Thesis — The Great Exhibition of 1851 was a showcase of nineteenth-century England's industrial and technological superiority.

But this method (discussed in detail at the end of chapter seven) presumes that a writer knows a great deal about a subject to begin with.

Finding a thesis

When, as often happens, you face an area of knowledge new to you, you may not know enough about it initially to ask the right questions—ones that will lead to a thesis statement. In such a circumstance, you can do two things. First, you can gain an overview of your subject by reading a general description of it in an encyclopedia or other appropriate reference work. (Up-to-date subjects may not have made it into an encyclopedia; you may have to read periodicals and journals.) Then you can examine your subject with the assistance of a *system of invention.* Both library research and systems of invention are discussed in more detail in the section entitled "Invention for Informative Writing" later in this chapter.

Using the modes to shape a thesis

Once you have a general idea of what aspect of a subject you intend to treat, you can begin thinking about how to present it clearly, accurately, and appropriately. The modes can help you in shaping a thesis that serves your particular informative aims.

If, for example, you want to explain what Gothic architecture looks like, you might formulate a thesis statement in the descriptive mode. It would indicate the dominant features of Gothic architecture:

Descriptive mode (characteristics) — Gothic architecture

Gothic architecture is characterized by its ribbed vaults, pointed arches, stained-glass windows, lofty pinnacles, and flying buttresses.

This simple thesis sentence commits you to a discussion of each of the features mentioned *in the order mentioned:*

Thesis: Gothic architecture is characterized by

1. ribbed vaults,

2. pointed arches,
3. stained-glass windows,
4. lofty pinnacles, and
5. flying buttresses.

Yet even though the proposed informative essay is predominantly descriptive, you may want to briefly explain what Gothic architecture is before examining its particular features. Other parts of a rapidly developing outline can be filled in:

Working title The Characteristics of Gothic Architecture
    A.   Introduction
        1.   What Gothic architecture is
        2.   When and where it flourished
Thesis   3.   *Thesis:* Gothic architecture is characterized by
    B.   Ribbed vaults
        1.   Form
        2.   Function
    C.   Pointed arches
        1.   Form
Points of   2.   Function
development D.   Stained-glass windows
        1.   Form
        2.   Function
    E.   Lofty pinnacles
        1.   Form
        2.   Function
    F.   Flying buttresses
        1.   Form
        2.   Function

If your reader needs to know the history of Gothic development, your thesis will reflect the narrative mode as it explains how and why the style grew:

Topic Gothic architecture

Draft Gothic architecture grew out of the prevailing Romanesque style
statements of European architecture then dominating in the 12th century. Strongly influenced by Norman architecture the Gothic building first appeared in Ile-de-France, then quickly spread over the rest of Europe. It was the dominant style for 400 years.

Thesis From its initial appearance in Ile-de-France during the 12th century, Gothic architecture rapidly spread to England,
Narrative Germany, and Spain to become the dominant style for 400
mode years.

Here, the example shows how a single thesis statement can be drawn from several related ideas. The final thesis commits you to examining the spread of Gothic architecture over the European continent during a 400-year period. The subject is still huge. Subsequent reading may convince you to deal with the development of Gothic architecture in one country only.

Thesis statements may also be derived from the remaining modes and their variants, depending upon your readers' needs and your interests:

Classificatory mode (major styles) The major styles of Gothic architecture are the high, the rayonnant, the flamboyant, the decorated, and the perpendicular.

In this classificatory thesis statement, the general architectural style is broken into the major substyles named by historians of architecture:

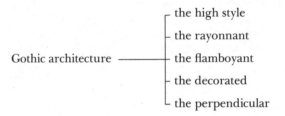

Gothic architecture
- the high style
- the rayonnant
- the flamboyant
- the decorated
- the perpendicular

A thesis statement this well informed can come only after some particular research. That may be the case with the following example as well, a thesis that combines comparison/contrast and the evaluative mode:

Evaluative mode (major achievement) The major achievement of the Gothic style was to supersede the dark, fortress-like Romanesque style with an architecture capable of creating buildings with vast, well-lit spaces and dynamic, vertical structures.

The thesis statement in informative writing helps the writer to discover what to say about a subject and how to control it. For the reader, the thesis is a concise preface to the information contained in the subsequent report.

The Components of a Report

Opening paragraphs
The opening paragraph may be the most important part of a report because it contains the thesis and important background information. When the full paper will be short, the first paragraph ought to spell

out the topic and the order of development and—at the same time—snare a reader's attention. In a longer report, several paragraphs may share introductory responsibilities. In any case, don't dawdle. The pace of exposition should be rapid:

Background   The Greek defense of Eastern European civilization against the Persian armies of Xerxes has traditionally been portrayed as a David VS Goliath struggle. Vastly outnumbered, the Greeks yet managed to thwart Xerxes' effort to annex their homeland to his already sprawling empire in the fifth century B.C. How did 110,000 Greeks repulse a reported 1,700,000 Persians? *An*

Thesis   *analysis of the four major battles of the war—Thermopylae, Artemision, Salamis, and Plataia—shows that the Greeks enjoyed better weapons, morale, strategy, and luck.*

The remainder of this essay would expand upon the thesis, answering the question that probably snared the reader's attention: "How did 110,000 Greeks repulse a reported 1,700,000 Persians?" If the report is thorough or the subject complicated, additional background material would have to be provided to set the major facts and events in an appropriate context. Here the context would be historical and the mode, consequently, narrative:

Background material

> In 490 B.C., the Persian monarch, Darius, launched an invasion of the Greek mainland to put an end to an irritating Greek influence in the Aegean area, but his forces suffered a humiliating defeat at Marathon (490 B.C.). Enraged, Darius plotted a full scale invasion. . . .

Then the sequence of the battles would be chronicled, one by one, in sufficient detail to explain the strategies of the opposing forces:

The body of a report

> For days, neither fleet would take the initiative to battle in the narrows but when the Greek navy faked a retreat, the Persians attacked to prevent its escape and fell into a trap. They were drawn steadily into the narrows while the Greek ships backed water. The long lines of Persian triremes were squeezed so that maneuvering became nearly impossible—and still the Greek ships continued to back off. Suddenly, a swell rolled through the narrow channel as it did every morning. The Greeks expected it; the Persian pilots did not. The swell threw the Persian formations into confusion, and then the Greeks attacked. . . .

Yet even vivid accounts of the battles might not, in themselves, adequately answer the question in the opening paragraph. Additional paragraphs of classification and evaluation might be required:

Classification   Persian triremes were constructed for speed and built high for the positioning of archers. Greek ships (which numbered approximately 400) were low and stoutly built to withstand the ramming techniques favored by Greek sailors. Unlike the Persians, Greeks preferred to board enemy ships and engage in hand-to-hand combat.

Evaluation   A second problem Xerxes faced stemmed from the composition of his army. Aside from the Persian contingents and the elite Immortals, most of Xerxes' grand army consisted of conscripts from various conquered parts of his empire. As C. Hignett observes, "unwilling subjects would not make good soldiers or sailors."

The conclusion
When all the battles have been reported and analyzed and all the significant material facts studied, the author is prepared to conclude with a list of those factors which most adequately explain the surprising successes of the Greek forces. The summary and conclusion follow easily and naturally from the body of the essay. They tend to classify and evaluate:

> That the Greeks had been able to thwart Xerxes' designs on their homeland is attributable to footsoldiers better armed and armored than their Persian counterparts, to Persian strategies which consistently failed to take advantage of superior numbers, to Greek strategies that capitalized on the terrain and conditions of battle, to the better morale of the Greek armies, and finally, to luck. With the advantage of hindsight, the Greeks in 480 might have considered their victory inevitable instead of impossible.

The complete version of this research report appears in the section on the research paper later in this chapter.

Sources for Reports

The information in reports and research papers is usually borrowed from a wide range of reference materials and secondary sources: books, magazines, newspapers, dictionaries, almanacs, bibliographies, and encyclopedias.

Some writers treat source materials uncritically, assuming that whatever gets into print must be reputable. It isn't so. When investigating a subject, you can make judgments about the quality of your sources. Within reason, you should try to learn as much as you can about the reliability of information you are borrowing.

Evaluating sources
How can you decide whether that book on the shelf, that microfilmed newspaper, and that battered magazine are reputable sources? With books and articles, you can begin with an author's credentials and reputation. Have you encountered the author's name in preliminary

readings? Has she been cited in bibliographies? Do her educational credentials fit the work she has written? In many cases, you won't have easy access to this information. But when you do, you can make some important assumptions and judgments.

Consider, too, the date of publication of your source. An old book is not necessarily an outdated book. But be sure to check (in a library card catalog) that you are using the latest edition. Or consider whether recent events, discoveries, or scholarship has put limits on what the older book can now tell you.

Dates of publication

Consider the publisher. Academic publishers (presses affiliated with universities) specialize in academic pieces, carefully researched and documented. Many commercial firms have equally high standards. Some publishers specialize in particular fields or particular kinds of books. In these areas, they are likely to be especially competent. Other publishers are interested in popular literature, in preparing simplified explanations of more complex materials. Their books distill the more detailed and firsthand efforts of other writers and publishers to make them available to a wider, less-specialized readership. In most cases, you will want to avoid citing such "popularizations" when more substantial materials are available.

Publishers

How thoroughly a source is documented may indicate something about its reliability. Not all facts and information need to be documented. News articles, features, reviews, and texts generally avoid a detailed citation of sources. But other kinds of informative discourse should make it possible—within reason again—for a reader to check upon sources, to retrace the steps that led an author to new knowledge. Documentation also tells a reader where more detailed information on a particular aspect of a subject may be found.

Documentation

When using a book, check its index. The index—especially one prepared by the author himself—can indicate how thoroughly a book treats a subject and how careful the author is. A secondary source that lacks an index can be almost useless to a researcher. On the other hand, not every type of resource can be easily indexed.

Index

When dealing with magazines and newspapers, check their circulation. Numbers alone don't make a reputation. But a large circulation usually indicates that many people regard the source as important and reliable. When you are trying to establish the feelings or opinions of groups or factions, large circulation publications can provide insights into public tastes and morals.

Circulation

The audience of periodicals and newspapers is also one criteria by which to evaluate their reliability and usefulness. The more "popular" a publication is, the less likely it is to explain all the complications or details in any given situation. Truly new ideas generally make their first appearances in works aimed at specialists. Gradually the information passes on to more popular sources. Thus a magazine like *Popular Science*

Audience

may carry articles on the potential uses of nuclear fusion, but the ideas themselves will have originated in scientific journals too technical for the average reader. Medical innovations discussed in *Time* may have first appeared in the *New England Journal of Medicine*. In general, you should rely on the most specialized source of information you can handle intelligently.

Coverage

When assessing a source, consider its depth of coverage. In many research situations, the more thorough the better. A newspaper covered by long dark columns of print may seem less inviting than one ornamented with pictures, boxes, and white space. But chances are good it will tell you more about any given event than its gaudier (or more stylish) competitor. The same may be true of magazines.

Primary and secondary sources

Consider how close the source you are evaluating comes to the subject itself. Sometimes a work may be of such substantial reputation that it becomes, itself, the topic of other studies. It is a primary source, a classic statement, a major article, a critical landmark. Other works make no pretense of examining primary materials or of advancing the commentary on such materials. Such summary works can be extraordinarily useful to you—encyclopedias fall into this category. But depending upon them too heavily and too often may cut you off from more formidable sources responsible for changes in ideas and perceptions.

Librarians

Finally, in determining the quality of a source of information, don't ignore librarians. Ask for their advice, especially when working with reference materials (encyclopedias, dictionaries, handbooks, bibliographies, catalogs, etc.). Because librarians work with books every day, they know what books have served users well in the past. And it's their job to help. Take advantage of the knowledge librarians have. They are resources too.

Documentation

Common knowledge

When you borrow information from a source, you must credit it unless the facts or ideas you cite are "common knowledge." When several different sources provide you with the same facts, figures, or ideas, you may assume that those facts, figures, or ideas are common knowledge within the field even though they may be new to you. Yet even in such cases, it may be advisable to identify a source for the sake of a reader who might want to follow up on your information.

When to quote

You must credit sources for borrowed material *even when you do not quote directly or word for word.* When you do quote directly, it should be because the citation is a classic statement of the point under discussion, a famous comment on it, a useful starting point for discussion, a controversial statement, a useful summary of facts and ideas, or an authoritative support for your assertion. You should not quote material to add to the length of your text or to avoid putting an idea or concept into your own words.

In this paragraph, for example, the sentence in quotations adds little in the way of support or information:

> Chimpanzees have long memories, a sign of mental process. In tests conducted by Robert M. Yerkes, a chimp would watch a trainer bury food and then be brought back to the same area four days later. The chimp would then locate the food, dig it up, and eat it. An experiment by Earnest Hooton suggests that chimps can also remember faces. *"I have recorded the chimpanzee's ability to recognize persons . . . over periods of several months or even longer,"* Hooton reports.[3] The chimpanzee's ability to remember simple tasks and stunts makes him the popular choice for circus acts the world over.
>
> [3]Earnest Hooton, *Man's Poor Relations* (New York: Doubleday, 1942), p. 55.

A revised version would retain the citation to *Man's Poor Relations*, but avoid the direct use of Hooton's language:

> . . . Experiments by Earnest Hooton suggest that chimps have the ability to remember faces for months or longer.[3]

A source is quoted directly to better effect in the following passage. Note especially the phrase introducing the quotation. Most matter directly quoted should be introduced by a phrase of explanation:

> Are chimps intelligent enough to communicate with humans? In dozens of cases, chimpanzees have been taught to form and utter simple words. In one case, a pet chimp named Vicki was taught, in a few days, to say *mama* whenever touched by her trainer. But though Vicki could say the word when prompted by her trainer, she had no idea what the word meant. Spoken language is not part of the chimp's natural endowment. As Dr. Philip Lieberman explains in his book, *The Speech of Primates,* "the ability to talk depends on our having a mouth, tongue, larynx, and pharynx that are adapted towards speech production."[2]

It is hard to underestimate the importance of introducing or identifying quoted material. Your readers should always know when you are about to present material borrowed from a source. Many tag lines are available to you:

Introducing quoted material

> As Dr. Curie observed, " . . .
>
> Yet a noted critic suggests that " . . .
>
> In *Shakespeare's Patterns of Self-Knowledge,* Dr. Soellner points out that " . . .

Nelson Rockefeller, vice-president during the Ford administration, once remarked " . . .

In all cases, remember that the introductory or explanatory phrase and the quotation itself must form a complete, grammatical sentence:

And yet if, as Edgar Allan Poe believed, "perverseness is one of the primitive impulses of the human heart," then perhaps we should expect violence and vandalism in even the most affluent neighborhoods.

Sometimes a quote may have to be shortened or modified to fit a particular context. Ellipses (. . .) indicate words left out:

The President claimed that "despite the increases we see now in domestic raw material prices . . . the rate of inflation will slow by the end of the year."

Words or phrases not part of the original expression appear between square brackets:

Swift's irony is apparent when Gulliver comments that "he [the emperor of Lilliput] is taller by almost the breadth of my nail, than any of his court, which alone is enough to strike an awe into the beholders."

To acknowledge that an obvious error in the quotation is not your own but the work of the original author, you can follow the error with the expression *sic* in brackets:

The student reported that she had taken "four years of excellerated [*sic*] English" in high school.

Since the formalities of documentation and footnoting vary from field to field, you may need to find out which system to use in any report that requires citations. The research paper in the last section of this chapter follows the *MLA Handbook for Writers of Research Papers, Theses, and Dissertations;* these Modern Language Association guidelines are followed in the humanities. But the sciences often employ simpler systems of documentation.

Two guidelines

In handling citations, two general guidelines are worth remembering. First, don't be intimidated. Footnotes and other types of documentation serve the practical purpose of acknowledging your sources. These references indicate that you have done your work. They give support to assertions. They tell a reader where to go for more information. While tedious to assemble and type, footnotes do matter.

Secondly, use common sense in citing sources. A four-page report with forty notes is as wrongheaded as a forty-page essay with four. Document those portions of an essay that you borrowed directly (quotations) or indirectly (ideas, concepts, terms). If an entire paragraph in your essay follows from what you read in a book or article, place a note at the end of the paragraph, not after every sentence. Combine notes whenever you can. Don't be reluctant to write brief explanations in your notes where they are needed and appropriate, but don't distract your reader from your text unnecessarily.

1. Take the editorial page from a daily newspaper (preferably a large metropolitan one) and prepare analytical summaries of the editorials, identifying the major point or argument in each piece and the major supporting arguments or details. Then prepare chronological or narrative summaries of all the letters to the editor. These summaries should be very short. Your audience: a high government official who needs an efficient summary of public opinion. Length: as short as possible.

2. Write a narrative summary of a chapter or section from a textbook other than this one. Limit the summary to a single typed page. What is the dominant mode in the chapter? What other modes are employed?

3. Write a summary of a complete article or essay from a college anthology or serious periodical. Use the summary form you think most appropriate.

4. In an encyclopedia, examine the entry under some very general topic: chemistry, United States, politics, Judaism, literature, economics. How is the general subject broken down into more specific ones? What principles of division are used? How might you use the entry to narrow a topic to the point that you might give an aspect of the subject reasonably through coverage in 1,000 words?

5. Examine the table of contents of several textbooks or other volumes that you would classify as reference material. What principles of division are operating in the structure of the book? What mode of development predominates? Is the book chronological (narrative), analytical (classificatory), descriptive, or evaluative?

6. Practice writing lead-ins to quoted materials by trying this exercise. Take a very short letter to the editor or a paragraph from an editorial and write a line-by-line summary or evaluation in which you quote directly a substantial portion of the original. Underline those phrases that lead into the quoted sentences. Sometimes you may have to modify the quotation slightly by dropping a word or words (indicated by ellipses: . . .) or you may make brief additions (indicated by brackets: [ ]). Here, for example, is the first paragraph from an editorial that appeared in the *New York Times,* January 23, 1980:

The good name of Andrei Sakharov is in no way tarnished by the Soviet government's spiteful withdrawal of his state awards and banishment from Moscow. Nor is he diminished by an attack that accuses him, in effect, of meddling in his country's affairs. The persecution of this brilliant and gentle physicist is the domestic analogue of the Soviet assault on Afghanistan. Both are clear tokens that every kind of independence is too easily trampled by the Soviet rulers.

A summary of it (quoting *much* more heavily than a typical summary would) might look like this:

> Condemning the internal exile of Russian physicist Andrei Sakharov, the *New York Times,* in an editorial of January 23, 1980, observes that his "good name . . . is in no way tarnished by the Soviet government's withdrawal of his state awards." The editorial points out that he is not "diminished by an attack that accuses him, in effect, of meddling in his country's affairs." The *Times* explores the political situation that may have prompted the Soviet government's action by suggesting that "the pursuit of [Sakharov] is the domestic analogue of the Soviet assault on Afghanistan." Sakharov's exile and the foreign incursion are, the *Times* notes, "clear tokens that every kind of independence is too easily trampled by the Soviet rulers."

Writing Assignments

7. Choose a set of encyclopedias and read several biographies, observing the length, arrangement, content, and style of these entries. Then, using these biographies as models, write the life story of someone you know well (it can be yourself). Your finished informative essay should be suitable for inclusion in the reference work. Both the length and the audience of your piece should approximate that of the encyclopedia that has served as your model.

8. Have you got a special skill or talent—something you do more expertly than most people? Write a short (500 words) informative essay in which you define the skill and describe some of the particular techniques that helped you master it.

You are more likely to educate your reader if you choose a subject you really know something about. Don't feel obligated to claim expertise in an area that is conventionally honored, such as sports, music, or handicrafts. If your unique talent is setting up a lab experiment, analyzing math problems, or finding intriguing sources for papers, write about that. And do it in the kind of detail that will make a reader appreciate, for example, the skill it takes to set up a problem and then solve it.

Your readers for this piece are nonspecialists with yet enough knowledge of your area of expertise to appreciate your achievement.

Briefly define any terms that might puzzle your readers because of their special or unusual meanings.

9. Write a short, informative pamphlet entitled "Practical Tips on Studying" in which you give down-to-earth advice that typical study guides seldom provide: how to cram effectively, how to stay awake through an all-nighter, how to find out what a teacher really wants. Be tough, realistic, sober. Organize the material in a way that will make it possible for a reader to find what she needs without having to read the entire pamphlet if she doesn't have time. Use headings where appropriate. Provide examples. Audience: inexperienced students in need of practical advice.

10. After reading the section "Invention for Informative Writing," begin a research project in some subject area of interest to you and of potential interest to a reader. The purpose of this paper is informative; you are to discover what is already known about a given subject and present that information in a clear and lively fashion. *Research Assignment*

Historical topics work well for this assignment. Choose some person, event, phenomenon, or object from the past and explain it to a contemporary reader:

Mary Tudor	Caravaggio
zeppelins	Robert Boyle
building the New York subway	Monitor VS Merrimac
Krakatoa	panoramas in the nineteenth century
woman suffrage	Canadian federation

Your topic does not have to be historical. You may instead choose to explain the structure of some discipline, or describe the features of some art or industry, or evaluate the significance of some religious, political, or social movement.

Make this an extended effort, the length determined by your instructor. Document your work carefully. Your audience for this research paper will be your classmates.

Demonstrating

An informative aim is also served by writing that demonstrates what a writer believes to be true in a given situation. A scientist advancing an hypothesis based on data gathered over years will present a clear and accurate account of the evidence that proves her case. A govern- *Informing VS persuading* ment agency announcing a new policy or regulation may justify its action by presenting an analysis of current conditions in need of improvement. A student preparing a poll to determine whether campus opinion favors reestablishing the draft will be sure that his sample is adequate, representative, and random. In these cases, and in many situations involving the demonstration of ideas, a writer walks a thin line between informing and persuading. The scientist, the bureaucrat, and the student may all be eager to win the approval of a particular audience. The consequence may be a Nobel prize, a promotion to GS-16, or an *A* in journalism. Consequently their informative pieces will probably contain persuasive elements.

In the best of all possible worlds, writers drawing conclusions in cases such as those named above might rely solely on the evidence they present to speak for them. The scientist's hypothesis either explains a phenomenon or it doesn't. The bureaucrat's new regulation is a needed one or it isn't. The poll shows that students either favor the draft or they don't. In pursuit of both reasonable conclusions and the approval of colleagues or teachers, the writers in these cases need to present their facts reasonably, accurately, and clearly, not cleverly.

Limits on proofs and demonstrations

If it were possible to split the human mind neatly between its faculties of reason and emotion, then you might find that essays of demonstration appeal to the rational side, the side that asks for figures, reasons, proofs, examples, and conclusions. But such a simple division does not withstand analysis. Even the best evidence may fail to tell the whole truth in areas of thought and behavior that go beyond rigid logic and mathematical calculation. And that includes most areas. Good as scientific instruments are, their accuracy has limits. Noble as a government policy may be, it may cause new problems hurtful to the nation in unanticipated ways. Careful as a poll may be taken, it may convey only a part of what students are thinking about the draft.

In some situations, writers simply cannot deal with all the facts, contingencies, and objections presented to them; yet they must arrive at some conclusions. Proving an idea under these circumstances involves selecting the most significant information and presenting it entirely, accurately, fairly, and with the understanding that the materials and conclusions presented have limits. Not every circumstance, situation, and perspective can be accounted for in every attempt to provide reasons for understanding the validity of a concept or proposal. But even within such limits, a writer with an informative (rather than a persuasive) aim writes for the sake of a conclusion he believes to be true. He says to his audience, "Let me show you" not "Don't you agree?"

Because the accuracy of human instruments of measurement and assessment is limited, it should not surprise us that two writers starting with the same evidence and the same good intentions may arrive at opposite conclusions. Between what is observed and what is concluded, between general principles and particular applications of them, there's always a leap, an uncertainty that limits what we can know and agree upon. As Hamlet observes, somewhat pessimistically, "there is nothing either good or bad, but thinking makes it so."

Two reviewers may read the same book, compose equally detailed analyses based on identical criteria, and arrive at opposite opinions of the book's worth. Which is right? If they both argued accurately, they may both be right. But the one who will be believed will be the one who presents the most convincing evidence in the clearest fashion.

A writer may go to great lengths to explain his method so that readers understand the limits and share the criteria that operate within a demonstration. For example, Anthony Lewis, reviewing a controversial book critical of the US Supreme Court *(The Brethren: Inside the Supreme Court* by Bob Woodward and Scott Armstrong), begins this way:

An example of demonstration

> Credibility is hard to measure when the issues are not black and white and when the affected institution cannot answer back. What a reviewer can do is look closely at a passage that makes a relatively definite and verifiable allegation. I shall do that here with the passage, already much noted, charging that Justice William J. Brennan, Jr. voted against his judgment of the merits in a case, making the fifth vote for the majority, in order to curry favor with a colleague, Justice Harry A. Blackmun. It is a serious charge. How serious, how convincing, how fair are the authors in making it?
>
> —"Supreme Court Confidential," *The New York Review of Books,*
>   February 7, 1980

Lewis then carefully examines the issue, assembling facts, tracing allegations, questioning some of the parties involved in the dispute. He finds the authors of *The Brethren* wanting, and then explains the point of his method and draws some conclusions:

> I have taken much space to explore a charge that is only a small part of a large book. But there is no way other than detailed analysis of particulars to appreciate the difficulties of this book—the difficulty, especially, of knowing what is true, what can be relied upon.

....

> But it is possible to reach a conclusion about the way *The Brethren* presents this episode [involving Justice Brennan]. It makes a serious charge without serious evidence—almost offhandedly, in two pages. It gets facts wrong. It gives the impression of relying on a conversation between Brennan and a law clerk that the law clerks of that term say never took place. If the passage was not meant to rely on such a conversation with a clerk, then it grossly and deliberately misleads the reader. In sum, the treatment of *Moore* v. *Illinois* leaves doubts not only about the authors' understanding but about their scrupulousness.

While there are persuasive elements in Lewis' review, they do not overwhelm what gives every appearance of being a careful and sober demonstration.

**From analysis
to persuasion**

How easy and tempting it is to veer from a demonstrative and analytical purpose should be evident from this less serious extract from an unfavorable review of *The Wizard of Oz*. The writer begins with a controlled, informative analysis of the plot of the film to support the opening contention that *The Wizard of Oz* is not an artistic achievement. But then notice how, near the end of the paragraph, the informative analysis becomes a persuasive one. The writer shifts to a different, satirical tone:

Analysis | Clearly, *The Wizard of Oz* cannot be considered a great film. To begin with, the plot makes no demands of us, presents us with no real moral choices because the characters and events of the film are part of a dream world. Neither witches nor wizards exist and, hence, neither can threaten us in our lifetimes. Nor can we regard them as metaphors for other malevolent forces. The film lacks the depth that would invite or permit such careful scrutiny. Yet even if we are willing to accept Dorothy's dream world as a representation of our own society, we cannot be moved by the sentimental issues the plot raises. Who really
Shift in tone | cares whether a weepy girl and her mangy dog find their way back to Kansas, especially when Munchkinland looks a whole lot better than Auntie Em's ramshackle farm? Yet the director would have us cower when the Wicked Witch of the West threatens Dorothy and "Your little dog too!" Blah.

In the first part of the paragraph, the writer counts on a reader understanding and accepting the argument presented. The aim is to prove, informatively. But when he calls Dorothy "weepy" and Toto "mangy," he is assuming an audience willing to agree with him—or one that can be manipulated into agreement by the unspoken suggestion that folks who don't find the characters as silly as he does are probably weepy and mangy themselves. The proof has become abuse.

Thesis Statement

Proving something

The thesis of an informative essay or *report* commits you, as we have seen in the preceding section, to providing a certain amount of information on a subject. The thesis in an essay of *demonstration* commits you to proving something:

Report: Statistics show that Houston is the fastest growing urban center in America.

Demonstration: Statistics suggest that Houston will face enormous economic, social, and political problems in the next twenty years unless its growth rate is curtailed.

Both types of essays use information, but while the report is content to convey the information clearly and accurately, the demonstration uses the information to comment on it, expand on it, rearrange it in order to explain and prove a conclusion.

In preparing an essay that proves something, you do not start off knowing what your thesis statement will be. The thesis statement in your finished essay summarizes the results of your investigations and discoveries:

> Students on this campus who favor the draft tend to feel that women ought not to be drafted; but those who oppose the draft would favor the drafting of women should the system be reestablished.

But you do not begin your work with this information in hand. Instead your writing process begins with a question: **The initial question**

> How do students feel about renewing the draft?

You then narrow the question, or break it into its significant parts:

> How do male students feel about renewing the draft? Female students?
> How do male students feel about drafting women? Female students?
> Do students who approve of draft renewal favor drafting women?
> How do students who oppose the draft feel about proposals to draft women?

And so on. Then you sample student opinion, asking the questions you need to complete your study. Finally you write the paper that begins with the thesis sentence that summarizes your findings.

Similarly in a demonstrative paper on a literary topic, you would begin with a question that may have arisen while you were reading:

> Does Shakespeare use economic imagery as consistently as Ben Jonson?

The topic is enormous and the field of Shakespeare studies a thriving one. So you would want to read secondary sources to find out what scholars and critics have already said about the playwrights' use of economic imagery. These scholarly opinions could constitute part of the evidence for (or against) your case. Then you might choose to read selected plays, guided by your knowledge or by the suggestions of scholars and critics, noting as you read how economic terms and situations are handled. You may discover that certain words have economic significance in the plays—gold, usury, prodigality, liberality—and decide to systematically study how each playwright uses them. If such were the case, your analysis would be assisted by a concordance—an alphabetical index of all the words used in a work.

The legwork done, you gather and review your evidence. You rethink your hypothesis in light of the new information. Finally you are ready to state the thesis of the paper, knowing that you have the evidence to back it up:

> Despite prevailing critical opinion to the contrary, I believe that Shakespeare's economic imagery in *Timon of Athens* is more consistent than Jonson's in *Volpone*.

As a result of the investigation and research, the thesis statement has become more precise and more challenging.

Processes of Demonstration: Induction and Deduction

Writers proving a thesis use induction and deduction.

Induction is a process of examining particular events, experiences, details, or facts, and drawing conclusions from them. In skeletal form, an inductive conclusion is reached like this:

Hypothesis: Chills cause colds.

1. Charlotte caught a cold after a chill.
2. David caught a cold after a chill.
3. Alec caught a cold after a chill.

Conclusion: Chills cause colds.

In practice, inductive demonstrations usually move more rapidly and less formally, and not infrequently the conclusion is stated first, with the evidence trailing after:

> *Most of the more complex emotions are common to the higher animals and ourselves.* Every one has seen how jealous a dog is of his master's affection, if lavished on any other creature; and I have observed the same fact with monkeys. This shews that animals not only love, but have desire to be loved. Animals manifestly feel emulation. They love approbation or praise; and a dog carrying a basket for his master exhibits in a high degree self-complacency or pride. There can, I think, be no doubt that a dog feels shame, as distinct from fear, and something very like modesty when begging too often for food. . . .

> Several observers have stated that monkeys certainly dislike being laughed at; and they sometimes invent imaginary offences (italics added).
>
> —Charles Darwin, *The Descent of Man*

Reduced to an outline that shows its logical arrangement, Darwin's inductive paragraph looks like this:

Evidence
1. Animals love and desire to be loved
   a. A jealous dog
   b. A jealous monkey
2. Animals feel emulation
   a. A dog carrying a basket
3. Animals feel shame and modesty
   a. A dog begging for food
   b. A monkey's displeasure at being laughed at

⇄ Conclusion: Most of the more complex emotions are common to the higher animals and ourselves.

Deduction is a process of examining general principles and drawing from them conclusions about particular events, details, or facts. The basic structure of deduction—as it typically operates—is simple: **Deduction**

General principle: Chills cause colds.

Particular event: └→Charlotte is chilled.

Conclusion: └→Charlotte will get a cold.

Quite often, the general principles in a deductive chain are not stated completely or explicitly. And arguments move without clear transitions from one conclusion to another. Like inductive demonstrations, deductive reasonings in prose are considerably more complex than a diagram may suggest:

> A struggle for existence inevitably follows from the high rate at which all organic beings tend to increase. Every being, which during its natural lifetime produces several eggs or seeds, must suffer destruction during some period of its life, and during some season or occasional year, otherwise, on the principle of geometrical increase, its numbers would quickly become so inordinately great that no country could support the product. Hence, as more individuals are produced than can possibly survive, there must in every case be a struggle for existence, either one individual with another of the same species, or with the individuals of distinct species, or with the physical conditions of life. It is

the doctrine of Malthus applied with manifold force to the whole animal and vegetable kingdoms. . . .

—Charles Darwin, *The Origin of Species*

Darwin's deductive argument moves like this:

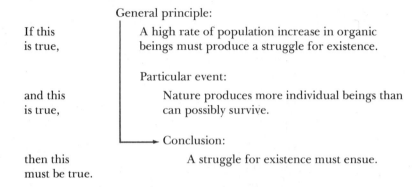

General principle:

If this is true,
A high rate of population increase in organic beings must produce a struggle for existence.

Particular event:

and this is true,
Nature produces more individual beings than can possibly survive.

Conclusion:

then this must be true.
A struggle for existence must ensue.

Relationship of induction and deduction Induction and deduction are closely related, in theory and in practice. The process of induction establishes the general principles by which deduction operates:

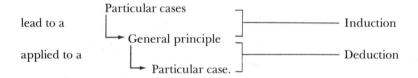

lead to a

Particular cases

General principle

applied to a

Particular case.

Induction

Deduction

Here's a particular example:

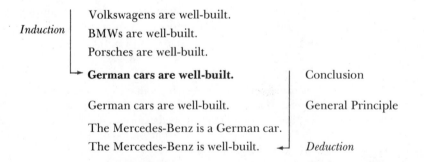

Induction
Volkswagens are well-built.
BMWs are well-built.
Porsches are well-built.

German cars are well-built. Conclusion

German cars are well-built. General Principle

The Mercedes-Benz is a German car.

The Mercedes-Benz is well-built. *Deduction*

Logical Problems

Questionable conclusions   The inductive and deductive examination of the relationship between colds and chills presented earlier reached shaky conclusions:

1. Chills cause colds.
2. Charlotte will get a cold.

Most people believe chills cause colds because they have themselves contracted a cold after a soaking or a night in an unheated room. So when they meet someone shivering from a dip in an icy lake, they prescribe a quick leap into a hot tub to stave off the inevitable symptoms.

Now, while chills may create bodily conditions conducive to colds, their actual cause is probably a virus. Hence the conclusion of the inductive process—namely, that chills cause colds—is false. Consequently the premise or general principle from which the deductive proof operates is questionable too:

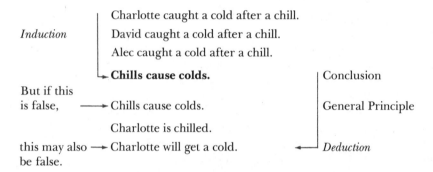

Unfortunately, the habits of mind that produce the hasty conclusions represent the way many of us reach conclusions daily. When you write to prove a case, it is your responsibility to use induction and deduction more carefully than you might in less formal situations.

And that is not especially difficult. While formal rules of logic can be complex and intimidating, the practical logic employed by most writers is little more than applied common sense.

For example, if you are working inductively, you would pay special attention to your facts and how they are related. How many cases have been examined to reach a conclusion? Three people catching a cold following a chill might suggest a relationship worth investigating, but you must also be willing to consider the possibility of other factors. Were the three exposed to some common source of infection? Were the three in close contact? Did they contract the cold from each other? The more cases you investigate, the more convincing the conclusion you may eventually be able to draw. And the more general the conclusion, the more massive the evidence to support it will have to be. Someone trying to prove that Gary, a twenty-year-old male with a dozen traffic tickets and two wrecks to his credit, is a reckless driver will have an easier time of it than someone else trying to demonstrate that most twenty-year-old

Weighing your evidence

males are reckless drivers. Many cases would have to be examined, many insurance records studied, and many factors considered before a conclusion could be stated.

Gathering facts

You would also want to be careful about the way facts are gathered and presented. Whether drawing conclusions about the theme of a poem or the causes of urban blight, you want to take a comprehensive view of your subject. If you read only half of the poem or record the opinions of business persons only, you will come away with partial and distorted pictures of the situation unless you can be certain that the portions you examined accurately represent the whole. And that is usually a risky assumption.

Surveying populations

When surveying large populations for the purpose of gauging public opinion, professional pollsters go to great lengths to be sure that their sample populations represent a cross-section of the society—racially, ethnically, politically, religiously, and economically. If a pollster like Gallup or Harris posed a political question to a group of liberal Democrats, then the poll would reflect the opinion of liberal Democrats only—not of any larger population. Yet even that conclusion could be unrepresentative if the question asked concerned social security taxes and all the polled liberal Democrats happened to be younger than thirty.

The inductive leap

When working inductively, you must also be concerned with the inevitable gap that exists between your facts and the conclusions you draw from them. By examining particular cases, you are attempting to draw conclusions that predict the future. But conclusions aren't always reliable. There's always the possibility that, despite dozens of supporting examples or hundreds of years of precedents, the next example or next year will contradict a seemingly sound prediction:

> Pope Pius X was Italian.
> Pope Pius XI was Italian.
> Pope Pius XII was Italian.
> Pope John XXIII was Italian.
> Pope Paul VI was Italian.
> Pope John Paul I was Italian.

leap

> Pope John Paul I's successor will be Italian.

but

> Pope John Paul II is Polish.

Such uncertainty always limits the reliability of inductive studies that cannot control all variables and study all examples of a given phenomenon. And that is most of them.

With deduction—the process of working from general principles to conclusions about particular cases—the conclusions are certain if the premises from which they are derived are accepted as true and if the structure the reasoning follows is valid. The most familiar expression of deductive reasoning is the syllogism, and this syllogism is still the most famous: **Syllogisms**

1. All men are mortal.

2. Socrates is a man.

→ Socrates is mortal.

If the first statement is accepted as true and it can be demonstrated that Socrates is, indeed, a man, then with certainty it can be stated that Socrates is mortal.

Writers seldom resort to full syllogisms, even when demonstrating propositions they believe are true. Instead they rely on their ability to identify and articulate premises and principles that their readers will agree to. Such principles are often shortened syllogisms: *Socrates will die because he is a man.* We will explore the significance of premises more thoroughly in the next section.

When premises are not self-evident, you may have to demonstrate their truth or acceptability before using them to develop an argument further. In the evaluative mode, for example, the statement of criteria is, in fact, a statement of premises. As we have seen in an earlier section, if a reader agrees with the stated principles, then the demonstration can proceed. But if he objects to the initial premises, all subsequent arguments based on them will fall on deaf ears.

Whether working inductively or deductively, you should present as many points of view as possible or as necessary in demonstrating a conclusion or proposition. In such a demonstration, you may not have time or space to explain every detail or every consideration, but in such cases you have recourse to documentation. Let a footnote or a textual citation refer the interested reader to materials—reports, encyclopedias, almanacs—that provide the appropriate facts, numbers, or background. Include in the text of your demonstration the most significant materials: those which explain your conclusion. But don't ignore materials which limit it. When persuading, you sometimes muzzle the voices of the opposition; when informing, it is your responsibility to let all voices be heard. Here, for example, a distinguished scholar openly acknowledges disagreement in his field over a significant issue: **Using documentation as evidence**

> The term "Renaissance" has given rise to an unending debate among
> the historians of the last hundred years or so, and there has been a
> great variety of opinions concerning the significance and characteristics

of this historical period, its relation to the periods preceding and following it, and the precise time of its beginning and of its end. Depending upon one's views, the Renaissance would seem to have lasted as much as four hundred years, or only 27 years, not counting the view of those scholars who think that the Renaissance did not exist at all. As we may see from Professor Ferguson's and Professor Weisinger's studies. . . .

—Paul Oskar Kristeller, *Renaissance Thought II*

Defining terms

As Professor Kristeller's paragraph above suggests, definition is another major concern in demonstration. To return to an earlier example, a writer plotting the relationship of chills to colds would have to begin with a precise definition for each word. Will a chill in the study be defined as simply a feeling of discomfort caused by a cold environment, or must the chilled subject display goose bumps and shivers? What is a cold? Sniffles for a day? Or a two-week bodily upset marked by a rise in temperature, nasal constriction, a runny nose, watery eyes, and general misery?

Definitions become more critical as issues and proofs grow more complex. The lengthy and bitter debate over abortion in the United States turns upon the definition of the fetus. Is it or is it not a human being with all the attendant rights? Similarly, how the government defines *poverty* or *unemployment* determines large (and expensive) aspects of public policy.

Qualifiers

For a writer trying to share acquired knowledge accurately, the handiest tool is the qualifier—a word or expression that fences in facts and conclusions. "Within these particular limits or under these conditions," a qualifier suggests, "this conclusion holds true. Outside these limits, you are on your own":

Conclusion Colgate with *MFP* has been shown to be an effective decay-preventive dentifrice that can be of significant value . . .

Qualifier . . . when used in a conscientiously applied program of oral hygiene and regular professional care.

—Statement printed on a tube of Colgate, citing the Council of Dental Therapeutics, American Dental Association

Fact The EPA estimate with manual transmission is 19 MPG, with a highway mileage of 28 MPG . . . .

Qualifiers . . . Remember the circled EPA estimate is for comparison; your mileage may vary depending on speed, weather, and trip lengths. California figures are lower, and your actual highway mileage will probably be lower than the highway estimate.

—Ad for a Triumph TR-7

Too many qualifiers can make a piece seem timid and gutless. But when the purpose of an article is to inform or demonstrate, you use qualifiers of this kind whenever the situation demands:

perhaps	possibly
it seems	often
it is possible	rarely
sometimes	generally
in most cases	almost
in many cases	frequently

Being skeptical

When writing or reading informative discourse, you have the right to be skeptical. When Jefferson penned the Declaration of Independence, he declared that "All men are created equal." Declarations—like manifestoes and proclamations—are generally more expressive and persuasive than informative. In its original context (one that required persuasion), Jefferson's statement could boldly distribute the blessings of equality. But set into an informative context, the document must face a stern interrogation:

"All men are created equal!"
"Does that include women?"
"Ah, no, not exactly."
"And blacks?"
"Well, to some degree, but . . ."
"And how about those white males who don't hold property?"
"No, not exactly . . . "

The significance of an assertion, conclusion, or statement of fact often resides in its qualifiers.

"In this life, we want nothing but Facts, sir; nothing but Facts!" a stern citizen in Charles Dickens' novel, *Hard Times,* declares, as if facts existed clear and certain in a simple and predictable world. They don't.

For Discussion

1. Review the ways ideas or facts are demonstrated in several disciplines: mathematics, sociology, chemistry, physics, history, philosophy, literary criticism. In which fields do demonstrations tend to operate inductively? Deductively? How are the processes interrelated?

2. Examine film or book reviews in several publications. Do the reviews tend to demonstrate or persuade? Can you identify particular habits of structure or language that distinguish an informative/demonstrative review from a persuasive one? Can you always make such a distinction?

3. Examine what would be involved in proving what should be done

about a complex social problem. What would you have to do, for example, to demonstrate that building a nuclear power plant would not harm the environment? That cutting taxes would stimulate growth? That capital punishment does deter crime?

Exercises

4. Find two reviews of the same book, one that is favorable and one that is not. (You can find reviews by checking *Book Review Digest* or *Book Review Index* in the reference room of a library.) Examine the methods each writer employs to reach a conclusion. Then, in a short essay, evaluate their methods. Which reviewer is more convincing?

5. Examine the qualifications used by advertisers in magazine ads or television commercials. Using evidence gathered from these sources, draw some conclusions about the ways advertisers use or abuse the language.

Writing Assignments

6. Under what circumstances might certain acts ordinarily considered offensive or criminal be justified? Choose a "crime" (murder, arson, treason, fraud, theft, bribery) and write a series of premises that state conditions under which the act ceases to be criminal:

Murder
1. Murder in self-defense is not murder.
2. Murder that prevents a war is justified.
3. Murder that brings down a dictator is justified.
4. Etc.

After preparing your list, discuss which premises might be accepted by a general audience. Choose a premise that would not be immediately acceptable, and prepare a short essay (500 words) defending it. Or attack a premise that might be readily accepted by a general audience. (How would you define a general audience?)

7. Survey the opinion of a small group (your class?) on some controversial political or social issue. Then write a short piece reporting your findings and explaining what factors (other than a lack of sufficient numbers in your sample) might prevent you from assuming that the opinion of your subjects represents American public opinion at large on that issue.

8. Study some convenient group of persons, places, or things to prove or disprove a belief you have about them:

Women have better study habits than men.

Downtown grocery stores have higher prices overall than suburban markets.

Catholics are more conservative politically than Protestants.

Choose a hypothesis that will require your respondents to answer more than one question, or which will require you to research more than one question. Then, carefully defining all critical terms and explaining the circumstances that limit the accuracy of your conclusions, write a short report that presents the facts you have gathered and supports or denies your hypothesis. Length: 400–600 words. Audience: your classmates or coworkers. Use diagrams, charts, or graphs if appropriate.

Research Assignments

9. Examine some political, military, or social decision of the recent past that is widely regarded as a mistake by the public today, but which you tend to believe may have been correct. Using the full resources of the library—books, periodicals, encyclopedias, newspapers—investigate that decision. Why was it made? What was the political atmosphere in which it was made? What have been the real consequences of the decision? The imagined consequences?

Examine the evidence as fairly as you can in light of your initial hypothesis—that the action may have been justified. If you believe that the evidence is with you, prove your case. If the evidence goes strongly counter to your original belief, be prepared to modify your position. The essay you write is to be a *demonstration from the facts*. It should not be an exercise in persuasion.

10. Coolly and rationally, demonstrate that some widely-held belief you know to be incorrect *is* incorrect. Use whatever evidence and resources you need to document your case: figures, statistics, authorities, documents, personal experience. The essay should, ideally, deal with a serious misapprehension about some aspect in your major field of study.

11. Examine the initial critical reception given to your favorite film or twentieth-century novel. You will need to find out when the work was first published or released. Then consult digests of book and movie reviews (the librarian can direct you to the appropriate sources) to gather evidence on the work's popularity with reviewers and critics. If the initial reviews were favorable, write an informative essay detailing what pleased the critics. If the initial reviews were negative, demonstrate why you think they are in error. Remember that you are demonstrating, not persuading. Stick to the facts and evidence. Length: 500 words.

Exploring

A special kind of informative writing is the *discursive* or *exploratory* essay. The English noun, *essay*, descends from a French verb, *essayer*, which means "to try." In its purest state, the exploratory essay is a trying out, an attempt by a writer to discover the dimensions of a problem, to explore the implications of an idea, to take the risk of unveiling private thoughts in the public arena. When a writer tackles a truly difficult problem—some political or social issue, a philosophical dilemma, a question of values—we are often grateful just for his attempt to organize its complications, spell out the contradictions, enumerate the possible solutions. A writer in the process of exploring takes the risk of discovering new ideas or placing old ones in a new perspective:

> It would not be difficult to come to an agreement as to what we understand by science. Science is the century-old endeavor to bring together by means of systematic thought the perceptible phenomena of this world into as thoroughgoing an association as possible. To put it boldly, it is the attempt at the posterior reconstruction of existence by the process of conceptualization. But when asking myself what religion is, I cannot think of the answer so easily. And even after finding an answer which may satisfy me at this particular moment, I still remain convinced that I can never under any circumstances bring together, even to a slight extent, all those who have given this question serious consideration.

Thesis statement
> *At first, then, instead of asking what religion is, I should prefer to ask what characterizes the aspirations of a person who gives me the impression of being religious. . . .* (italics added)
> —Albert Einstein, "Science and Religion"

Thesis Statement

The exploratory or discursive essay ends where the demonstrative essay begins: with a question. In the demonstrative essay, that initial question or hypothesis is resolved before the piece takes shape; the reader may never see the question that initiates the investigation. In exploratory writing, the question is the heart of the matter and can remain that. A demonstrative essay is stable and conclusive; a discursive essay is open-ended and often inconclusive. By its very nature, exploration encourages speculation, digression, and risk.

Like Einstein's piece, many exploratory essays evolve from a question:

> Can America's mainstream culture, made pervasive by the electronic media, absorb all the diverse groups that live here, that are passionate about maintaining their identity?
>
> —Paul Cowan, "A Fight Over America's Future"

What does laughter mean?

—Henri Bergson, *Laughter: An Essay on the Meaning of the Comic*

Why did so many drive all night, take plane trips they couldn't afford, set out from half a continent away without money or comforts or plans, solely to attend the funeral of Elvis Presley?

—Molly Ivins, "Why They Mourned for Elvis"

In preparing an exploratory essay, you may want to begin with just such a large and puzzling question. And then you will have to think about it. The essence of exploration is the eagerness to get to the heart of a matter, sometimes by direct and logical routes, sometimes by what seem like digressions and detours. Where informative and demonstrative essays encourage tightly focused thesis statements, exploration allows you to examine the larger issues and the timeless questions if you choose to:

Pilate saith unto him, What is truth?

—John 18:38

What Is Thought?

—Title of an essay by John Dewey

But explorations do not have to operate on this scale, nor do they have to begin with questions.

Old beliefs, stereotypes, maxims

Many fine discursive essays grow from a desire to explore once again an old belief, saying, stereotype, or maxim to find how it applies to new times and situations:

No young man believes he shall ever die. It was a saying of my brother's and a fine one. There is a feeling of Eternity in youth . . . . (italics added)

—William Hazlitt, "On the Feeling of Immortality in Youth"

If only it were that simple. There may really be high schools where *life approximates an Archie comic,* but even in the Fifties, my . . . high school was not one of them. (italics added)

—Ellen Willis, "Memoirs of a Non-Prom Queen"

Or they develop from a willingness to explode current notions, to see what happens if we stop thinking in conventional ways:

Current beliefs

A building, we suppose, is an individual container, housing an office, a factory, a school, or a residence . . . . Suppose, however, that the factory, office, residence, and school are components of a single continuous structure . . . .

—Walter Karp, "Omnibuildings"

Why Smaller Refrigerators Can Preserve the Human Race

—Title of an article by Appletree Rodden

Personal exploration   Many exploratory essays deal with contemporary social or political issues because these are the problems that press against us: can we live without oil? What happens if inflation doesn't stop? What is the future of a liberal arts education? But explorations can be more personal; in such cases, the exploratory essay moves into the realm of the self-expressive:

> What is the effect of property upon the character? Don't let's touch economics; the effect of private ownership upon the community as a whole is another question—a more important question, perhaps, but another one. Let's keep to psychology. If you own things, what's their effect on you? What's the effect on me of my wood?
>
> —E. M. Forster, "My Wood"

Two Exploratory Structures

It is possible to construct structural models of the exploratory essay. According to one such formulation, in James Kinneavy's *A Theory of Discourse,* the process of exploration has five steps:

1. a review of the current situation or beliefs,
2. an explanation of the problems inherent in the current situation or beliefs (why is the status quo threatened?),
3. a crisis (what *in particular* makes change in the current situation necessary and desirable?),
4. a consideration of alternatives (what changes are possible? what solution might solve the problem?),
5. a testing of solutions (what are the limitations of the proposed solution? will it work?).

Applied to a particular situation, this model might produce an essay which, in summary form, would look something like this:

1. Current belief   The author of *Crisis in Housing* argues that, currently, most Americans dream of owning their own home someday. But inflation has caused the prices of new homes

2. The problem   to skyrocket out of the reach of the average American wage-earner. Even in households where both spouses work, the income may not meet mortgage loan requirements. Moreover, there is an actual shortage of new housing units, the housing industry being unable to keep up with demand or needs.

3. The crisis	As a result, Americans are angry and clamoring to Washington for help. But politicians seem incapable of controlling spiralling costs and declining output.
4. Alternatives	More government money for mortgage loans is one proposed solution, but freeing up capital for loans could drive up prices even more without increasing the housing supply. More assistance to builders is another solution, one limited by the availability of land and material resources. Perhaps the best solution, the author argues, is for Americans to lower their expectations, to resign themselves to row houses, rental apartments, or close-quartered condominiums.
5. The solution	Such a solution would cause political difficulties for its advocates. Many American habits would have to change. But less grandiose housing can still provide adequate privacy, security, and comfort in a rapidly changing world. Americans must alter their expectations.

The model produces an intelligent, formal essay by giving the act of exploring a dependable, repeatable sequence.

"The free play of ideas"

But in other circumstances, particularly personal ones, exploratory essays can and perhaps should be more than exercises in pinning ideas to a preexisting frame. The essay is the type of informative writing most adapted to the personal voice. At its best, exploration is the human mind working, and the exploratory essay captures in language that mental labor, its wit, weariness, inventiveness, and concern. It involves a writer in what Matthew Arnold called "the free play of ideas." Because the mind does not always work in straight lines, the exploratory essay can ramble, digress, and even contradict itself as it seeks answers or raises more questions. Its structure may twist and turn, finding a place for digressions and flashes of insight:

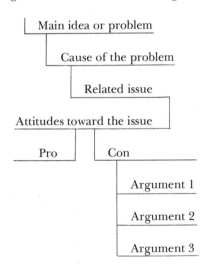

For cohesion, such an essay relies on the compelling personal voice of its author and various techniques of transition—often the ones that do not involve enumeration or surface structuring. This type of essay, too, falls easily into persuasion and special pleading. But essentially readers are informed and enlivened by the experience and ideas they share with a fellow human being. They may even discover some truths:

> In many ways writing is the act of saying *I,* of imposing oneself upon other people, of saying *listen to me, see it my way, change your mind.* It's an aggressive, even a hostile act. You can disguise its aggressiveness all you want with veils of subordinate clauses and qualifiers and tentative subjunctives, with ellipses and evasions—with the whole manner of intimating rather than claiming, of alluding rather than stating—but there's no getting around the fact that setting words on paper is the tactic of a secret bully, an invasion, an imposition of the writer's sensibility on the reader's most private space.
>
> —Joan Didion, "Why I Write"

> Now, anyone who has been compelled to think about it—anyone, for example, who has ever been in love—knows that the one face that one can never see is one's own face. One's lover—or one's brother, or one's enemy—sees the face you wear, and this face can elicit the most extraordinary reactions. We do the things we do and feel what we feel essentially because we must—we are responsible for our actions, but we rarely understand them. It goes without saying, I believe, that if we understood ourselves better, we would damage ourselves less. But the barrier between oneself and one's knowledge of oneself is high indeed. There are so many things one would rather not know!
>
> —James Baldwin, "The Creative Dilemma"

Values

Conflicts of values

Some explorations begin with a particular issue or question. Should a nuclear power plant be built? Should the federal government regulate athletic scholarships in college? Is abortion ethical? How ought the US to deal with illegal immigrants? Debate over such questions can heat up quickly as proponents and opponents pile facts, figures, personal experiences, and second-hand horror stories onto the fire. The discussion of issues is quickly consumed in a blaze of charges, counter-charges, angry words, and insinuations. When you examine such issues, you can waste time and energy explaining and defending particular details when the basic problem or issue stems from a conflict of values. You may never resolve or even understand a problem unless you first trace disputes back to their roots, where the real issues tangle.

Values are the principles—spoken or assumed—on which a society or any group acts. They shape the premises of deductive reasoning and serve as the foundations of public policies.

Values and premises range from the fundamental to the frivolous, from the abstract to the concrete. We make dozens of decisions a day upon unspoken principles we've learned through experience:

Hot soup tastes better than cold.

Russian novels are better than French.

Cotton underwear is more comfortable than polyester.

Honesty is better (in the long run) than cheating.

Better to bear the troubles we have than risk new ones.

These principles are usually unexamined. We are hardly aware that we are operating according to a system of values when we heat a cup of soup or get dressed in the morning.

Systems of value

Other, more serious values or principles of action can define an ethical attitude or a national consciousness:

An eye for an eye!

Turn the other cheek.

The business of America is business.

Bigger is better.

Smaller is more efficient.

The smaller the group to which a set of values adheres the easier it is to define precisely where conflicts may arise. Americans, in general, might agree that Jefferson's words speak best of the values held by the nation:

We hold these truths to be self-evident, that all men are created equal, that they are endowed by their Creator with certain unalienable rights, that among these are Life, Liberty and the pursuit of Happiness.

—The Declaration of Independence

But Americans, as individuals and "interest groups," act and respond according to principles as varied as the make-up of the population:

America, love it or leave it.

Trees are more useful than parking lots.

Get it while you can.

Do it to others before they do it to you.

No nukes.

Black is beautiful.

Make love, not war.

We do it all for you.

We don't care. We don't have to care.

Similarly, large groups may commit themselves to abstract principles expressed by single words: *fraternity, liberty, justice, equality, freedom, truth, beauty*. But particular cases involving any one of these concepts may find a value pitted against itself:

> *Justice* demands the death penalty in this case.
>
> In the name of *justice,* how can we take the defendant's life?

Thus, when you are exploring an issue, you need to give serious consideration to the values at the heart of the debate or controversy. These premises tell you where to begin your work:

Rejected value Alone on a mountain top no one ever believed that *Man is nothing but the product of economic forces* or that production per man hour is a reliable index of human welfare. And surely no
Rejected value man on a mountain top ever believed that *Good and Evil are nothing except the prejudices of a given society.* Such dismal, such deadly opinions are possible only to those who do not know
Source of human beings because *they do not know themselves* and do not
false values know themselves because *they have never been alone with themselves.* This will never be a world in which a good life is
Problem possible for most people as long as dismal and deadly opinions predominate. And the nature writer, like the poet and the priest, is their enemy. (italics added)

> —Joseph Wood Krutch, "Some Unsentimental Confessions of a Nature Writer"

When exploring an issue, you may discover that a given value is less important than its relationship with other values. Speaking about systems of value, a Belgian philosopher puts the matter this way:

Value hierarchies

> Value hierarchies are, no doubt, more important to the structure of an argument than the actual values. Most values are indeed shared by a great number of audiences, and a particular audience is characterized less by which values it accepts than by the way it grades them.
>
> —Ch. Perelman and L. Olbrechts-Tyteca, *The New Rhetoric,* trans. John Wilkinson and Purcell Weaver

Thus, in examining a dispute—an issue, let us say, of whether a nuclear power plant should be built—you may discover that while both sides claim to value business growth, a clean environment, energy independence, prosperity, and public safety, they would establish different hierarchies if asked to rank their values from the most important to the least:

Proponents	*Opponents*
1. energy independence	1. public safety
2. prosperity	2. clean environment
3. business growth	3. business growth
4. public safety	4. energy independence
5. clean environment	5. prosperity

Understanding that energy independence VS public safety is a major source of conflict, you could then begin looking for solutions that addressed both concerns. Or you might look for an area of relative agreement: in this case, business growth.

In exploring values and value hierarchies, you may choose to adopt certain principles as your own: "Clearly then, in this situation we must assume that . . . ." Or you could state values hypothetically to test them: "If, for the moment, we assume . . . ." Or you may concede that values under exploration are not your own: "A second group of public officials believes that government funding of college programs at any level implies the right to regulate at every level . . . ." You help your reader if you make it clear where you stand.

For Discussion

1. Can you identify certain situations that stimulate exploration? What prompts you to explore a problem? Under what circumstances do you think about pressing problems, either personal or societal?

2. Many television and radio talk programs justify their existence by claiming to foster debate and exploration. Do you think this is true? Cite examples. What structure do these explorations take? Are such programs useful?

3. Discursive essays seem to have been more popular in the eighteenth and nineteenth centuries than they are today. Can you suggest why? Can you name any essayists you read regularly? Where do most serious essays appear today? Examine the sources and credits of the essays in a college anthology. Where were the articles first published?

4. In class, choose a controversial issue and then make a list of the values in conflict. Break into groups and discuss the values, ranking them from most important to least. Compare your value hierarchy with those of the other groups. Be prepared to defend your ranking.

5. Make a list of the values of a group to which you belong. Then arrange the values in a hierarchy from most important to least. Do your own values conflict at any point with the values of the group or organization?

6. Exploratory essays have a finality to them that the process of exploration does not. Yet they can be more tentative than informative, demonstrative, or (as we shall see) persuasive pieces. Examine a college anthology and try to find essays you would classify as exploratory. (Many anthologies do not have this category.) You can usually determine what aim an essay serves by examining its title and first few paragraphs.

7. Prepare a list of questions in the local or national news today that might serve to stimulate an exploratory essay.

8. Take one of the questions from Exercise 7 and examine it from the point of view of the formal exploratory process:

> 1) current beliefs
> 2) explanation of the problem
> 3) crisis
> 4) alternatives
> 5) testing of solutions

Then write a short essay that follows the step-by-step organization. Use "Crisis in Housing" as a model.

9. Take one of the questions raised in Exercise 7 and think about it from a personal point of view. What is your own reaction to it? What is your solution? Is your solution a gut reaction? A plausible alternative to the current dilemma? Have you had a personal experience with the problem?

Write a paragraph that summarizes your feelings. Do not follow the formal exploratory pattern.

Writing Assignments

10. In an essay of 500–600 words, challenge a value that most of your colleagues in school or at work accept. On what is that value based? What are the consequences of it? What are the alternatives to it?

11. Examine a currently stable situation, personal or societal, and then explore what would happen if an element responsible for that stability were withdrawn. For example:

> What happens if an international crisis forces Americans to cut their energy use in half in one month's time?
>
> What would happen if a major industry in your town or state folded or moved away?
>
> What would you do if you were unable to go to college?
>
> What would you do if a sudden debility prevented you from enjoying the life and recreations you currently do?

Direct this essay (even a personal one) to a wide and serious audience. Do not spend too much time in the narrative mode (first I would . . . then I would . . .). Be rigorous and analytical.

12. In a carefully researched and documented article, explore a major problem in your intended field of study. That problem may be theoretical (what role do business courses have in higher education?); technological (what is the future of fusion research?); or practical (what can an English major do after college?).

Research Assignment

You may want to initiate your exploration by interviewing someone more knowledgeable about the area of study you are just entering. Ask for suggestions about books and articles that address the problem. Explore the problem in the library. Then write your full-length report, following the formal structure for exploration as much as possible.

If you have not declared a major field, use this assignment as a way of exploring an area that might intrigue you.

Some General Comments on Style

Keep it simple, keep it clear. That's the essence of well-fitted informative prose. In many cases, reports and summaries can be almost stark: their sentences short, clear, repetitive; their transitions obvious and basic; their vocabulary concise and unobtrusive. Similarly, demonstration, whether inductive or deductive, should focus on clear statements and clear arrangement, not on subtle devices, strategic parallels, or clever alliterations. Exploratory pieces, moving toward a persuasive aim and often carrying a first-person point of view, may properly indulge in more studied uses of language, but the basic informative aim should not be obscured.

Keep it simple and clear

Informative discourse tends to be "front-loaded." That is, the important information is delivered quickly by sentence structures that emphasize facts:

> NEW YORK (UPI)—A spokesman for the New York Yankees said Monday that an incident on the Yankees' bus in Chicago, during which a girl reportedly had her bottom autographed by the team, had been twisted around and blown completely out of proportion.
>
> —*The Daily Texan,* August 14, 1979

The opening sentence of the news story is deliberately structured to provide the necessary facts at the proper moment. The subject is comic, but the reporter reserves the chuckles to the readers. He or she makes no comment.

Though the language of most informative, demonstrative, and exploratory writing should be clear and simple, that is not to imply it should be artless. Just the opposite: when you are informing, your sentences must work overtime to clearly identify issues or explain facts. Modifiers should be direct and purposeful. Opening paragraphs and topic sentences tell what is to follow, and then the essay delivers on those promises gracefully and efficiently. There's no need for informative prose to sound like the regurgitations of a machine.

Achieving clarity

Informative writing makes heavy use of surface devices to fit the parts of an article together. Since clarity is usually a primary virtue, any device that signals or emphasizes what direction a writer is taking is useful. Titles of informative essays ought to be factual. If a report can be conveniently divided into parts under headings and subheadings helpful to the reader, the division ought to be tried. Enumeration may be practical too.

The highly-structured patterns of organization discussed in chapter 10 help fit informative essays together by putting facts and ideas in clear and consistent relationships. And devices of transition that stand at the leading edges of paragraphs are often the kind most helpful to readers scanning an article for information.

What is generally regarded as colorful or emotive language is best left out of most kinds of informative writing. A writer, informing, should be wary of revealing or, worse, conveying a bias in the presentation of material. Even slight modifications can turn a news item, for example, into an editorial:

> NEW YORK—A harried spokesman for the New York Yankees admitted Monday that the disgraceful incident on the Yankees' bus in Chicago, during which a girl had her bottom autographed by a giggling, leering, sophomoric team, had perhaps been overblown.

Tone

But informative writing is not without variations in tone. A serious subject, like death, might evoke in some contexts sentences that are stately and a vocabulary that is somber:

> When we look back in time and study old cultures and people, we are impressed that death has always been distasteful to man and will probably always be.
>
> —Elizabeth Kübler-Ross, *On Death and Dying*

Yet other treatments of the subject are possible. The scientist, for example, who regards death as a mechanical process will describe it in cold language, without passion or solemnity:

> Thus the matter of life, so far as we know it (and we have no right to speculate on any other), breaks up, in consequence of that continual

death which is the condition of its manifesting vitality, into carbonic acid, water, and nitrogenous compounds.

—Thomas Henry Huxley, "On the Physical Basis of Life"

Nor does informative writing avoid all devices of amplifying language. Similes and analogies, for example, are useful ways of conveying the meanings of difficult concepts:

Similes and analogies

> Thus the study showed that the earth's shape was not simple and round, but more geometrically complex. The earth is shaped like a pear.

> An original work and its parodies are like a planet and its satellites. . . . There is no single, ideal relationship between an original and an imitative work; around any literary body there can be numerous satellites at different orbital levels, representing unique balances between the forces of imitation and creation.

So when you inform, you can do so in a wide range of attitudes and styles. You can treat a subject from a distance in prose that is taut and cold:

> Muhammed Ali predicted several of his early victories. He advanced from Golden Gloves champion to Olympic gold medalist to heavyweight champion. He acquired significant public attention with his two victories over Sonny Liston and convincing defeats of other fighters—including former champion, Floyd Patterson—over the next three years. He was less successful, though, in dealing with the courts.

Or you may develop a fondness for your subject, and find a way of giving it a personal touch that demonstrates your care and concern. Your informative aim will be no less well served:

> If any man could be said to have controlled his destiny, it seemed Ali was the man. Audacity helped turn his early prophecies into actual victories. They came so easily, those initial successes: Golden Gloves champ, Olympic gold medalist, and finally, heavyweight champ. Until Ali became the champion, he was, to many, just a loudmouthed boy from Louisville, but once he cooled Sonny Liston and snatched the title, he acquired an attentive audience. Ali continued to "shock the world!" as he put it after the first Liston fight, by taking out Liston in one round during their rematch. The blows Ali leveled at Liston would overwhelm Floyd Patterson (a former champ) as well. For the next three years, no one could touch Ali. In the ring he was invincible. In the courtroom, though, he was helpless.

—Lon Cargill, "To an Athlete Dying Middle-Aged"

Invention for Informative Writing

**Finding
subject matter**

In recent years, specialty magazines have proliferated. Drugstore and supermarket racks overflow with monthly journals on subjects as narrow and specific as running, jogging, macrame, amateur rocketry, Texas football, scuba diving, and many more. Until you have paged through one of the issues, you might wonder how the editors of any one of these publications can fill their pages month after month. What can you say about running twelve issues a year, year after year? Yet the success of specialty magazines proves that not only can the editors find new material, but the material is interesting enough to persuade consumers to fork out $2.00–$3.00 each month to read it. How do the editors do it?

A glance through the table of contents of one such magazine is enlightening. Here are some of the regular features which every issue of one specialty magazine, *Runner's World,* includes:

> Byline [identifies contributors to the issue]
> From the Editor
> Runner's World Update [news briefs]
> Readers' Forum [reports on running]
> For the Record [recent running records]
> Around the Country [upcoming competitive events]
> Medical Advice
> Best of Times [recent race timings]
> Running Shorts [anecdotes]
> Olympic Update
> Dear Runner's World [letters]

These regular features and the general sections used by most serial publications—journals, magazines, newspapers, newsletters—are ways of generating subject matter. Each issue of *Time,* for example, has sections on the nation, the world, sports, the law, the economy and business, theater, books, cinema, science, and art, along with other features. The editors know that they will have to fill up each category with some event or development of the past week. That simple commitment generates pages of information from equally simple questions: what happened this week in sports? In the nation? In the theater? What happened in the world of economics and business? In the world of science?

Forms and structures

Forms and questionnaires are probably the most familiar kind of slot-filling device used for generating informative discourse. When you fill out a form, you are generating the information the carefully controlled questions and spaces demand:

```
┌─────────────────────────────────────────────────────────┐
│                                                         │
│   Name: _____  Date: _____  │
│                                                         │
│   Address: _____ │
│                                                         │
│   Place of employment: _____ │
│                                                         │
│   Number of years employed: _____ │
│                                                         │
│   Amount of loan requested: _____ │
│                                                         │
│   Reason for loan: _____ │
│                                                         │
└─────────────────────────────────────────────────────────┘
```

Some types of informative discourse follow clearly defined forms and structures. In such cases—lab reports, book reports, summaries—the form will determine your subject matter. Similarly, structural devices such as the four-to-seven paragraph essay can generate ideas and subject matter:

> 1) introduction/thesis,
> 2) example #1,
> 3) example #2,
> 4) example #3, #4, #5, etc.,
> 5) conclusion.

Confronted by this structure, you know you must have a beginning paragraph that states a thesis. You are committed to finding three to five examples (or arguments or reasons or details) that support the thesis. And then you conclude. And in this elementary way, the essay is built. The model for exploratory writing discussed in this chapter is another such structural aid to invention, as are the six parts of the classical oration:

> 1) the exordium,
> 2) the exposition,
> 3) the proposition,
> 4) the argument,
> 5) the refutation, and
> 6) the conclusion.

The classical oration

The Journalist's Questions and the Modes

But not all ideas can be generated nor all topics developed in these slotted ways. Returning to the table of contents of *Runner's World*, we find that regular features make up only a part of the publication. The magazine also examines particular, nonrepeating topics that demonstrate how even a simple action like running can be amplified, developed, and complicated:

A Simple Guide to Carbohydrate Loading
The Man Who Preserves Bodies
Weight Training for Women Runners
Two Steps Ahead of the Running Boom
The Runner's Diary
Putting Your Finger on the Source of Pain
America's Golden Girl
The AAU Championships

—*Runner's World,* August 1979

Running is no longer just moving fast. For *Runner's World,* it is everything associated with running: the people, the events, the locales, the history, the techniques, the psychological motivations. It involves reflections on the act of running and anecdotes about great milers and distance runners. It is the examination and definition of types of running skills and competitions. It is the evaluation of running performances and equipment. And more.

We can generate topics of this variety in a systematic way by using and combining two familiar devices: the journalist's questions and the modes of discourse. Satisfactory news stories generally provide answers to these basic questions:

The journalist's questions

Who?
What?
Where?
When?
Why?
How?

These same questions can generate material for other kinds of informative writing. In many cases, these questions will uncover all the aspects of a topic you can conveniently handle.

General subject: Running

Running ⟶ Who?
Who are the top runners in America today?

Running ⟶ What?
What are the major races this month?

Running ⟶ Where?
In what cities or regions did running first attain its new status as America's most popular sport?

Running ⟶ When?
When did Jesse Owens win his Olympic gold medals? What were the circumstances?

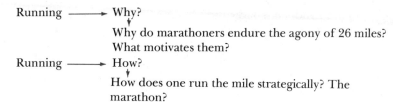

Running ⟶ Why?
                 Why do marathoners endure the agony of 26 miles?
                 What motivates them?

Running ⟶ How?
                 How does one run the mile strategically? The
                 marathon?

If these questions do not raise enough interest or insight into a topic themselves, you can plot *who, what, where,* and *when* against the modes to produce a matrix that explores a subject from yet more perspectives. (*How* and *why* are not included because *how* is considered under the category of narration/process and *why* under evaluation.) A full matrix of modes and questions would look like this:

The modes and the questions

	Description	Narration	Classification	Evaluation
WHO?	1	2	3	4
WHAT?	5	6	7	8
WHERE?	9	10	11	12
WHEN?	13	14	15	16

Applied to a general topic, the matrix generates questions like these in each of the numbered categories:

General topic: Shakespeare

1. (who/description) What did Shakespeare look like? Are there any life portraits of him? What evidence do we have on his appearance?

2. (who/narration) What were the major events in Shakespeare's life? His career? Whom did he marry? For what reasons? Did he have children? A mistress? What can we tell about his life from his literary works?

3. (who/classification) What was Shakespeare's social position? His religion? His economic status? What position and status did his profession have in England?

4. (who/evaluation) Where does Shakespeare rank among English poets and playwrights? Where among world authors?

5. (what/description) In what form were Shakespeare's plays published? What is a quarto? A folio? What does the Shakespeare First Folio contain?

6. (what/narration-process) In what order were Shakespeare's

plays produced? How did Shakespeare compose a play? How did he reshape his sources?

7. (what/classification) What kinds of plays did Shakespeare write? What distinguishes the types? How were his plays like/unlike those of his contemporaries?

8. (what/evaluation) Which of Shakespeare's plays are his best? Which work most successfully on stage today? Why? What do literary critics say about the plays?

9. (where/description) Where were Shakespeare's plays performed? What were his theaters like? What was their size? Shape? Capacity? Audience?

10. (where/narration) How was an Elizabethan play staged? What can we learn about staging from the plays as we have them?

11. (where/classification) How was the Elizabethan stage like/unlike the modern stage? What types of theaters did the Elizabethans have?

12. (where/evaluation) What advantages did Shakespeare's stage have over contemporary structures? What disadvantages?

13. (when/description) What characterized the English Renaissance? What was England like socially, economically, politically, architecturally, artistically, musically in Shakespeare's time?

14. (when/narration) What do we know about the history of Shakespeare's acting company? How did it acquire its theater? What political and social events in London affected Shakespeare's troupe?

15. (when/classification) How did the English Renaissance resemble developments on the continent of Europe? What other periods of theatrical activity in England parallel the time of Shakespeare? What are the characteristics of such times?

16. (when/evaluation) What were the accomplishments of the English Renaissance? Its failures?

This lengthy roster of questions is offered only as an example of the kinds of inquiries you can make when prompted by the modes and the journalist's questions. You may never need to examine a subject this thoroughly to discover the perspective you want to follow. Yet despite the length of the roster of questions, it is not exhaustive. And there is overlap in the coverage at some points. With some general topics, certain categories might suggest no questions at all. Any questions you do ask will suggest additional limitations. No matter. The categories succeed if they suggest to you some aspect of a subject worth your extended attention.

What does the reader need to know?

In answering any one question (or a related group of them) developed by an aid to invention, the writer aiming to inform needs to remember one fundamental question: what does my reader need to know? Not every aspect of a subject is equally important to every audience, nor is a writer obligated to anticipate every potential question. For example, when Jimmy Carter began his campaign for the presidency in late 1975 and early 1976, the great question was "Jimmy who?" People wanted to learn about the man, his education, politics, family, religion, properties, and more. But after Carter was elected, the *who* in the news stories was answered by the simple term *President*. And the nation's attention turned to *what* Jimmy would do, and *how*.

The process of invention for informative discourse is simplified if you can determine at the outset what information readers don't have but need.

Reading and the Library

Reference works

Use the library as a stimulus to thinking. When you have a question or idea, go there to discover what others have said about it before writing on the subject yourself. An encyclopedia entry can quickly deepen your knowledge of a subject, answering economically questions you hadn't even thought to ask, opening avenues for further exploration. Dictionaries and handbooks can do the same. The definition or origin of an unfamiliar word encountered in your reading may key you in to an idea or individual worth more detailed attention:

> *Orrery* . . . (Named after Chas. Boyle, Earle of Orrery, for whom a copy of the machine invented by George Graham *c* 1700 was made by J. Rowley, an instrument maker.) A piece of mechanism devised to represent the motions of the planets about the sun by means of clockwork.
>
> —Oxford English Dictionary

From here, you may be off to one of the various dictionaries of bibliography to discover what you can about Messrs. Graham, Rowley, and Boyle. And then perhaps you will want to thumb the card catalog to find information on the modern equivalents of orreries, planetariums. And soon you've got an essay.

Occasionally, browse the shelves of a library reference room or section. Examine the interesting volumes and the dull ones, the atlases, corporate financial reports, lists of peerage, naval records, medical treatises, charts and maps. You will find unusual volumes such as William Walsh's *Handy Book of Curious Information* or Tom Burnam's *Dictionary of Misinformation*. You'll find lists of world records, museum catalogs, handbooks of etiquette, collections of mythology, and compendiums of folklore, mythology, and symbols. There are lists of famous men and indexes to famous women, various guides to who's who and who was who. There are abstracts of history and outlines of Western thought, dictionaries and encyclopedias of religions, science, arts, and sports. And you will find shelf after shelf of technical information, from the decisions of the Supreme Court to catalogues of economic statistics. You may even discover a dictionary of fictional detectives, and more—lots more.

Newspapers, books, magazines

Old newspapers, books, and magazines can stimulate the imagination too. If you are interested in some person, event, product, style, fad, fashion, or problem of the past, read about it in a periodical contemporary with it. Your favorite movie may be *The Wizard of Oz* or *On the Waterfront*. How favorably was it reviewed when it was introduced? You could find out by consulting books on film history. But why rely on a secondhand source? Find a magazine or newspaper from 1939 or 1954 that contains a review and find out for yourself. And that periodical itself—the news it contains, its advertisements, its graphics—may suggest ideas to you about the film that the book about films may ignore. Just browsing through old magazines can be a lesson in styles and values. How has sports coverage changed? What was the world doing the week you were born? How much did cars cost in 1932? Essays are brewing.

Similarly, flipping through a yearbook or almanac—those vast compendiums of facts, tables, summaries, and dates—can alter your perspectives and get you thinking. How populous a nation is Israel? Forty million? Fifty million? Consult an almanac for the surprising figure. How does the United States rank as a producer of oil? Pretty low, no doubt. But you better check the facts. Which is the richest nation on earth? That's easy. Or is it? Check it out. How old is Elizabeth Taylor? Where was Dwight Eisenhower born? How many tons of wheat were produced in Canada last year?

Don't ignore card catalogues and bibliographies as aids to invention. Subject catalogues can be an especially productive vein when you are mining for suggestions to enrich an essay. And don't ignore the librarians either. They aren't in the library to find topics for you, but they can direct you to places where topics might be found.

Exercises

1. Examine the table of contents of a specialty magazine that intrigues you. Then classify the major articles and departments according to the journalist's questions that they answer: Who? What? Where? When? Why? How?

2. Construct a list of sixteen questions that might be generated from a topic of your choosing by using the matrix for informative writing. From the sixteen questions, choose four or five that might be tied together to form a single essay.

3. Browse the reference room in a local library to find three intriguing reference works you have rarely or never used. Examine these works and find at least three topics or subjects you might want to find out more about. List the topics.

4. Choose a topic from exercise 3 and write a 500-word report on it, supplementing the information gained from the initial reference work with at least three additional sources.

5. In the library reference room, examine a copy of Constance Winchell's *Guide to Reference Books*. Using this work and any library skills you can muster, choose a question from the list below and spend no more than an hour trying to answer it. Whether you find the answer or not, write up a short report (100–200 words) explaining your research strategy. Compare your library strategy with that of classmates. Then tackle a second and third question.

   a. What does "as plain as Dunstable Way" mean? What is the first recorded use of the phrase?
   b. What Indian tribes lived in the county you were born in? What language did they speak?
   c. Where could you find a book or article to tell you how to feed and care for a baby owl?
   d. What was the price of a new Plymouth in 1954? How wide were lapels in that year?
   e. You are taking a camping vacation through Texas, Louisiana, Mississippi, Alabama, and Tennessee. Find some books to give you information about campgrounds (maps, facilities, prices, days open, etc.).
   f. About how many automobiles were on American farms in 1920? How many tractors?
   g. What was the dollar value of US exports in military sales to Latin American countries in 1960 and 1966?
   h. How many bookstores (approximately) are there in Paris? In New York?
   i. How does it happen that Christians pray with their hands pressed together?
   j. How did pockets get invented?

6. What happened the week that you were born? Write an informative essay on this topic that draws on materials from several newspapers and magazines.

7. Use the library as a resource for narrowing down one of the following questions to a manageable size. Then form a tentative hypothesis and outline an essay.

    a. What is philosophy?
    b. What defines classical music?
    c. How are diseases controlled?
    d. How have movies developed?
    e. How has the Democratic party changed?
    f. What controls the weather?
    g. Who were the Morgans?
    h. How did the Olympics develop?
    i. How does printing work?
    j. Who were the Romans?

Your instructor may suggest other general questions.

The Research Paper

What a research paper does

    More than once in your academic career you will probably be asked to write a research paper. Depending upon the discipline (history, psychology, English, anthropology, etc.) and the particular assignment, a research paper may be designed to convey information, to demonstrate assertions, or to explore new ideas. Or it may combine the basic aims of informative writing discussed in this chapter.

    The process of writing a research paper is often more formal than writing another kind of essay. Your instructor may ask you to keep a record of your research procedures in a journal or to prepare a detailed outline and preliminary drafts. You may be asked to turn in all your drafts and notecards when the paper itself is due. The following section deals with some of the formalities of producing the research paper.

    But don't allow composing a research essay to become a purely mechanical exercise ten pages long. Rather, consider what you are doing in terms of the aims discussed in this chapter. How can you convey information about your subject that is clear, surprising, and thorough? What must you do to prove adequately the basic assertions you make about your subject? How can you reshape what you have learned about the past into practical and innovative suggestions for future action?

Invention and your thesis statement

    To do a research paper well, you will have to transform the mechanical procedures into a process of discovery. You'll want to begin with one of the techniques of invention described in this chapter. Then you can formulate a thesis statement or a working hypothesis. But as you do your research, you will probably discover that your subject or thesis is changing, revealing new aspects, becoming more refined, altering your preliminary opinions and assumptions. If your essay is a demonstration or exploration, you may not discover what you want to say until after you have finished your research.

Using
source material

Real research involves more than rehashing the facts and ideas you've borrowed from a dozen books. You want to take that source material and shape it into a useful summary of events, a convincing body of evidence, or an intriguing assessment of present and future. The sample research paper in this section borrows facts and materials about the Persian Wars from eight sources. The author himself has contributed no new material facts to his presentation of the subject. He couldn't. Instead, the borrowed facts are used to explain a question that initially puzzled the author: how did the underdogs in that war, the Greeks, manage to win? Each source contributes an idea, a fact, or a description to answer the initial question. Systematically, the author assembles the material, looking for areas of agreement and disagreement in the various sources until, *at the end of the research process,* he can write the statement that gives the essay its confident thesis: the Greeks enjoyed better weapons, morale, strategy, and luck. The material facts of the essay (who? what? where? when? how? why?) are borrowed; the idea that gives them shape, interest, and cohesion is provided by the author whose aim is to inform and to demonstrate.

Length: Narrowing Your Subject

What you do in an investigative paper is in part determined by expectations of length and comprehensiveness. An essay of 5000 words can be more ambitious in its choice of topics than one of 500. Most college research papers fall between 1500–2500 words.

Given this typical length, you should try to avoid general topics and massive subjects: health, the Roman Catholic church, Shakespeare, modern architecture. You could stuff whole encyclopedias with information on those subjects. You might begin a paper wanting to write about some such topic, but quickly narrow your ideas down to some specific aspect or idea that you can hope to learn about in a few weeks or months:

> health
> Paracelsus and the treatment of miners' diseases in the sixteenth century

> the Roman Catholic church
> art treasures in the Vatican

> Shakespeare
> the books Shakespeare may have read

```
┌─ modern architecture
└─► Le Corbusier and Modern French Architecture
```

How do you narrow a general topic to a thesis statement? The sections on informing, demonstrating, and exploring suggest techniques appropriate to each of the types of informative writing. The best general advice is to examine a reference work that provides a concise overview of your subject.

You may find it an advantage to choose a research topic with a little bite to it, so that the thesis statement requires you to demonstrate or prove something:

> Nursery rhymes foster sexist attitudes.
>
> Producing oil from shale would have disastrous environmental consequences.
>
> The shopping mall is destroying neighborhood shops and businesses.
>
> The weather, more than the English, defeated the Spanish Armada in 1588.

By identifying an issue clearly and argumentatively, you know exactly what you must prove and what kinds of facts, documents, and proofs you must muster to establish your position. Moreover, you are more likely to grab your reader's interest with an idea that challenges conventional beliefs or attitudes.

Researching a Topic

Encyclopedias

Begin your research with encyclopedias or other general reference tools. Such works will give you a compact summary of your topic and place your narrow inquiry within a larger context. Even if you are writing only about the cost of extracting oil from shale, it would be useful to you to know something about the costs of oil exploration and the economics of buying foreign oil. An encyclopedia would probably provide you with this needed background information (though figures and facts on a subject like this are quickly outdated). Don't limit yourself to general encyclopedias if one geared to your subject is available. There are full encyclopedias that deal with individual religions, sciences, disciplines, and crafts. There are massive dictionaries of biography as well, which can supply you with facts you need about particular individuals:

> The New Catholic Encyclopedia
> Grove's Dictionary of Music and Musicians
> The Encyclopedia of Philosophy
> The Encyclopedia of the Social Sciences

Encyclopedia of the American Revolution
Dictionary of National Biography (Great Britain)
Dictionary of American Biography

Use a reference work fitted to your time and purposes. If you want quick information, works like the *New Columbia Encyclopedia* or *Collier's Encyclopedia* might be your most efficient choice. For more detailed information, you might turn to the *Encyclopaedia Britannica*. Remember, though, that an encyclopedia or general reference work is a beginning, not a conclusion, to research.

For more information, proceed to the card catalog in the library. **The card catalog** Card catalogs sometimes lump authors, titles, and subjects together. Some libraries separate subject listings from author/title cards. A subject listing can be a fruitful source of references and ideas.

When browsing the card catalogue, be critical. Don't just list the **Bibliographies** first five or ten books in the drawer. Examine the entries to determine **and indexes** whether individual books are worth the effort it will take to retrieve them from the shelves. Cards in the file can tell you the subtitle of the book, its length, date of publication, publisher, general contents, and whether it has illustrations, an index, and a bibliography. *A bibliography and index are especially important to a researcher.* The bibliography may lead you to more source material. An index will key you in to exactly the part of a book you are interested in. (You needn't feel the obligation to read whole books while doing investigative writing.)

From the card catalog, move your search for sources to the various indexes of newspapers and periodicals. Such indexes do what catalogues cannot: they clue you in to recent articles in publications large and small. Some indexes are general, others are tied to particular interests and disciplines. The most familiar index is probably the *Readers' Guide to Periodical Literature,* but be aware of the *Humanities Index,* the *Social Science Index,* the *Biography Index,* and the *New York Times Index.* Your librarian will be able to suggest other works useful to you in pursuing a particular inquiry.

Once you have assembled a list of potential sources for your carefully focused topic, you are ready to begin reading and taking notes.

Taking Notes

Some people keep notes on cards, others in notebooks, still others **Note cards** on loose-leaf sheets. Some take relatively few notes, preferring to copy large quantities of materials and then to fill the margins with commentary or other marks. The note card methods are still probably the most efficient and economical. Cards are easily sorted, compact, and less prone to getting misplaced than notebooks or sheets of paper.

Howsoever you take notes, be sure to carefully record somewhere (preferably on a card—one source per card) all the data you will subsequently need for your footnotes and bibliography:

name of author(s)
title and subtitle of the book or article
name of periodical, newspaper, or reference work
publisher (for books)
place of publication (for books)
date (of publication or issue)
page numbers or section numbers

Many researchers keep at least two sets of cards. Cards of the first type record only the pertinent bibliographical information:

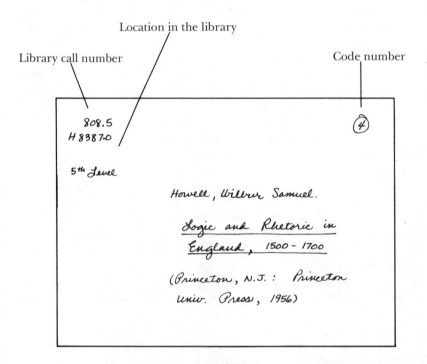

Location in the library

Library call number

Code number

808.5
H 8387.0

5th Level

Howell, Wilbur Samuel.

Logic and Rhetoric in
England, 1500 - 1700

(Princeton, N.J. : Princeton
Univ. Press, 1956)

④

Information gathered from the cited work is recorded on a second set of cards cross-referenced to the first by a code number or a short title. Notes can be organized by the source or, more efficiently, by your subject:

Note Card Organized by Source

Howell, *Logic & Rhetoric*   ④

There are three patterns of
traditional rhetoric:

1. the Ciceronian   (five parts)
2. the Stylistic   (heavy emphasis
   on style)
3. the formulary (heavy emphasis
   on examples)

                           pp. 6-7

Note Cards Organized by Subjects

Rhetoric: Ciceronian

   Ciceronian rhetoric is based
on the writings of Cicero and
Quintilian. It emphasizes the
traditional five parts of rhetoric:
invention, arrangement, style,
memory, and delivery.
                    Howell, pp. 6-7

> Rhetoric formulary (definition) ④
>
> _Formulary rhetoric_ "is made up of compositions drawn to illustrate rhetorical principles and presented as models to students to imitate in the process of developing themselves for the tasks of communication."
>
> Howell, p. 138

This method saves you the time it would take to record bibliographical information on every note card. The cross-reference directs you from your notes to their source. When you are done with your research, the first set of cards can be put in alphabetical order and typed up as your bibliography. You may find it practical to keep bibliographical information on three-by-five-inch or four-by-six-inch cards, and notes on larger five-by-eight-inch cards.

Plagiarism

Be sure that your notes reflect your own version of source material, not a simple paraphrase. If you do paraphrase, be sure that the paraphrased material does not subsequently find its way into your own essay unacknowledged. That would be plagiarism—claiming someone else's thoughts and language as your own. One way to avoid plagiarism while taking notes is to read your source, section by section, and to write your comments or summary with the book or periodical closed. Then open the material and check the accuracy of your comments. Be sure to keep track of page numbers throughout this process. Put a page reference next to every significant line or paragraph in your notes. Doing this will save you much time later when you write up your footnotes.

Quoting accurately

When you find material in your source that merits direct quotation, copy it word-for-word, figure-for-figure, letter-for-letter, complete to any errors in the original (which you can indicate with a [_sic_] to show that the error is not yours). Quotations should be scrupulously accurate.

Other sources

Finally, don't assume that printed materials can be your only sources of information. When your subject requires them, conduct interviews, watch films, cite television programs, observe events yourself, or record your own experiences. These too can be part of your record of research.

Preparing the Essay

When you have gathered what seems to be an adequate amount of information, read through all of your notes to determine what you actually have. Fill any obvious gaps with another afternoon's work in the library. Then prepare some preliminary outlines to see how your materials fit together. These should be short, rough, and tentative:

Topic: the causes and consequences of the Great Fire of London, September 1666

Preliminary outline

A. Introduction
B. How the fire started
   1. Accidental?
   2. Deliberate?
C. The fire itself
   1. Where
   2. When
   3. What it destroyed
   4. How it was stopped
D. Consequences
   1. Rebuilding of the city: Sir Christopher Wren
   2. Safer, healthier atmosphere
E. Conclusion

Adequate research

After examining several such schemes of organization, you can pick one that works best and begin fitting your information together. If you have kept your notes on cards, you can gather related slips and organize them into piles keyed to particular points on the outline. Ideally, several sources will contribute to each section and paragraph of the finished work. If you have too much information, you must decide what to leave out. Don't include any materials in a report that contribute little or nothing to the idea you are developing no matter how interesting they may be or how much time you spent collecting them. On the other hand, when your research has been inadequate, admit it and spend some more time in the library. Don't fill cavities in your work with stuffing.

After fitting your materials to your rough plan of development, you may want to construct a more detailed outline to guide you through the writing of your first draft. This outline may consist of phrases or, even more formally, of complete sentences. You may even choose to indicate precisely where you will insert particular citations or direct quotations.

Your outline prepares you to write the first draft of your essay. More than some other types of writing, research papers often require formal introductions, clearly articulated patterns of organization, and detailed conclusions.

The Final Version

When, after one or several drafts, you are finally ready to produce "the paper," review any particular instructions your teacher has given you about format.

Research papers sometimes include a separate title page, an outline, an abstract, footnotes, and a list of sources. Not all of these elements are always required. Check with your instructor.

Footnotes

Your teacher may specify whether footnotes are to be placed at the bottom of the pages of your text, or gathered together at the end of an essay (as in the sample paper). In either case, footnotes are numbered consecutively through the piece, not page-by-page. Footnotes placed at the bottom of a page are easy to find but hard to type. And they can distract a reader. Footnotes at the end of an essay are more convenient for the typist and the writer, and not especially troubling to a reader. But if your essay has its notes on a separate sheet at the end, don't staple it together. Use a paperclip so that a reader can remove the page of notes and place it alongside the text for reference while reading.

Use a handbook or research paper guide for advice on documenting unusual sources. In most cases, the form for documentation will be relatively straightforward.

Sample Footnotes

—Book with one author:

> [1] Preserved Smith, The Enlightenment, 1687–1776 (1934; rpt. New York: Collier Books, 1962), pp. 202–03.

(Note that this footnote indicates that the work was originally published in 1934 and is examined in a later printing. This is important information since it tells your reader that the source is approximately half a century old.)

> [2] Smith, p. 208.

(This note is to the same work cited in footnote # 1. Since the full title and publishing information are given directly above, there's no need to repeat that information here, or in subsequent references to the work.)

—Book with two authors:

> [3] R. Ernest Dupuy and Trevor N. Dupuy, The Encyclopedia of Military History (New York: Harper & Row, 1970), p. 71.

—Book with multiple authors:

> [4] M. H. Abrams, et al., The Norton Anthology of English Literature, 3rd. ed. (New York: Norton, 1974), pp. 294–295.

—Book with a translator:

> 5 Alexander Solzhenitsyn, <u>August 1914</u>, trans. Michael Glenny (New York: Farrar, Straus and Giroux, 1971), p. 21.

—An edition:

When you are citing the editor's work, the editor's name comes first.

> 6 G. N. Garmonsway, ed., <u>Aelfric's Colloquy</u> (New York: Appleton-Century-Crofts, 1966), p. v.

Place the author's name first when you are citing the actual text of the work.

> 7 Jane Austen, <u>Pride and Prejudice</u>, ed. Mark Schorer (Boston: Houghton Mifflin, 1956), pp. 5-9.

—An article in a collection:

> 8 Kellogg W. Hunt, "Early Blooming and Late Blooming Syntactic Structures," in <u>Evaluating Writing</u>, ed. Charles Cooper and Lee Odell (Urbana, Ill.: <u>NCTE</u>, 1977,) p. 91.

(Since Urbana is not so well known as New York, London, or Chicago, it is followed by an abbreviated designation of state: Ill.)

—A reference book:

> 9 "Calligraphy," <u>The New Columbia Encyclopedia</u>, 1975 ed.

(Since encyclopedias are alphabetically arranged, no page number is necessary in the footnote.)

—A magazine article:

> 10 Anthony Lewis, "Supreme Court Confidential," <u>The New York Review of Books</u>, 7 Feb. 1980, p. 3.

> 11 "The Pope in America," <u>Time</u>, 15 Oct. 1979, p. 14.

(No author is listed here because the article in *Time* is unsigned.)

—A journal article (numbered by volume, not by individual issue):

> 12 Evan Carton, "Complicity and Responsibility in Pandarus' Bed and Chaucer's Art," <u>PMLA</u>, 94 (1979), 60.

—Newspaper articles:

> 13 Patrick Malone, "Players Risking Further Injury," <u>Austin American-Statesman</u>, 2 Sept. 1979, Sec. J., p. 11, col. 4-5.

> 14 "Ensure Protection for Whistle Blowers," Editorial, <u>Austin American-Statesman</u>, 9 March 1980, Sec. C., p. 2, col. 1.

(an unsigned editorial)

—A movie:

> 15 Franco Zeffirelli, dir., <u>Romeo and Juliet</u>, with Leonard Whiting and Olivia Hussey, BHE Verona Productions, 1968.

—A television program:

16 <u>CBS</u> <u>Evening</u> <u>News</u>, writ. and narr. Walter Cronkite, 22 June 1980.

(You may include director and producer in the note if that information is important.)

—A personal interview:

17 Personal interview with Jimmy Carter, 13 May 1980.

Bibliography

A bibliography is an alphabetical list of the sources consulted in compiling a research or investigative paper. Because the list is alphabetical, an author's last name or the first key word in the title comes first in the entry; there are other differences between footnote and bibliography form too, particularly in punctuation. Include in your bibliography all the items that you cite in your footnotes plus every additional work that contributed to your understanding of the subject. Don't pad bibliographies.

Selective and annotated bibliographies

There are two special types of bibliographies you should be aware of: *selective bibliographies* and *annotated bibliographies*. Selective bibliographies list the most important or best works on a given subject. In a sense, the bibliography you prepare for a research paper will be selective since you will exclude sources that you consulted but which did not prove useful. Annotated bibliographies are lists of works on a subject with commentary. An annotated bibliography can be a helpful research tool since its comments may direct you to exactly the materials you need. Moreover, it may tell you what sources are not reliable or up-to-date.

Sample Bibliography Entries

(Be sure to check the sample research paper for the proper arrangement of bibliography entries.)

—Book with one author:

Smith, Preserved. <u>The</u> <u>Enlightenment,</u> <u>1687–1776</u>. 1934; rpt. New York: Collier Books, 1962.

—Book with two authors:

Dupuy, R. Ernest, and Trevor N. Dupuy. <u>The</u> <u>Encyclopedia</u> <u>of</u> <u>Military</u> <u>History</u> <u>from</u> <u>3500</u> <u>B.C.</u> <u>to</u> <u>the</u> <u>Present.</u> Rev. ed. New York: Harper & Row, 1970.

—Book with multiple authors:

Abrams, M. H., et al. <u>The</u> <u>Norton</u> <u>Anthology</u> <u>of</u> <u>English</u> <u>Literature</u>. 3rd ed. New York: Norton, 1974.

—Book with a translator:

> Solzhenitsyn, Alexander. <u>August 1914</u>. Trans. Michael
> Glenny. New York: Farrar, Straus and Giroux, 1971.

—An edition:

> Garmonsway, G. N., ed. <u>Aelfric's Colloquy</u>. New York:
> Appleton-Century-Crofts, 1966.

> Austen, Jane. <u>Pride and Prejudice</u>. Ed. Mark Schorer.
> Boston: Houghton Mifflin, 1956.

—An article in a collection:

> Hunt, Kellogg W. "Early Blooming and Late Blooming Syn-
> tactic Structures." In <u>Evaluating Writing</u>: <u>Describing</u>,
> <u>Measuring</u>, <u>Judging</u>. Ed. Charles Cooper and Lee Odell.
> Urbana, Ill.: <u>NCTE</u>, 1977, pp. 91-104.

—A reference book:

> "Calligraphy." <u>The New Columbia Encyclopedia</u>. 1975 ed.

—A magazine article:

> Lewis, Anthony. "Supreme Court Confidential." <u>The New York
> Review of Books</u>, 7 Feb. 1980, pp. 3-8.

> "The Pope in America." <u>Time</u>, 15 Oct. 1979, pp. 12-35.

—A journal article:

> Carton, Evan. "Complicity and Responsibility in Pandarus'
> Bed and Chaucer's Art." <u>PMLA</u>, 94 (1979), 47-61.

—Newspaper articles:

> Malone, Patrick. "Players Risking Further Injury." <u>Austin
> American-Statesman</u>, 2 Sept. 1979, Sec. J, p. 11, col.
> 4-5.

> "Ensure Protection for Whistle Blowers." Editorial. <u>Austin
> American-Statesman</u>, 9 March 1980, Sec. C., p. 2, col. 1.

—A movie:

> Zeffirelli, Franco, dir. <u>Romeo and Juliet</u>. With Leonard
> Whiting and Olivia Hussey. BHE Verona Productions,
> 1968.

—A television program:

> <u>CBS Evening News</u>. Writ. and narr. Walter Cronkite. 22 June
> 1980.

—A personal interview:

> Carter, Jimmy. Personal interview. 13 May 1980.

A complete sample research paper follows.

Mark Kusner

History 306

Professor Mulderig

March 23, 1981

Why Xerxes Lost:

An Account of the Persian Wars

Thesis: The Greeks thwarted Xerxes' attempt to conquer
the Greek mainland because they enjoyed better weapons, morale, strategy, and luck.

  I. Background of Xerxes' invasion, 480–79 B.C.

     A. Darius' plans for an invasion

     B. Xerxes' plan

        1. Bridge across the Hellespont

        2. Channel through the Athos peninsula

     C. Xerxes' problems

        1. The size of his army

        2. The composition of his army

        3. The navies

 II. The Battles of Thermopylae and Artemision

     A. Greek strategy at Thermopylae

     B. Sea maneuverings at Artemision

     C. Greek defeat at Thermopylae and withdrawal
        at Artemision

     D. Consequences of the battles

III. The Sea Battle at Salamis

     A. Greek strategy at Salamis

     B. The Persian defeat

     C. Xerxes' return to Persia

 IV. The Battle at Plataia

     A. Greek strategy at Plataia

     B. The Persian defeat

  V. Conclusion

                           i

Why Xerxes Lost:

An Account of the Persian Wars

The Greek defense of Eastern European civilization against the Persian armies of Xerxes has traditionally been portrayed as a David VS Goliath struggle. Vastly outnumbered, the Greeks yet managed to thwart Xerxes' effort to annex their homeland to his already sprawling empire in the fifth century B.C. How did 110,000 Greeks repulse a reported 1,700,000 Persians? An analysis of the four major battles of the war—Thermopylae, Artemision, Salamis, and Plataia—shows that the Greeks enjoyed better weapons, morale, strategy, and luck.

In 490 B.C., the Persian monarch, Darius, launched an invasion of the Greek mainland to put an end to an irritating Greek influence in the Aegean area, but his forces suffered a humiliating defeat at Marathon (490).[1] Enraged, Darius plotted a larger expedition, combining land and sea forces, to crush his Greek foes. The invasion was three years in preparation when, in 487, Egypt revolted against Persian dominance. Darius was compelled to delay his planned attack. He died in 486, bequeathing his kingdom and his design for conquering Greece to his son, Xerxes. Xerxes quickly suppressed the Egyptian uprising in 485. Then he turned his attentions to the Greeks.

The new monarch had to be persuaded to undertake his father's invasion, but the advice of relatives and counselors convinced him to continue the expensive and elaborate preparations.[2] A bridge was built across

1

Quadruple space

Triremes **defined**

the Hellespont to expedite troop movements, and a
channel wide enough for two triremes (warships with
three tiers of oars) was cut through the peninsula of
Athos to protect the fleet from stormy bluffs around
Mt. Athos where a Persian navy had foundered in 492.[3]
Stores of grain and supplies were assembled along the
projected route of march from Asia right on into
European and Greek soil.[4]

Herodotus identified

 The actual size of Xerxes' invasion force is a
matter much disputed by historians. Herodotus, a
Greek historian whose account of the Persian Wars is
generally reliable, gives an unacceptably high figure
for the size of Xerxes' army:

**Quote indented
ten spaces**

  What the exact number of troops of each nation was
  I cannot say with certainty—for it is not
  mentioned by anyone—but the whole land army
  together was found to amount to 1,700,000.[5]

Triple space

Herodotus' error has been explained in a variety of
ways, and Xerxes' army trimmed by subsequent
historians to approximately 210,000 men— still a
formidable power.[6] This size was one of Xerxes'
problems. His army moved slowly, hampered by poor
communications and the need to find large supplies of
food in unfriendly territories.

 A second problem Xerxes faced stemmed from the
composition of his army. Aside from the Persian
contingents and the elite Immortals, most of Xerxes'

grand army consisted of conscripts from various conquered parts of his empire. As C. Hignett observes,
"unwilling subjects would not make good soldiers or
sailors."[7] Moreover, these men were not well-armed,
despite the Persian experience of losing at Marathon
in part because of the superiority of Greek weapons.[8]
Xerxes did possess a superb cavalry.

Herodotus also exaggerates the size of the Persian
navy, reporting a figure of 1207 triremes.[9] But even
a more conservative estimate of 600–800 ships gives
Xerxes a fleet considerably larger than any the Greeks
would have been able to muster. And Xerxes had in his
service the finest sailors in the world, the Phoeni-
cians.[10] Persian triremes were constructed for speed
and built high for the positioning of archers. Greek
ships (which numbered approximately 400) were low and
stoutly built to withstand the ramming techniques
favored by Greek sailors. Unlike the Persians, Greeks
preferred to board enemy ships and engage in hand-to-
hand combat.[11]

The first two major battles of the war took place
almost simultaneously in August, 480 B.C.: the defense
of the pass of Thermopylae and the naval engagement
at Artemision.

The Persians marched with ease through northern
Greece, following a strategic Greek retreat from the
pass of Tempe.[12] The Greeks chose instead to hold a
narrower and more defensible position at Thermopylae,
one supported by a fleet at nearby Artemision.[13] The
pass, only fifty feet across at its narrowest, guarded

**Note the phrase
introducing the
quotation**

**First and second
battles**

the entrance to central Greece. The decision to defend the pass was strategically sound since it pitted
the numerically superior Persians against the local
geography. For all the vast numbers of his army,
Xerxes could march against only a fifty-foot front,
leaving the rest of his army inactive. But the Greeks
failed to support their brilliant move with enough
troops.

Only 7000 Greeks under the Spartan king, Leonidas,
were sent to Thermopylae, with the promise of more
troops to follow. A thousand of these men were deployed to defend a little-known track over Kallidromos
by which Thermopylae could be turned. The decision to
fortify Kallidromos so lightly proved fateful since
it was Xerxes' subsequent discovery of this route that
led to Leonidas' defeat.[14]

Yet fortune seemed to smile on the Greeks. The
Persian navy approaching Artemision was caught in a
storm at Cape Sepias and heavily damaged. Herodotus
reports that as many as four hundred triremes may have
been lost during the storm (probably another exaggerated figure), while the Greek fleet, adequately
sheltered, sustained no significant damage.[15] On land
the assault on Thermopylae began with little success.
Wave after wave of Xerxes' conscripted troops failed
to daunt the stout Spartan line, and his Immortals
fared no better. The pass held.

At Artemision, the fleets finally engaged. The
Persians, with their superior numbers, tried to out-

flank the Greeks who successfully maintained a close
and defensible formation. The battle lingered on until night, when the fleets disengaged. Maneuvering to
surround the Greeks at night, the Persian ships were
again caught in a storm and battered, if Herodotus'
account is to be believed.[16] Fierce fighting resumed
the next day, with neither side gaining an advantage.

In the meantime, the dogged Persian assault on the
Spartans at Thermopylae continued without success
until Xerxes, learning of the pass at Kallidromos,
sent 10,000 of his elite fighters up the path where
they crushed the small number of defenders. When
Leonidas learned of Xerxes' circling maneuver, he sent
the main body of his troops into retreat, remaining
to defend Thermopylae to the death with 300 Spartans
and 1100 other soldiers. The Greeks fought bravely,
but were soon surrounded and slaughtered.[17]

The battle at Artemision was well into its third
day when news of Thermopylae's fall reached the
fleets. Their position now made untenable by Persian
control of the coast, the Greeks were forced to dis-
engage at sea and retreat to guard the island of
Salamis, leaving the Persians in control of the central portion of the country. Yet the Greeks had not
been overwhelmed. They had seen at Thermopylae and
Artemision that the superior numbers of the Persians
were of no advantage in certain situations and that,
in future battles, victory would be possible if the
Greeks capitalized on their advantages in geography

**Preliminary
conclusions**

and armaments. Even the slaughter at Thermopylae was not without significance, as Grundy observes:

Triple space

> To contemporary Greeks, and to Greeks of after time, Thermopylae seemed, if not the most important, the most impressive page in the history of the race. It was regarded as an act of pure self-sacrifice, whose splendour was such as to place it outside the range of any logical discussion as to its practical strategic value. The sole motive which was attributed to the gallant band who fought the last fight was a stern, unyielding sense of duty, such as might serve as a pattern to all after-time.[18]

Triple space

The third battle

Triumphant in Attica, Xerxes soon moved to destroy the Greek forces on Salamis, the island to which the Athenians had evacuated following the first two battles. But the Greeks saw an opportunity for victory against the reinforced Persian navy if they could draw Xerxes' ships into the narrow waters between Salamis and the mainland, thereby compressing their line of contact, as had been done with the Persian troops at Thermopylae.[19] Then the Greeks could employ their superior arms in close-quarter fighting. The plan hinged on drawing the Persians into the narrows. For days, neither fleet would take the initiative to battle in the narrows, but when the Greek navy faked a retreat, the Persians attacked to prevent its escape and fell into the trap. They were drawn steadily into the narrows while the Greek ships backed water. The long lines of Persian triremes were squeezed so that maneuvering became nearly impossible—and still the Greek ships continued to back off. Suddenly, a swell rolled through the narrow channel as it did every morning. The Greeks expected it; the Persian pilots did not. The swell threw the Persian formations into confusion, and then the Greeks attacked in the tight quarters that best suited their mode of battle.[20] While Xerxes watched from a throne overlooking the channel, the Greeks forced the Persians into retreat. They had used the enemy's numbers to their own advantage and dictated the terms of battle.

The victory destroyed Xerxes' will to personally oversee the campaign, and he returned to Persia, leaving a still formidable army and navy under the command of his general, Mardonius. Mardonius' army, made up of the best troops from the original expedition, freed of excess baggage, commanded by a true military man, may have posed a greater threat to the Greeks than Xerxes' grand army.

The Greeks spent a disorganized winter before preparing to battle the Persians again, but at length, Sparta and Athens joined forces to challenge Mardonius.[21] In the summer of 479 B.C., the two armies once again faced each other, the habitually outnumbered Greeks taking up their position three miles east of

The last battle

Plataia in a rocky, hilly area that limited the mobility of the Persian cavalry. For days, as at Salamis,
neither army attacked. But when a Greek movement in-
advertently exposed supply lines to the Persian
cavalry, the Greek position became untenable and a
retreat was ordered. Mardonius mistook the Greek
retreat for a rout, and launched a rash and disorderly
charge that he hoped would achieve a spectacular and
complete victory.[22] Once again, the Persians fell
into a trap, this one engineered by the Spartan commander, Pausanias. Though they fought bravely, the
Persians were slaughtered by the better-armed Greeks.

Note form of quote here

"As at Marathon," Peter Green observes, "it was spear
against scimitar, metal breastplate against quilted
cuiras, bronze helmet against leather cap."[23] Mardonius was slain, and victory fell to the Greeks.
Several lesser battles ensued, including a sea struggle at Mycale (also a Greek triumph), but Plataia
effectively ended the Persian Wars.

Conclusion

That the Greeks had been able to thwart Xerxes'
designs on their homeland is attributable to foot
soldiers better armed and armored than their Persian
counterparts, to Persian strategies which consistently
failed to take advantage of superior numbers, to Greek
strategies that capitalized on the terrain and conditions of battle, to the better morale of the Greek
armies, and finally, to luck. With the advantage of
hindsight, the Greeks in 480 might have considered
their victory as inevitable instead of impossible.

Notes

— Indent five spaces

[1]N. G. L. Hammond, A History of Greece to 322 B.C., 2nd ed. (Oxford: Clarendon, 1967), p. 217.

[2]Peter Green, Xerxes at Salamis (New York: Praeger, 1970), pp. 51–52.

Footnote numbers raised a half-space

[3]C. Hignett, Xerxes' Invasion of Greece (Oxford: Clarendon, 1963), p. 92.

[4]Jacob Abbott, History of Xerxes the Great (New York: 1852), p. 90.

[5]Francis R. B. Godolphin, The Greek Historians, I (New York: Random House, 1942), p. 412.

[6]A. R. Burn, Persia and the Greeks (London, St. Martin's, 1962), pp. 328–29 and Green, pp. 58–59.

[7]Hignett, p. 92.

[8]Hammond, p. 216.

[9]Godolphin, p. 418.

[10]Hammond, p. 242.

[11]Hammond, p. 241.

[12]Hammond, p. 227.

[13]Hignett, pp. 114–15.

[14]Green, pp. 116–17.

[15]Hignett, pp. 172–75.

[16]Burn, pp. 398–99; Hignett, pp. 187–88.

[17]Green, pp. 141–42.

[18]George B. Grundy, The Great Persian Wars and Its Preliminaries (1901; rpt. New York: AMS Press, 1969), pp. 313–14.

[19]William L. Rodgers, Greek and Roman Naval Warfare (Annapolis: 1937), p. 86.

[20]Green, pp. 193–94.

[21]Rodgers, pp. 98–99.

[22]Rodgers, pp. 101.

[23]Green, p. 266.

Bibliography

Abbott, Jacob. History of Xerxes the Great. New
    York: 1852.

Burn, Andrew Robert. Persia and the Greeks: The
    Defence of the West, c. 546—478 B.C. New York:
    St. Martin's Press, 1962.

Godolphin, Francis R. B. The Greek Historians: The
    Complete and Unabridged Historical Works of Herod-
    otus, Thucydides, Xenophon, Arrian. 2 vols. New
    York: Random House, 1942.

Green, Peter. Xerxes at Salamis. New York: Praeger,
    1970.

Grundy, George Beardoe. The Great Persian War and Its
    Preliminaries: a Study of the Evidence, Literary
    and Topographical. 1901; rpt. New York: AMS
    Press, 1969.

Hammond, N. G. L. A History of Greece to 322 B.C.
    2nd ed. Oxford: Clarendon, 1967.

Hignett, Charles. Xerxes' Invasion of Greece. Ox-
    ford: Clarendon, 1963.

Rodgers, William L. Greek and Roman Naval Warfare.
    Annapolis: 1937.

Quadruple space

Indent five spaces

151

Sample Page with Notes at the Bottom

486, bequeathing his kingdom and his design for crushing Greece to his son, Xerxes. Xerxes quickly suppressed the Egyptian uprising in 485. Then he turned his attentions to the Greeks.

The new monarch had to be persuaded to undertake his father's invasion, but the advice of relatives and counselors convinced him to continue the expensive and elaborate preparations.[2] A bridge was built across the Hellespont to expedite troop movements, and a channel wide enough for two triremes (warships with three tiers of oars) was cut through the peninsula of Athos to protect the fleet from stormy bluffs around Mt. Athos where a Persian navy had foundered in 492.[3] Stores of grain and supplies were assembled along the projected route of march right on into European and Greek soil.[4]

The actual size of Xerxes' invasion force is a matter much disputed by historians. Herodotus, a Greek historian whose account of the Persian Wars is generally reliable, gives an unacceptably high figure

Quadruple space

[2] Peter Green, Xerxes at Salamis (New York: Praeger, 1970), pp. 51-52.

[3] C. Hignett, Xerxes' Invasion of Greece (Oxford: Clarendon, 1963), p. 92.

[4] Jacob Abbott, History of Xerxes the Great (New York: 1852), p. 90.

Reasons for Writing

Persuasion

Persuasion and Choice

Writing that focuses on subject matter is informative. Writing that focuses on the reader with the purpose of changing opinions, modifying values, or encouraging action is persuasive. In many writing situations—political, social, ethical, religious—you use persuasion to get people to agree that a given decision or action is the best option, the one most likely to succeed. Where the facts are questionable, where systems of value held by people of different nationality, upbringing, age, race, religion, sexual orientation, political philosophy, taste, and profession seem irreconcilable, it is the task of persuasion to demonstrate a common ground, if not in facts, then in feeling and in human nature. You use persuasion to defend ideas you believe in strongly or to oppose those that seem incorrect or harmful.

Informative and demonstrative essays are sometimes regarded as products of the rational faculties of men and women; persuasion is as-

What persuasion does

sociated with emotion, a less noble trait in some opinions. Yet it may be argued that persuasion—at its best—unites the logical and emotional faculties of the human character for the tasks of judging the past, assessing the present, and mapping out the future. A distinguished philosopher and rhetorician puts the issue in these words, worth more than casual attention:

> Only the existence of an argumentation that is neither compelling nor arbitrary can give meaning to human freedom, a state in which a reasonable choice can be exercised. If freedom was no more than necessary adherence to a previously given natural order, it would exclude all possibility of choice; and if the exercise of freedom were not based on reasons, every choice would be irrational and would be reduced to an arbitrary decision operating in an intellectual void. It is because of the possibility of argumentation which provides reasons, but not compelling reasons, that it is possible to escape the dilemma: adherence to an objectively and universally valid truth, or recourse to suggestion and violence to secure acceptance for our opinions and decisions.
>
> —Ch. Perelman and L. Olbrechts-Tyteca, *The New Rhetoric,* trans. John Wilkinson and Purcell Weaver

For Perelman, persuasion provides the alternative to a distasteful choice between authority and anarchy. Persuasion is an exercise in freedom and choice:

	FREEDOM	
This is the TRUTH. You have *no choice* but to accept it.	Domain of ← *Reasonable* → Choice (Persuasion)	There is no TRUTH. *No choice* you make is right or wrong.
AUTHORITY		ANARCHY

Thesis Statement

When your aim is to persuade, you ordinarily do not have to search for a thesis. You start out with an idea to defend, a political candidate to campaign for, a product to sell, a charity to assist, a program to recommend. You know what you want to accomplish at the outset. What you seek are the means to advance your thesis, the arguments that will make readers agree with and act upon your recommendations.

This does not mean that you are wedded inseparably to your initial thesis. As you seek out materials to support your arguments, you may find your own beliefs changing and maturing. Or you may not discover what you actually want to say until you start writing. But in many argumentative situations, it makes sense early on in the composing process to formulate a thesis clearly stating where you stand on an issue. The thesis guides your work by indicating what you have to prove:

> The United States should remain an island of plenty in a sea of hunger. The future of mankind is at stake. We are not responsible for the rest of humanity.
>
> —Johnson C. Montgomery, "The Island of Plenty"

> . . . in practice women are still kept in their place just as firmly as the animals are kept in their enclosures. The barriers which keep them in now are invisible.
>
> —Brigid Brophy, "Women Are Prisoners of Their Sex"

Both these examples are of theses that actually appear in the finished persuasive piece. You may find that your working thesis is considerably bolder than the statement that finally appears in your essay:

> *Working thesis:* The best way to solve the energy crisis is to fire every bureaucrat in the Department of Energy.

> *Final thesis:* A major stumbling block to the production of energy in the United States is the Department of Energy. Congress should consider curtailing its activities or abolishing the agency entirely.

On the other hand, with some audiences, the less cautious, more aggressive statement may fly better.

In most informative writing, the thesis appears early on in a piece, often in the first paragraph. That can be the case with persuasive writing too, but writers will often delay the statement of their opinion until after they have explained and demolished opposing opinions or until after they have fully examined a situation. This thesis, for example, appears in the next-to-last paragraph of an essay in which its author, a Chicano, narrates his experiences with affirmative action:

Placing your thesis

> Affirmative Action programs *are* unfair to white students.
>
> —Richard Rodriquez, "None of This is Fair"

The thesis (which is also a conclusion) gains power from the tale the writer has carefully told.

Thesis statements in persuasive pieces are often preceded by explanations or qualifications:

I am not arguing that . . .

I do not mean to say that . . .

Do not think that I am advocating . . .

While I may seem extreme at this point, what I am really saying . . .

The qualifiers may, of course, follow the statement of a thesis, giving the author an opportunity to win a reader's attention with the bold statement and his respect with the qualified one. Sometimes no thesis is ever stated explicitly; many advertisements work on this principle. Their implicit message is "Buy X," but we are never told as much. Instead we may be treated to descriptions of wealth, power, machismo, or elegance in some way connected to the product or service being offered.

In a satire (an argument that makes its point indirectly, through wit and ridicule), a thesis may be presented, but it often says just the opposite of what we are being led to believe. For example, the narrator of Jonathan Swift's *A Modest Proposal* suggests that the best way of alleviating Ireland's poverty is to make better use of its children:

> . . . the remaining hundred thousand may, at a year old, be offered in sale to the persons of quality and fortune through the kingdom; always advising the mother to let them suck plentifully in the last month, so as to render them plump and fat for a good table. A child will make two dishes at an entertainment for friends. . . .

From this startling suggestion, his argument proceeds methodically, exposing indirectly the greed and cruelty of Ireland's oppressors.

Developing the Argument: The Appeals

With a clear sense of what you want your readers to believe or do, you can begin shaping the arguments that will achieve your purpose. There are three basic persuasive appeals that work together in arguments: the logical, the emotional, and the personal.

The Logical Appeal

In informative writing that moves toward a conclusion or explores an idea, the reader, in effect, accompanies the writer along the paths that lead to a conclusion. The truth arrived at is carefully and systematically demonstrated. In persuasive discourse, the writer begins with a truth, idea, or belief which, for him, is established. He wants the reader to share his belief and to act on it, but not necessarily to acquire it through a complete and systematic demonstration. Consequently, he provides readers with only as much fact and reasoning as are necessary to move them to agree.

At first glance, you may find this a doubtful method. Only as much truth as necessary? Doesn't that imply concealing inconvenient facts and evidence, suppressing what is not favorable to one's side? In practice, that does happen. An advertiser will note that his car has more leg and shoulder room that the competition's but not mention deficiencies in hip and trunk room. A political group will praise the benefits of an enlarged and improved system of urban mass transit while minimizing the impact the accompanying tax increase will have on family budgets. A real estate agent will praise the location and charm of an old house, ignoring its damp basement and lack of insulation. In such cases, the selective presentation of facts, evidence, and logical arguments is unfortunate, and unfair to those who must act upon such evidence.

As much truth as necessary

In other cases, a reader has neither the patience nor the need to hear the full, systematic demonstration of a fact. Nor when a question is complex is it always possible to say that a principle, idea, belief, or course of action is fully agreed upon and convincingly demonstrated. The length of persuasive appeals is effectively limited in many cases by circumstances. A sermon can last only so long before even the most pious congregation begins yawning and coughing. A politician can afford to buy only a limited amount of space in the newspaper. A student is limited to three, five, maybe ten pages to explain his opinion that *Hamlet* is a failure, or defend his belief that class conflict is the most basic human struggle.

Limits of length and time

These constraints of length and time may seem artificial, but they are typical of the practical limitations placed on writers. We cannot always say as much as we'd like to, so we must select the most powerful examples, the most convincing statistics, the most comprehensive arguments to lead toward conclusions our audience will agree to. Most of us, for example, regard essay examinations as exercises in informative writing. Asked a question, we are expected to provide a detailed, specific answer. But essay questions are usually open-ended; they could be answered at much greater length than the allotted time permits. What does the writer do? He chooses to present the *best* of what he knows to speak for *all* of what he knows about the subject. He makes his choices to persuade the teacher that he understands the subject. In a similar way, when writing persuasively, you do not need to present every fact and every argument to defend a proposition if you take care to show the unconvinced reader the best arguments and best points. Sometimes though, readers *are* moved by the sheer weight of accumulated facts and evidence.

The same kinds of factual materials and logical procedures (induction and deduction) available to the writer working informatively are

Induction and deduction

available to the writer persuading and are subject to similar demands for accuracy and careful qualification. In fact, the power of persuasive writing is enhanced by its relationship to informative discourse because, in practice, readers are rarely conscious of distinctions between the two aims. The logical and documentary evidence in a persuasive piece can be as thorough and factual as that in a report or an essay. But the persuasive writer has additional appeals by which to make a case.

The Emotional Appeal

For as long as feelings, intuitions, and emotions remain a part of human character, emotional appeals will speak powerfully and legitimately to audiences. George Campbell, a famous rhetorician, answers those who believe that logic and reason provide the only grounds for argument:

Feeling and emotion

> The coolest reasoner always in persuading addresseth himself to the passions some way or other. This he cannot avoid doing, if he speak to the purpose. To make me believe it is enough to show me that things are so; to make me act, it is necessary to show that the action will answer some end. That can never be an end to me which gratifies no passion or affection in my nature. . . . So far therefore it is from being an unfair method of persuasion to move the passions, that there is no persuasion without moving them.
>
> —George Campbell, *The Philosophy of Rhetoric* (1776)

There is no persuasion without the moving of some feeling or emotion. And there are some subjects which virtually require an emotional consideration. You could, for example, provide logical reasons for relieving the misery of victims of fire, plague, famine, or political upheaval. But pity arising from a description of their plight is a more potent mover of action. There are strong logical reasons for and against capital punishment or abortion, but the reasons stand cold and partial without the human consideration, the brow wrinkled in pain that is part of both issues on both sides of the question. Deny feeling in an argument and you deny human nature.

Aristotle and the emotions

The earliest rhetoricians recognized the power language has to raise and control the attitudes of an audience. Aristotle in his *Rhetoric* discusses emotion and teaches the orator how to arouse specific feelings. Among the emotions he finds it useful for a writer to control are anger and mildness, love and hate, fear and confidence, pity, indignation, envy, emulation, and contempt.

Fear

These emotions can be aroused in many ways, often quite powerfully by using the narrative and descriptive modes. To rouse a patriotic fear, a writer might describe the weapon systems under development by the enemy and then evaluate them through a comparison with domestic armaments. To engender another type of fear, a TV advertiser might present a 60-second drama in which an otherwise handsome young man or woman loses a date because of warts, a pimple, foot odor, body odor, mouth odor, dandruff, or itchy skin. The narrative warns its audience that such are the consequences of failing to use some particular product. To move readers to pity, a writer might describe in unflinching **Pity** detail the plight of refugees in Asia or the conditions of a ghetto apartment in Watts or Hough. To incite envy, a writer might compare the **Envy** murder and assault statistics of London with those of New York, Chicago, or Atlanta. And so on.

An audience will also respond to devices of language that suggest **Allusions** that a writer shares concerns and experiences with the readers. Particular allusions can signal that a writer knows what an audience wants to hear. Students in the late 1960s, disgruntled by the Vietnam War and the establishment, recognized their complaints and aspirations in the words and images of Charles Reich:

> The new lifestyle is no longer on just a few campuses, it is to be found in every region in the country; it is even invading the countryside. And wherever it goes, underground newspapers, free schools, rock music, clashes with the law, rejection of the machine go too. Before long, the sideburns, beards, and long hair will mean votes as well. Nineteen sixty-eight was the year of Chicago. Nineteen sixty-nine was the year of Woodstock. That speaks of the distance we have come, and the speed with which we are traveling. The new consciousness is sweeping the high schools, it is seen in smiles on the streets. It has begun to transform and humanize the landscape.
>
> —*The Greening of America*

But the allusions and ideas speak less forcefully to the 1980s. New words and ideas have supplanted them. Chicago is just a city again to most people and Woodstock a pleasant memory.

Yet allusions to past experiences, personal or historical, can persuade powerfully. In most cases, writers seek to contrast a simpler, better past with an unsatisfactory present or future. For such an allusion to work, both writer and reader must agree on the value of the past. The father who wishes to deny his daughter a car to drive to school may allude to a past *he* values: "In my time, I walked five miles to school through snow drifts two feet high." Unfortunately, his daughter probably doesn't see the value of returning to that time. More persuasively, a writer may argue for change in the present to recapture the values of the past:

> Obviously, small structures tend to be more humane than large ones. The one-room schoolhouse, the family-run grocery, and the corner

drugstore are on a human scale; those who are part of them know each other. In a small organization, moreover, everyone can feel that he is somebody.

But is smallness possible in the last third of the twentieth century?

—Anthony Lewis, "A Plague of Giants"

Once again, the device fixes an identification between writer and reader that can be developed throughout the essay. Both writer and reader are made to share the vision of a better past.

Wit and ridicule

Not to be ignored as powerful emotional tools appropriate in some circumstances are wit and ridicule. When we can provoke readers to laugh at an opposing position, belief, or argument, we have all but sewn up our case. No feeling is more willingly shared than good humor. A reader hastens to join in the fun, lest he become a butt of ridicule himself:

Admittedly, in addition to covering you on board the aircraft, this policy also protects you "while traveling to and from the airport by taxi, bus, or limousine." (The presumption here must be that late for a flight and driving your own car, you might easily end up splattered against an abutment—but that in the hands of a professional, who cares not a zit whether you make your flight or not, the risk is slight.) And, yes, the policy also covers loss of sight (as in the case of a stewardess accidentally ramming a plastic fork into your eye).

—Andrew Tobias, "American Express Flight Insurance, Don't Leave Home *With* It"

Unfortunately, many writers grow heavy-handed when using humor. John Dryden provides what is probably the finest analogy to explain the difference between a target toppled by clumsy ridicule and one laid low by a perfectly aimed dart:

There is . . . a vast difference betwixt the slovenly butchering of a man, and the fineness of a stroke that separates the head from the body and leaves it standing in its place.

—*A Discourse Concerning Satire* (1692)

Cutting wit leaves your opponents laughing helplessly at themselves, and your reader chuckling with you. Don't be hesitant to employ humor when persuading. But exercise judgment. If you attack an opponent for some personal failing over which he has no control, or come across to the reader as cruel or cynical, your wit may turn on you.

Self-interest

Implicit in Campbell's defense of the emotional appeal quoted earlier in this section is yet another persuasive technique: the argument from self-interest. No one, Campbell suggests, can be persuaded or moved by a proposal "which gratifies no passion or affection in [his] nature." To maneuver a reader into agreement with you, you must do more than present the reasons why a given action, thought, belief, or policy is advantageous to the general public. You must show how—in particular—it benefits the readers or the groups they belong to:

> Hence a wise leader cannot and should not keep his word when keeping it is not to his advantage or when the reasons that made him give it are no longer valid. If men were good, this would not be a good precept, but since they are wicked and will not keep faith with you, you are not bound to keep faith with them.
>
> —Machiavelli, *The Prince*

> And so we arrive at the real issue in foreign assistance, skittishly avoided for so long: After all the political and economic arguments, dealing with hunger and malnutrition is a moral issue—that demands a moral response. Why should it be so difficult to justify? We often hear that national policies should flow only from self-interest. We somehow have failed to recognize that "doing good for the sake of doing good" *is* self-interest. To most people, ethical concerns are of value.
>
> —Alan Berg, "The Trouble with Triage," *New York Times,* June 15, 1975

Machiavelli persuades a prince that, for his own good, he need not be any more honest than the people he rules. Berg defends American foreign assistance by suggesting that the American people will profit from doing good.

An appeal to self-interest can make even a radical change in policy or behavior acceptable if the proposed new order offers the hope for a better future:

> One day the South will know that when these disinherited children of God sat down at lunch counters they were in reality standing up for the best in the American dream and the most sacred values in our Judeo-Christian heritage. . . .
>
> —Martin Luther King, Jr., "Letter from Birmingham Jail"

The Personal Appeal

The personal appeal, traditionally called the ethical appeal, describes how a writer uses his or her own personality to persuade by ma-

The personal voice

nipulating vocabulary, point of view, and degree of formality. A writer, in effect, creates a personality within a piece of writing. When persuading, you ordinarily want your personality within the prose to be one most readers would be eager to agree with. This personal voice can be especially appealing when it is but one of several inducements to agree:

> Neither by my habits of life, nor by vigour of age, am I fitted for the task of authority, or of rule, or of initiation. I do but aspire, if strength is given me, to be your minister in a work which must employ younger minds and stronger lives than mine. I am but fit to bear my witness, to proffer my suggestions, to express my sentiments . . . to throw such light upon general questions, upon the choice of objects, upon the import of principles, upon the tendency of measures, as past reflection and experience enable me to contribute.
>
> —John Henry Newman, *The Idea of a University*

In the passage above, the writer conveys the impression of honesty and reason by claiming limitations on what he can do, know, and express. A reader will listen to a writer who argues with such integrity.

In most persuasive writing, you want to seem authoritative and ethical. Being authoritative simply means sounding like you know what you are writing about. (It does not mean you should use twenty-dollar words and ponderous phrasing.)

Authority
Sometimes a writer imports "authority" into an argument by naming or citing the works of competent men or women who support an idea under discussion. When such authorities are actually experts in their field and are quoted within the area of their expertise, then their presence adds weight and prestige to both the argument and its advocate, the writer. The citation of authorities is one of the most common of persuasive techniques. Politicians frequently begin speeches by calling up the memory of some distinguished predecessor: Washington, Jefferson, Lincoln, King, Anthony, Roosevelt. Scholars usually preface their analyses with reviews of work done by previous scholars. Preachers and ministers cite the Bible or the church as their ultimate authorities. Little kids argue from the authority of their parents: "Oh ya? Well my father says. . . ."

Reputable sources
In scholarly or scientific writing of the kind discussed in the previous chapter, the citation of reputable sources is expected and essential. In persuasion, the importation of an expert's words can be an embellishment, one of the many devices to convince a reader that some idea or topic deserves attention. The previous section in this chapter ("The Emotional Appeal"), for example, contains several citations of authorities with credentials as writers, rhetoricians, or polemicists: Aristotle, George Campbell, John Dryden, and Machiavelli. The long (and diffi-

cult) quotation from Campbell early in the section is an attempt to defend emotional appeals by citing an expert from the eighteenth century. Most readers would not recognize the name or know much about Campbell. They rely here on the author to play fair and to cite a reputable thinker.

Similarly, Aristotle makes an appearance in connection with a list of emotions. The list is neither unique nor essential to the discussion of persuasion. Anyone could sit down and compile such a list on his own. But mentioning Aristotle, a name almost everyone recognizes and respects, helps to emphasize the antiquity and importance of the appeal to emotions. Both Aristotle and Campbell could be eliminated from the previous section. But because they are worthy experts cited appropriately and offered in good faith, they add to the demonstration, as do Dryden, and the rest.

But sometimes writers defend a position by soliciting the support **Endorsements** of personalities who have little to offer their argument other than a famous name or accomplishments in an unrelated area. We see such endorsements all the time in politics and advertising. A movie star sits on the podium nodding her approval while a presidential candidate blasts nuclear power plants, explains a matter of foreign policy, or argues the advantages of fiscal restraint. What does the star know about the technicalities of these matters? Little more than the average member of the audience. But the star adds glitter and glamour to the candidate's campaign. Anxious campaign managers hope some of the star's charisma will rub off on the sometimes plodding candidate. Similarly, we see sports figures endorsing products they may know little about or experts in one area flying their banners in fields they hold no expertise in. Yet viewers and readers are impressed by such endorsements. They regard the stars as people who have made it, whose opinions are worth something. "If it's good enough for Farrah Fawcett, it's good enough for me," they think. Or, "If you can't trust Henry Fonda or Jimmy Stewart, who can you trust?"

When you cite an authority in an argument, you should be willing to defend the legitimacy of that source. Occasionally, you may choose to cite an authority outside his area of expertise simply because of the interest such an inclusion will generate: Einstein on playing the violin, Bella Abzug on millinery, Dr. Spock on civil disobedience. But at critical moments in the defense of an argument, the experts recruited should be the real thing. Otherwise an opponent or critic can destroy your position by simply examining and exposing the credentials of those people you relied on.

How do you convey competence and authority yourself? By using **Conveying** language that is simultaneously forceful, reasonable, and geared to your **competency and** degree of knowledge and your readers' expectations. A real authority, **authority** versed in the facts, familiar with the issues, confident of his abilities, and respected by readers, can write with something approaching arrogance:

> A man may take to drink because he feels himself to be a failure, and then fail all the more completely because he drinks. It is rather the same thing that is happening to the English language. It becomes ugly and inaccurate because our thoughts are foolish, but the slovenliness of our language makes it easier for us to have foolish thoughts. The point is the process is reversible.
>
> —George Orwell, *"Politics and the English Language"*

This is bold writing that reveals an author not afraid to make sweeping assertions or blunt conclusions: "The point is the process is reversible."

But most of us can't speak with the authority of an Orwell. To do so is to risk the contempt or hostility of an audience judging our expertise. In such situations, you carefully qualify what you know, identify with the concerns of your audience, and speak in a voice that asserts and soothes. You may use the pronoun *I* and narrate experiences shared by an audience you address informally as *you*. Or you may put yourself right into the audience by employing *we*. Or you may combine these techniques:

> Unfortunately *we* English teachers are easily hung up on this matter of understanding. Why should children understand everything they read? Why should *anyone*? Does *anyone*? *I* don't, and *I* never did. (italics added)
>
> —John Holt, "How Teachers Make Children Hate Reading"

The impression of ethical behavior

A more difficult matter to explain is how a writer creates the impression of moral judgment or ethical behavior. In many persuasive situations, the writer is virtually anonymous, an unfamiliar name attached to an editorial, a letter, a position paper, a legal brief. But even when anonymous, you should seem consistent and fair in dealing with fact and opinion.

Thus you ought to treat an opposing group or opinion with honesty and understanding when persuading. If you do, you will seem trustworthy and reasonable. In some cases, you may have to attack the opposition openly and harshly. Then, the attack should be directed at an issue and, as much as possible, away from the individuals who hold the position. Even when an opposition resorts to name-calling, distortions, and other questionable tactics, a writer interested in moving a neutral and initially impartial audience should avoid the ploys. They signal a loss of control.

Being consistent

In creating a personal appeal, strive to seem consistent. If you accuse the opposition of name-calling, bad faith, or arguing from tainted facts, don't resort to these tactics yourself. Nothing seems so inept as a writer raging against what he's guilty of himself; few arguments work so well as showing the opposition in the position of contradicting itself:

> Finally, in Ms. Bryant's own favorite Bible verse, I Corinthians 6:10, homosexuals are told that they will not "inherit the kingdom of God." Nor will "the immoral, nor idolaters, nor adulterers . . . nor drunkards . . . nor robbers," all of whom make life easy in the conservative Orange Juice churches because, of course, there are none of such. But those dots also mark the omission of the word "revilers."
>
> Revilers won't inherit the kingdom. And while Anita often stuck to the text, her husband, Bob Green, did some macho reviling of homosexuals. Out he goes. Now I'd better quit, stopping just short of reviling *him*. Otherwise the kingdom will have to get along without both Bob Green and me.
>
> —Martin E. Marty, "Anita Bryant Reads the Bible"

Finally, when appropriate, you should strive to seem humane, aware of frailties and weaknesses in others, and capable of concession, good will, and humor. Writers who can create such images have won a third part of their persuasive battle. Surely you have met people you've disliked so much, you disagree with everything they say. You even begin doubting your own positions when they coincide with their's. And just as surely, you have enjoyed the company of folks you want to agree with (even when you can't) simply because they seem so decent, wise, and intelligent. When persuading, you want your readers to regard you as one of these decent persons they hate to disagree with.

Strategic concessions

Fallacies

Certain types of reasoning and persuasion are considered inaccurate and fallacious. Yet these same argumentative fallacies can be persuasive traps of no small bite when sprung on uninformed or unsuspecting readers. To pretend that successful writers do not use these devices to persuade is naive. They may use them to embellish other, stronger arguments. They may slip into fallacious or unfair argument unwittingly, carried by the heat of debate or the scent of victory. Or they may use them because no better arguments are available.

Knowing some of the common faults a writer can fall into while arguing is a way of avoiding them and a way of discovering arguments to use against an opposition. Whenever your opponents employ an illegitimate argumentative device, they have furnished you with an argument of your own. All you have to do is point out the fallacy.

Hasty Generalization

Stereotypes

Logical demonstrations are commonly shortened in persuasive writing. As a consequence, writers may be tempted to generalize from too little evidence. One bad experience with a foreign car leads the writer to conclude that "foreign makes aren't all they're cracked up to be." Several unfortunate encounters with a particular group lead to the sorts of undocumented conclusions that create stereotypes:

> Women are fickle.
>
> Anglos are racist.
>
> Blacks are lazy.
>
> Men are insensitive.

Inadequate
information

Or a conclusion may be drawn from evidence skewed in other ways. Many people may be surveyed for an opinion sample, but if they are predominantly of one race, religion, income level, or political persuasion, no conclusion can be drawn about the more general population. A survey of two hundred people on the question of legalizing marijuana will turn out differently if all two hundred respondents are retirees in Miami Beach, ministers in small Texas towns, dockworkers in New Jersey, or freshmen at Ohio State. Conclusions drawn from any such survey would have to be carefully qualified to avoid charges of hasty or unwarranted generalization.

Faulty Causality

Superstition

A second fallacy attributable to mishandled facts is false cause—attributing an event or phenomenon to causes not responsible for them. In simple cases, false causes can seem almost silly. Most superstitions are steeped in this fallacy. You knock a post out from under your carport, and then discover it is Friday the 13th. And the day, not the six-pack you chugged down, gets blamed for the tottering roof. Or you kill a spider and then flunk an astronomy exam. Bad luck to kill a spider. And the poor squashed arachnid gets blamed for your academic mispreparation.

In more serious matters and more complex issues, causality becomes a major point of debate. Does cigarette smoking cause cancer? The debate has raged for years. Is atmospheric pollution the cause of lung disease, or are there other factors? What causes inflation? Too much government spending? Too much speculation on the gold market? Diminished productivity?

Either/Or

Attributing any complex event or phenomenon to a single cause is to eliminate all others. And that's always risky. Yet effective persuasion often requires that an issue be addressed forthrightly, and that means narrowing possibilities down to a single conclusion:

> The only way to stop inflation is to stop the growth of government!
>
> Television is responsible for the steady decline of writing skills among undergraduates.

Sometimes, however, a writer deliberately takes the risk of narrowing an issue in just this way in order to stir debate, to measure opinion, or to challenge a reader to act.

When issues are complex, some writers attempt to simplify issues for their readers by indulging in an either/or argument:

> Either we hang together or we shall surely hang separately.
>
> Give me liberty or give me death.
>
> Put up or shut up.
>
> America, love it or leave it!
>
> You are either with me or against me.
>
> To be or not to be, that is the question.

Reducing alternatives to just two simplifies the task of convincing. A question in these terms can then be portrayed in sharp contrasts, not in indiscriminate shades of gray. Yet many questions—perhaps most—have three, four, five sides or more. The solution to a problem may reside in a compromise, in a certain give-and-take between the extreme positions that can result from an either/or split. But compromises, like committees, are dull. They make for gutless, heartless debate. Here you must choose between heat and light—and perhaps the light of reason ought to prevail.

Compromise

Red Herring

A red herring is an argument deployed as a distraction from the main issue, a statement that throws a reader or opponent off the scent. Red herrings aren't always easy to sniff out, nor are they necessarily "illogical." The senator who asks how can we spend a billion dollars on an aircraft carrier when the streets of New York are crumbling away indulges in red herring—and a bit of grandstanding as well. But he raises an issue of priorities. The zealot who defends the legalization of marijuana on the grounds that it is less dangerous than alcoholic beverages already legal has introduced a side issue. The merits or dangers of marijuana must be debated on their own terms. Yet the alcohol digression may suggest ways by which the use of a potentially dangerous substance may be socially controlled. Red herrings do sometimes distract attention from a main issue but, as in the cases cited above, they sometimes lead to new positions and points of view. At that point they cease to be red herrings.

Ad Hominem

"When all else fails, sling some mud." That might be the motto of those who indulge in arguments that attack the personality or character of the opponents rather than what they say. Such attacks, called *ad hominem* arguments (literally, "to the man"), are something like killing the messenger who brings bad news. An attack on the character of someone who disagrees with you is fair only when character is at issue. In a presidential election, for example, a debate only over issues (which most candidates piously champion) would leave essential questions unanswered. The people need to know the character, the morals, the attitudes of the person on whom they are about to confer awesome power.

But even when character is not at issue, human nature makes it tempting to indulge in a little closet-cleaning, in exposing those skeletons our opponents would just as soon not mention.

Racism and sexism

"How can you endorse the economic programs of a peanut farmer from Georgia?" the outraged citizen asks. But if the programs are solid, does it matter what their author farms? *Ad hominem* arguments are often subtly racist and sexist. As such, they are reprehensible:

> Don't vote for me because I'm white. That's a side issue here. Vote for me because . . .
>
> He's a fine administrator, but do we really want a person of his sexual orientation?
>
> For a woman, she is a remarkably capable mechanic.
>
> A man can't possibly understand the feelings of women on this issue.

Name-calling

Ad hominem appeals are closely related to name-calling. Name-calling is bunching the opposition together under some fierce rubric and identifying particular opponents with these groups: reds, rednecks, petty bourgeois, filthy rich, fags, oil-barons, libbers, welfare cheaters, pointy-headed intellectuals, Bible-thumpers, Texans, stump-jumpers, swell-headed bureaucrats. Naturally, a writer carefully identifies the values of an audience before indulging in name-calling. No sense in railing against bureaucrats at a Washington dinner party or against Texans at a barbecue in Waco. In fact, there's usually little sense in railing against folks at all—except that, unfortunately, it sometimes works.

Ad Populum

Scare tactics

Then there's the argument *ad populum*—"to the people." When all else fails, scare the pants off 'em. Identify what a given audience fears most—their most rabid prejudices—and play upon those weaknesses. Threaten hoards of unfriendly soldiers landing in San Francisco. Suspect an FBI tap on every phone, chemicals in every preservative, atheists in every textbook, and cancer in everything. Tell them that the world's at an end now that the Jews hold Jerusalem, and blame the Arabs for every American business failure. All liberals are commies at heart, all conservatives are fascists, and worst of all, your deodorant spray is destroying the ozone. Instant panic. Instant victory for the ruthless persuader who doesn't give a darn for anything but winning—or instant defeat if his audience is wise enough to see through his ploy.

The Style and Language of Persuasive Writing

Perhaps only literary discourse shows a greater concern for the fit of its language than does persuasive writing. Some persuasive prose can be stark and impersonal, relying on content to achieve its end:

> Your payment for the entire amount must be received in our office on or before the due date or service will be terminated immediately.

But more often, writers eager to convince readers to take action are more inventive and self-conscious in manipulating language. Readers and listeners can be moved by the sound of words and the shape of sentences, as hundreds of advertising jingles and slogans attest:

> Reach out and touch someone.   **Slogans**
>
> Tippecanoe and Tyler too.
>
> You deserve a break today.
>
> Coke adds life.
>
> Winston tastes good, like a cigarette should.
>
> Nixon's the one.
>
> Why not the best?
>
> In your heart you know he's right.
>
> See the U.S.A. in a Chevrolet.

Add music and a convincing representative and you've customers and voters standing in line. Well-fitted language in persuasive prose connects and embellishes the logical, persuasive, and personal appeals a writer makes. You don't ordinarily want to rely on surface devices to win an argument, but you cannot ignore them.

The various devices of rhythm and repetition discussed in chap-   **Rhythm and repetition**
ters 8 and 9 are especially well-suited to persuasive appeals. Rhythmic language draws readers into an argument, highlights relationships between parallel ideas, and aids the memory. In 1979, the Chrysler Corporation used a highly rhythmic, cleverly repetitive style in ads designed

to persuade the public to support federal loan guarantees for the company:

> Does Chrysler have a future?
>   You can *count on it.*
>   Seventeen million Chrysler owners can *count on it.*
>   Our 4700 Chrysler-Plymouth and Dodge dealers can *count on it.* Our employees can *count on it.* Our suppliers can *count on it.*
>   The concerned citizens of 52 communities whose livelihoods are closely tied to Chrysler can *count on it.*
>   And the competition can really *count on it.*
>   We have in place for 1980 and 1981 the programs, the products and the management Chrysler needs to be competitive, to sell cars, to meet our obligations, to become profitable.
>   We've been in business for *fifty-four* years, and almost all *fifty-four* have been profitable.
>   We plan to be around at least another *fifty-four.*
>   You can *count on it.*
>
> —Newspaper ad, "Does Chrysler Have a Future?"

Observe how strategically and often the phrase "count on it" is used in the first part of the appeal. Then that phrase is interrupted by three occurrences of "fifty-four years." Finally, the blunt conclusion circles back to the major point: "You can count on it." With the future of a multi-billion-dollar company on the line, Chrysler's writers resort to the most emphatic rhetorical devices available to them.

Similarly, in the Declaration of Independence, with the future of a nation in the balance, Jefferson uses repetition and parallelism (related ideas expressed in grammatically similar constructions) to emphasize the number and seriousness of the crimes perpetrated by King George III against the American colonies:

> He has refused his Assent to Laws. . . .
>
> He has forbidden his Governors. . . .
>
> He has refused. . . .
>
> He has dissolved. . . .

These two examples show parallelism and repetition used to unusual degrees. In most persuasive situations, a writer will use the devices more sparingly to key in on points of emphasis.

Emotional motifs   Emotional motifs may likewise be used to shape the style of a persuasive essay. An abstract issue or concept can be given concrete form by introducing a human situation, narratively or descriptively. Here such a technique is employed to open and close essays on two sides of a controversial issue:

Introduction   Sarah sits in a drab room, alone and afraid. Fifteen years old. A runaway from a home where a stepfather beat and abused her. A chain smoker since age eleven. Unemployed. Uneducated. Now she is pregnant and needs an abortion. A man told her about a place where they did it "cheap." Sarah couldn't afford professional medical care, and no government agency would help. Her life is on the line in a cold, drab room because a repressive Congress has listened to the shrill threats of the anti-abortion lobby.

Conclusion   Sarah died in that drab room. And thousands of women like her—some even younger—will suffer the same fate if Congress does not remove its restrictions on government-funded abortions.

Introduction   Sarah would have been five years old this year. She would have been meeting new friends at the bright new kindergarten down the block. She would have been discovering books and learning songs, roughhousing with her brothers, learning the ways of the world. She would have been counting the days to her birthday, anticipating the party, the cake, and the gifts. Would have, because Sarah was aborted by a mother "too busy to be bothered with another child."

Conclusion   Abortion is morality at the cheapest rate, ethics by convenience. Sarah would be five now. But her mother chose to steal the time that belonged to the unborn child. And now Sarah has no choices. And what has her mother done with the time?

Needless to say, emotional motifs like these can be misused. Both examples totter on the brink of good taste and fair play; both might be rejected by most readers as too pat, too emotional. But in both cases, a complex problem is transformed by language into something a reader can feel.

Sometimes you may want to evoke an even more controlled response from readers, one that involves more than shared feelings and values. In such a case, you can employ rhetorical questions. Though manuals of style sometimes frown on the technique, rhetorical questions are used frequently by professional writers. A rhetorical question is simply an interrogative that a writer doesn't expect readers to answer on their own. Instead, he or she supplies an answer or implies strongly what the answer should be:

Feelings and values

Rhetorical questions

> Frequently I have been asked questions by students and young people who have been harassed because of their theology, their dress, and their

behavior. Why have "born-again" Christians been singled out? Why aren't dope dealers or pornographers kidnapped and deprogrammed? How would the public respond if a Protestant pulled his son out of a seminary and kept him incommunicado until he gave up his vocation? What would the Vatican do if a Catholic dragged his daughter from a convent? How would the Black Muslims react if their congregation was picked off one by one? Would Jews consider it just if Reform members grabbed Orthodox believers and put them through a crude form of behavior modification?

These questions, I think, deserve careful consideration—and honest answers.

—Michael Mewshaw, "Irrational Behavior or Evangelical Zeal?"

The author then supplies the principle that must guide the answers: America's constitutional commitment to religious freedom.

Questions raised in a persuasive argument have the advantage of focusing and summarizing issues. They make it possible too for a writer to state a position without explicitly endorsing it:

Can one be a liberal and yet endorse capital punishment?

Or they can state an issue in a way that makes a reader reluctant to disagree:

Can a reasonable person think otherwise? Is any other course of action even plausible?

Or they can provoke a powerful emotional response:

Hath not a Jew eyes? If you prick us, do we not bleed?

—William Shakespeare, *The Merchant of Venice*

Understatement and overstatement

Understatements and overstatements, often coupled with humor, can have remarkably persuasive clout. For example, Stuart Chase cleverly titles an examination of the advantages and disadvantages of modern technologies "Two Cheers for Technology." He has in four words quietly conveyed a great deal of his point. Samuel Clemens, in his essay, "The Lowest Animal," takes an opposite tack, avoiding all subtlety to enrich his claim that man is the lowest of animals:

Man seems to be a rickety poor sort of thing, any way you take him; a kind of British Museum of infirmities and inferiorities. He is always undergoing repairs. A machine that was as unreliable as he is would have no market. . . . He is but a basket of pestilent corruption provided for the support and entertainment of swarming armies of bacilli—armies commissioned to rot him and destroy him.

Well-placed ridicule goes a long way.

So do well-chosen words. Persuasive language tends to be highly connotative, the writer capitalizing on the associations that surround even abstract terms. A government employee handling documents becomes a "bureaucrat pushing paperwork" in the prose of a writer who dislikes bureaucracy. The Dallas Cowboys become the "Dallas Cryboys" if you are a sportswriter from Pittsburgh. If you distrust oil companies, you call the executives that run them "oil barons." "As American as apple pie" suggests the warmth and goodness of grandma and her cooking. Radicals, zealots, and dogmatists are people and words to be feared. Depending on your politics, right-wingers or left-wingers are threats, as are fanatics and vigilantes. Black power, white power, women's rights, gay rights, gray rights are all words keyed into emotions, as are the isms: Marxism, fascism, capitalism, terrorism, socialism, nationalism. The names of world figures—living or dead—provoke responses of varying intensity: Karl Marx, John Kennedy, Mahatma Gandhi, Eleanor Roosevelt, John Paul II, Jackie Kennedy Onassis, Billy Graham, Anwar Sadat, Leonid Breshnev, Truman Capote, Mickey Mouse. Places and times also create emotional atmospheres that a writer may have occasion to use. New York is the image of uncontrolled, threatening, yet vital urban life. Iowa is farms and hogs. Paris is glamour and amour. Moscow, the cold, suspicious walls of the Kremlin. The twenties in America were corrupt and violent, the thirties poor and radical, the forties a time of war and rebuilding, the fifties the age of Ike and "American Bandstand." The sixties have slipped into legend, a tumultuous period of war, assassination, revolt, and rock 'n roll. And the seventies?

Sometimes writers will choose to focus on a few features of an individual, concept, or idea and make them stand for the whole. Thus fundamentalist preachers become "Bible-thumping tent-warmers," football linemen "unbrained clots of muscle wrapped in polyester," and a president "that peanut farmer from Georgia with the Colgate smile." Such reductions can be enormously unfair, as the examples demonstrate. Use such devices and you may be guilty of an *ad hominem* fallacy. But there's no denying their effectiveness in shaping readers' attitudes. Just consider how the reductions employed in these sentences create less-than-subtle persuasive appeals:

> While the complaints against the instructor are serious, we must consider that they have been raised by a group of *C and D students.*

> The only groups opposed to reductions in military spending are the *flag-wavers* and the *cold warriors.*

> *Gun-toting* is outmoded in twentieth century America. We need gun control legislation.

Maxims and clichés   Finally, attitudes and values in persuasive writing can be shaped by a writer's choice and presentation of maxims and clichés. In general, you want to avoid clichés like the plague. The writer who unconsciously pens a cliché is trodding a well-beaten path, abandoning the adventure of discovery to rely on what's tried and true. Of course, avoiding clichés is easier said than done. And that's because clichés represent a comfortable, familiar, and reputable path from idea to expression. In that way, clichés are like wise sayings and maxims, which are common ideas uncommonly-well put:

> Hypocrisy is the homage that vice pays to virtue.   —La Rochefoucauld
>
> To err is human, to forgive divine.   —Alexander Pope
>
> All politics is applesauce.   —Will Rogers
>
> Familiarity breeds contempt.   —Aesop

Because maxims are wise and clichés comfortable, the writer who fits an adage to an appropriate contemporary situation or rekindles the glow in a dying expression will often please an audience by joining the old to the new. Sometimes it startles a reader to discover that a line of argument exploring a modern problem is drawn from an ancient commonplace. Sometimes clichés seem spanking new when the persuasive situation revives them, allowing the reader to appreciate the folly in beating a dead horse, the helplessness in being over a barrel, the good agricultural sense in making hay while the sun shines, the clawing velocity of letting the cat out of the bag, and the virtue in making a long story short. Sometimes an audience is simply happy to discover that what seems solemn and serious can be simple and humorous:

> Go to bed early, get up early—this is wise. Some authorities say to get up with the sun; some others say get up with one thing, some with another. But a lark is really the best thing to get up with. It gives you a splendid reputation with everybody to know that you get up with the lark; and if you get the right kind of lark, and work at him right, you can easily train him to get up at half past nine, every time—it is no trick at all.
>
> —Samuel Clemens, "Advice to Youth"

Invention for Persuasive Writing

Inventing persuasive arguments systematically has never been as easy as finding materials for informative writing. When arguing, we often expect the reasons we have for supporting a cause to reveal themselves somehow. And they often do. A favorable statistic is immediately translated by the classificatory mode into a formidable logical appeal. The anger or outrage we feel viewing an instance of injustice, intemperance, or incompetence becomes a description of the scene designed to anger or outrage our readers. Or we count on our good name to sway the reader into siding with us.

Yet some more systematic way of discovering persuasive arguments is useful at those times when we begin with an idea or opinion we already hold and must find good reasons to defend or advocate it.

Once again, as with informative writing, the modes can serve as tools for suggesting how an idea can be developed. In the matrix that follows, the modes are understood in a broad, general way. Description is to be regarded not only as a simple process of pictorial representation, but as any static representation of a thing. Thus facts, situations, circumstances, and examples can be aspects of description. Similarly, narration encompasses more than just stories or sequences of events; it also includes history, precedents, and matters of cause and effect. Classification is an appreciation of similarities, differences, definitions, and relationships. And evaluation, the most active mode, examines criteria, qualifications, limitations, benefits, and authorities.

To produce the matrix, we plot the modes against the types of appeals available in most persuasive situations and generate a series of questions:

	Description (analysis)	Narration (history)	Classification (theory)	Evaluation (criticism)
Logical appeal	1	2	3	4
Emotional appeal	5	6	7	8
Personal appeal	9	10	11	12

Thesis: _____X_____

1. (logical appeal/description) What are the facts, statistics, examples, circumstances, etc., that support your case? Which might be used against you? How might you anticipate the opposing arguments? How much evidence must you present to clinch your case?

2. (logical appeal/narration) What historical circumstances or precedents support your argument? What are the causes of the current situation or problem? What will be the effects of the situation continuing? What will be the effects of your proposal(s)?

3. (logical appeal/classification) What familiar and accepted values or ideas does your position support or advance? How does your proposal differ from others? How is it similar? How do your definitions of key terms differ from those of others?

4. (logical appeal/evaluation) How will your argument or proposal improve the current situation? How is your proposal superior to alternative arguments in its use of facts or evidence?

5. (emotional appeal/description) What can you portray that will support your position? What emotions (fear? anger? goodwill?) do you want associated with your argument? What emotions will counterproposals stir? How can you anticipate or circumvent these feelings?

6. (emotional appeal/narration) What unfortunate feelings, stereotypes, or beliefs have been aroused by the current situation? How would your proposal alleviate the unfortunate effects of the current situation? What emotional, physical, social, or economic pains or problems does your proposal address? Who have been affected or hurt by the current situation? What has happened to them? How are your readers likely to be affected by the current situation?

7. (emotional/classification) How would you compare and contrast the consequences of the present situation with the consequences of your proposal? What words, phrases, or concepts in the controversy you are addressing have powerful connotations? How can you exploit those terms?

8. (emotional/evaluation) How will others benefit personally from your proposal or argument? How does it affect or arouse their self-interest? How will your proposal make their lives or futures more secure, content, stable, happy, or predictable?

9. (personal appeal/description) What characteristics or experiences can you claim that make it appropriate for you to address the issue? Education? Practical experience? Familiarity with the persons, places, things involved? The trust of all parties involved in the dispute? What proves that you are concerned with the issue? What can you reveal about yourself to suggest your reasonableness? Will your audience believe you?

10. (personal/narration) How have you been affected by the current situation? What personal experiences or anecdotes explain your involvement in the dispute, argument, or issue?

11. (personal/classification) What knowledge do you have of the current situation and of alternatives to it? What social, political,

Reasons for Writing

religious, occupational, recreational, or other associations do you have that make you especially fit to address the topic? What other authorities can you introduce who support your case? How is your personal interest in the situation like or unlike that of your readers?

12. (personal/evaluation) What limitations do you have in presenting the argument? What particular knowledge, skill, or authority do you possess that makes you among the most able to present a case? What authorities who oppose your argument or point of view can you discredit?

These general questions are addressed to a persuasive situation in which the writer considers a question of future action: what shall we do to combat inflation? How do we solve the coming crisis in housing? With minor modifications, the questions also apply to problems or arguments that deal with the past or present: was the Vietnam War a worthwhile undertaking? Should President Carter have imposed wage and price controls in 1979? Should the government act against monopolies?

For Discussion

1. How often do you persuade? In what situations? To what kinds of audiences? Discuss the opportunities you have on any given day to persuade.

2. How many types of persuasion are you exposed to in a given day? Which seem to work the best? Do you resent any particular kinds of persuasion?

3. Do you know any currently debated issues in which one side takes what Perelman might classify as an authoritarian position? That is, does it claim to possess the whole truth in some area (politics, economics, psychology, religion, etc.), rejecting all others? Similarly, can you think of an issue over which some people take an anarchic position, that "one choice is as good as another"?

Exercises

4. Examine the lead editorials in a medium-to-large circulation newspaper until you find one you disagree with strongly. Then write an editorial of your own to counter it. Try to use as many appeals and devices of persuasion as you can, but emphasize the logical appeal. Wherever you can, point out flaws in the reasoning of the original editorial, turning its faults into arguments for your side of the question. Length: 200–300 words. Audience: the readers of the original editorial.

5. Defend some idea or proposal you strongly endorse by preparing a

list of single-sentence arguments generated by the matrix for persuasive writing. Do not write an actual essay; instead, when you have completed your list, decide which of the arguments could be developed convincingly into a full essay aimed at your classmates. Which would be the least effective? How does your audience affect your evaluation of the arguments? Would a different audience cause you to alter your approach to the subject?

6. Examine a major news story in *Time, Newsweek,* or *U.S. News and World Report* to determine whether its primary aim is informative or persuasive. Write a paragraph evaluating the neutrality of the news article. Cite examples (if any) of persuasive appeals intruding into informative writing. Be sure to consider any photographs, tables, charts, and headlines that accompany the text.

7. Classify the argumentative essays in a college anthology according to their dominant appeals (logical, emotional, personal). Can you always determine what the dominant appeal is?

8. Prepare advertising copy (approximately 200 words) for a book you have read recently. Describe the book and its author in terms that would make it appeal to a large, well-informed, and critical audience.

9. Write a job application letter. You are confident that you have the ability to do the job you are applying for, but you lack the required credentials and experience. Persuade the personnel manager to hire you. Your experiences applying for actual jobs may provide you with the details for this persuasive effort. Limit your letter to one single-spaced typed page or less.

Writing Assignments

10. Write a short informative article about some local or personal problem that has two clearly defined sides. (Should real estate taxes be raised? Should student government be abolished? Should the ERA be approved?) This first essay should be impersonal and factual.

Then, in a second piece, give the original report a persuasive slant. Introduce elements of emotional and personal appeal. Use devices of style, especially parallelism and repetition. But don't overdo it. Try to retain something of the structure of your original informative article and some of its details. Length: limit each article to 300–400 words. Audience: your classmates or colleagues.

11. Write an analysis of some printed advertisement, identifying what you think its major appeal is (logical? emotional? personal?) and then showing how the other appeals also operate on the page. Consider its visual content, its verbal content, and its effectiveness. Design your structure around a main idea that explains why the advertisement does or does not work.

If you wish, you may do a more complex analysis, comparing two ads for the same product, comparing ads for competing products, or comparing ads for products in different price ranges (expensive cameras/low-priced cameras; luxury cars/economy cars). Length: 500 words. Audience: a group of critical consumers. Design your article as an address or statement for this organization.

12. Write a persuasive essay defending an idea or concept you do *not* believe in or one you actually oppose. The paper may not be sarcastic or ironic. It must be truly persuasive and offered—for all your audience knows—in good faith. Length: 600–1000 words. Audience: your classmates or colleagues.

13. Argue for the side you stand with on one of these issues (or a topic suggested by your instructor):

   a. Should the federal government fund abortions for the needy?
   b. Should the US be content with parity in the arms race with the Soviet Union? Should the US participate in the arms race?
   c. Should the US have attended the 1980 Olympics?
   d. Should the oil business be controlled by the government?
   e. Should genetic research and experimentation be allowed to continue?
   f. Should pollution standards be relaxed in times of economic hardship to encourage production and jobs?
   g. Should the social security system be abandoned?
   h. Should students control their college curricula?
   i. Should students have the right to evaluate teachers?
   j. Should the US permit freer emigration from Mexico?
   k. Should affirmative action programs be expanded or abandoned?

Try to use all three of the appeals in some way in your essay. Length: 500–1000 words. Audience: a group of your classmates who haven't yet made up their minds on the issue.

14. Write two political pamphlets for or against an issue or candidate that you know well. One of the pamphlets is to be distributed among blue-collar workers; the second is to reach college students in your area. Let your perceptions of these audiences determine the style and length of your pamphlets.

15. Analyze the techniques of persuasion used by Brutus or Antony in Act III, scene i of Shakespeare's *Julius Caesar*. Or explain why Antony is more successful than Brutus in swaying the opinion of the mob angered by Caesar's assassination. If you examine Antony's eulogy, be sure to consider Caesar's will, his blood-stained robe, and his well-knifed corpse. How do they function as persuasive appeals? Length: as you like it. Audience: your classmates or coworkers.

7

Nouns, Verbs, and the Thesis Statement

Nouns and Verbs

Investors put their money where it will bring the best return. If you're investing time in learning to write well, bank on nouns and verbs. No parts of a sentence work harder. And when you control nouns and verbs, you hold the key not only to good sentences but to clear thesis statements.

Why? Because nouns and verbs form the core of ideas. Nouns are what you are talking about. Verbs are what's being done. Everything else is amplification and development. Get the nouns and verbs marching right—that is, clearly stating what you mean to say—and chances are the rest of your thoughts will file into line. Ignore these key components, and your ideas will scatter like dry leaves. Nouns and verbs are the blue-chip investments of written language.

Nouns

Nouns are words that name persons, places, things, and ideas. Nouns vary from the abstract to the specific. What is an abstract noun? That's a difficult question. In general, abstract words describe things we can't contact with the senses, that we can't picture or explain simply, that exist as ideas, not as particular objects. *Mammal,* for example, is an abstraction. You can define a mammal simply as a warm-blooded, milk-bearing, furred vertebrate, and point to hundreds of them. But none of the individual creatures fully represents what a mammal is; none defines the abstract term. Rather, each is a particular and specific variant of the concept: a chimpanzee, a dog, a platypus, a man. Yet even these terms are abstractions since that dog, for example, is likely to be someone's pet, a creature with idiosyncrasies, a residence, and a name. Grouping the nouns we've used here, we can list them from the general to the specific, from the abstract to the particular:

vertebrate

mammal

dog

beagle

Sluggo

Though a general term, *animal* at least has relatively familiar physical representations. What happens when we deal with concepts— like love, freedom of the press, intelligence, punctuality, honor, team spirit, naiveté, and democracy—that do not lend themselves to physical appearances? How is it that we even understand them? How do we talk about them? How do we define them? One way is through specific nouns and familiar situations. *School spirit* may be understood through the confetti choking the halls after a victory, or the torn program in a tearful cheerleader's hand after a defeat. *Punctuality* is your Uncle Joe punching the time clock at the mine the same minute every night for ten years. And *democracy?* Perhaps you recognize this famous definition penned by E. B. White during World War II:

> Democracy is the recurrent suspicion that more than half of the people are right more than half of the time. It is the feeling of privacy in the voting booths, the feeling of communion in the libraries, the feeling of

vitality everywhere. Democracy is a letter to the editor. Democracy is the score at the beginning of the ninth. It is an idea which hasn't been disproved yet, a song the words of which have not gone bad. It's the mustard on the hot dog and the cream in the rationed coffee . . . .

—"Democracy"

For many of us, the grand political concept, *democracy,* translates into just such petty, silly, simple things we'd never think of mentioning in our own essays on the subject. We would likely be much more serious than White. Yet how accurate he is. And how much trust he puts in the good sense and experiences of his readers.

In many situations, however, a definition like White's would be wholly unsatisfactory. You would find the color and charm of his prose out of place in a dictionary or encyclopedia. In an essay examining various systems of government, White's details might be a distraction. In establishing criteria for successful self-rule, White's definition might not apply outside the USA. In short, specific details aren't always the best way of developing a sentence or idea. When scientists formulate theories, theologians shape treatises, or philosophers explore concepts, they want their ideas to have general application. So the scientist discusses *gravity,* not the falling apple that initiated his speculations; the theologian expounds on *poverty,* not on the holes in his own robes. And the philosopher proves abstractly that *causality* does not exist, ignoring the bruise he suffered kicking the Coke machine. Their use of abstract nouns is appropriate and necessary.

Unfortunately, many writers rely on abstract words in situations where more particular language is justified. They labor to be dull because they believe that abstract nouns make them sound serious and intellectual. They find themselves writing long essays about the nature of love without ever mentioning that they have been in love. They criticize the system of grading used at their school, but never explain exactly what is wrong with it. They expound pompously on sportsmanship, never commenting on the nasty clip that prompted their essay. They don't realize that their own experiences can matter to other readers. The details go unmentioned, and the prose plods:

Specific details

> Sportsmanship is the key to athletic endeavor. No matter what the athletic endeavor you are engaged in is, it requires sportsmanship to make it really and truly worthwhile. We, as a society today, value sportsmanship and all that goes along with it. Sportsmanship is the key to success and to happiness. Without sportsmanship, we would not have athletic competition. . . .
>
> My neck snapped back and I was dazed for half a minute, sore for a week. The official missed the clip; no penalty was called; no points were scored because of it. All my opponent had done was hurt me. And for

what? For the pleasure of watching me stagger to my feet, head buzzing, wondering where I was? His coach, no doubt, had mentioned sportsmanship, but. . . .

Often, just one detail per page—just one—can make a huge difference to a reader searching for a spark of original insight, an idea treated in a slightly different way. Trust your readers to recognize common and specific things; whenever you can, fill your essays with nouns closest to your own experiences.

Verbs

Verbs are words that express action (to go) or existence (to be). Verbs give prose its energy. Lively verbs can animate dull subjects, while convenient but pale verbs will anesthetize even rollicking events. When is a verb lively? When it describes an action or state of being that is physical and particular, and when it accurately represents what its subject does:

The blood coagulated.
The coach bellowed.
The milk curdled.

The most common verbs are both the most important and the dullest. The language could not operate without constantly relying on variations of these:

Common verbs

to be	to have
to do	to make
to give	to say
to want	to go
to come	to get
to be able	to use
to happen	to occur

Because you cannot avoid using these verbs in most writing, you should employ them when you must, but substitute livelier actions whenever you can. Be reasonable. Don't strain your reader's patience with fruitless end-runs around the obvious. At times the basic verb is the best choice:

⌐I achieved completion of the job.
└►I did the job.

⌐I utilized the learning resources center.
└►I used the library.

One way of squashing the juices even out of lively verbs is to set them in unnecessary passive constructions. The basic English sentence moves directly from the doer of an action (subject) to what is done (verb):

S	**V**
<u>Lon</u>	<u>stubbed</u> his toe.

<u>Unions</u>	<u>changed</u> the American way of life.

Make the subject the thing acted upon, and you've got a passive construction:

> The toe was stubbed by Lon.
>
> The American way of life was changed by unions.

The resulting sentences are still accurate, but they're not quite as fit as the original versions. In fact, they've grown paunchy by the addition of an auxiliary verb (was) and a preposition (by). The energy of their actions dribbles out at the end of prepositional phrases: by Lon, by unions. The active forms avoid these weaknesses.

Yet the passive voice appears too often and too naturally in much good prose to stand universally condemned. Some notions require the passive voice; some situations favor it:

> The constable was robbed.
>
> We were stopped by an obstacle in our way, an angry mob.

In the first sentence, we cannot supply a precise doer of the action since the robber is probably unknown. Who robbed the constable? That's exactly the question. In the second example, while it may be true that the mob is doing the action (stopping), the writer probably wants to focus on the more particular subject: us. The mob is important because it is menacing the *we* of the sentence. The passive voice works well here, even adding a little suspense by delaying the appearance of the angry crowd until the end.

Even the examples we looked at to begin with might be better in the passive in certain situations. If the focus of a paragraph is on the American way of life, a writer might want to keep that idea at the focal point of sentences too. Hence, a writer might prefer "The American way of life was changed by unions" to the more active version, "Unions changed the American way of life."

Perhaps the best guideline here is to use passive verb constructions when you must, the active forms whenever you can. Let your subjects act, and let their actions be lively. As an exercise, occasionally pause after you have composed a page or two to review what you have produced. Circle your passive constructions (and other dull verbs, while you are at it). Then, wherever you can, tighten your prose with the appropriate turn of phrase:

> The Civil Rights Bill of 1964 ⟨was passed⟩ by Congress after ⟨it was⟩ lobbied for vigorously by President Lyndon Johnson. ⟨It is⟩ very likely that the act ⟨would not have been passed⟩ by the reluctant Congress without its ⟨having been supported⟩ by a President at the height of his popularity.

> Congress passed the Civil Rights Bill of 1964 after vigorous lobbying by President Lyndon Johnson. The reluctant Congress probably would not have passed the act without the prodding of a President at the height of his popularity.

Important Modifiers

Modifiers

Put a specific noun and a lively verb together and you've got the core of a great sentence. But you cannot even then ignore the words immediately surrounding that core, the faithful servants—articles, adjectives, and adverbs—that are in themselves powerful shapers of meaning. We sometimes treat these parts of speech like luckless draftees ready to be pressed into service as often and casually as needed. We do so at some risk. They are modifiers: words that limit, qualify, explain, specify, and amplify nouns and verbs. Just consider for a moment the influence even slight changes in modification have on an idea:

Boys plagiarize.	(Base idea)
All boys plagiarize.	(Not true!)
Most boys plagiarize.	(Prove this!)
Some boys plagiarize.	(OK, I'll agree.)
The boy plagiarizes.	(Which one?)
A boy plagiarizes.	(Be more specific.)

And yet many writers do use words like *all* and *most, the* and *a* almost interchangeably, ignoring the impact they have on the meaning of a sentence.

Here, for example, are three sentences that may seem synonymous on first glance. But consider the real differences the modifiers—*each, every,* and *all*—make:

Nouns, Verbs, and the Thesis Statement

Each bird flew away.
Every bird flew away.
All the birds flew away.

The first version emphasizes the action of individual birds. All the birds fly away eventually, but our attention is drawn to the acts of particular birds: each one flies away. In the second sentence, the emphasis remains individual: every (one). But there is now a slight shift toward a sense of the flock flying away together. The lash sentence completes this movement. Now we sense what the group did: all flew away. The differences between these sentences are subtle, but on occasion you may need to draw distinctions this fine. And the language provides you with the qualifiers you need to be precise.

There's another reason for concentrating on the basic parts of a sentence. As you experiment with nouns, verbs, and their modifiers you may gradually discover what you want to say in a concluding sentence, a transitional paragraph, or, perhaps most important of all, a thesis statement.

Shaping and Reshaping a Thesis Statement

A single example may serve to explain how paying attention to the main parts of a sentence can clarify or generate a thesis statement. We'll begin with the need to write an essay on the state of the free enterprise system for a government class. We've already got some thoughts on the subject which we get down on paper in no particular order and without regard—at this point—for substance or style:

Thesis statements

> Free enterprise is good and so is individualism. Most people agree. But they don't act that way. They want things done for them at the same time that they complain about how much government costs. They want to be protected by a government too, but that costs money and means rules and regulations that don't help individualism and free enterprise.

We can generate a whole paragraph of such thoughts in a few minutes. What we've got is not a developed paragraph, but strings of ideas. Some will help us formulate a thesis; others we'll discard. Reading over the jottings, can we identify some simple and basic relationships? Yes, if we first isolate the major nouns:

free enterprise
individualism
government
rules
regulations

Now we can sort out the relationships among these key nouns:

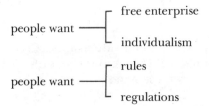

In this case, we have discovered a potential conflict between what it is that people want.

With the issues outlined in this stark fashion, we can begin sharpening the nouns and verbs. Several basic versions of the developing thesis are worth consideration:

Sharpening the thesis statement

> People want free enterprise and individualism, but they also want rules and regulations.

> Although most people want free enterprise and individualism, they also want rules and regulations.

> The rules and regulations people want don't get along with the free enterprise and individualism they also want.

Any one of these versions could be developed further in the direction of greater precision. We'll work with the third version, and immediately make one easy specification:

> The rules and regulations *Americans* want don't get along with the free enterprise and individualism they also want.

Get along with is a relatively vague, strung-out verb. What do rules and regulations do to the free market and individualism? A list of possible verb alternatives might help at this point:

> undermine?
> contradict?
> complicate?
> choke?
> destroy?
> weaken?

These aren't the only choices, or necessarily the best ones. But we have to commit ourselves eventually to some choice:

> The rules and regulations Americans want undermine the free enterprise and individualism they also want.

But now another consideration: can you *want* free enterprise the same way you *want* rules and regulations? Free enterprise and individualism are concepts you believe in. Here is a revised version of the thesis which reflects one more attempt at refining the basic idea:

> The rules and regulations Americans want undermine the *principles* of free enterprise and individualism they *believe in.*

Refining the basic idea

Where do the rules and regulations come from? The federal government? The state government? The schools and churches? The sentence can be modified one more time to reflect the writer's opinion:

> The *federal* rules and regulations Americans want undermine the principles of free enterprise and individualism they believe in.

Is the sentence finished? That's up to us. Does it say what we want it to? If not, more work is needed, especially since this looks to be a key sentence in the projected essay. We can make the sentence much more specific:

> The federal rules and regulations American truckers want contradict the principles of free enterprise and individualism they have come to represent in the public imagination.

Or we can make it sarcastic:

> The federal rules and regulations Americans cry for undermine the principles of free enterprise and individualism they so piously champion.

We can even make it a question:

> Do federal rules and regulations weaken the principles of free enterprise and individualism on which America was founded?

Essays spawned by these sentences would probably spend several paragraphs listing and complaining about superfluous regulations, several paragraphs explaining the tenets of free enterprise and individualism, and several exploring the contradictions between regulation and personal freedom. The paragraphs listing the virtues of individualism could slip into tedious sermonizing if we aren't careful. But our main idea, here at the outset, holds potential.

1. This section asks you to focus on individual words as you shape sentences: nouns, verbs, adjectives, adverbs, and articles. Do you

For Discussion

Shaping and Reshaping a Thesis Statement

compose sentences word by word? Or do you compose in larger units: phrase by phrase, or whole sentences at a time? If you compose in larger units, when do you think might be the opportune time to focus on individual words?

2. Most disciplines, professions, and interests use abstract terms that mystify outsiders. Can you name some abstract nouns of importance in a field you know well? Try to distinguish between abstract terms that describe concepts and technical terms that precisely name particular things.

Exercises

3. For three of the following terms, find two related words or terms more specific than the original. Then write a statement for each term that might serve as the main idea for an informative or persuasive article.

For example:

Original

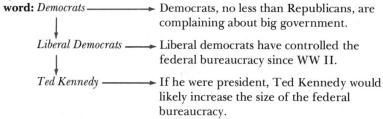

Suggested terms:

aircraft	doctors	women
team sports	immigrants	periodicals
religions	laws	psychology
thieves	presidents	mammals
dance	victory	mechanisms
tools	stimulants	pride

4. For three of the following words, find two terms *more abstract,* and construct a thesis sentence around each term.

For example:

Original

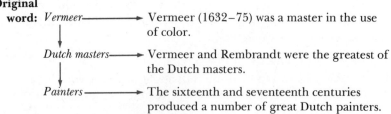

Nouns, Verbs, and the Thesis Statement

Suggested words:

Volvo	poison ivy	Julia Child
dollar	inflation	Karl Marx
Will Rogers	parliament	Milton Friedman
appendix	Nikon	*The Empire Strikes Back*
Chaucer	Mahler	felinophobia
martini	guillotine	Saudi Arabia

5. Examine a letter to the editor in the daily newspaper. Circle weak verb choices and passive constructions. Rewrite the letter in more vigorous language.

6. Examine the language of your textbooks or any documents or papers you may have received recently from a government or business office. Collect examples of prose that seem clotted or lifeless because of wordiness or poorly chosen nouns and verbs.

7. Define one of the following terms first as a dictionary might (maximum length: 50 words) and then by specifying details the way E. B. White defines democracy (aim for 200–300 words). You may want to review the section on definition in chapter two.

justice	science	truth
philosophy	music	commerce
economy	sociology	integrity
baseball	mathematics	senior citizens
prejudice	toleration	free enterprise
hope	the news	pain

8. Apply the following modifiers to some general assertion and decide which you could defend in an informative essay and which in a persuasive essay:

All _____ .
Most _____ .
Some _____ .
No _____ .

For example:

All attempts to legislate morality fail.

Most attempts to legislate morality fail.

Some attempts to legislate morality fail.

No attempts to regulate morality fail completely.

9. Following the method described in this chapter for shaping a thesis, develop a general idea into a specific main idea. Choose a general idea

from the area of politics, religion, economics, or sports. Come up with at least three workable versions of a given main idea.

Denotation and Connotation

Choosing accurate and specific language is complicated by the relationship words have to the world at large. Words have straightforward and explicit meanings—what we sometimes call "dictionary definitions." These definitions, which attempt to describe a thing or an idea in itself, represent the *denotation* of a word. But words also have meanings that exist in the thoughts and feelings and associations of individuals and groups. These additional layers of meaning, called *connotations*, surround a word and expand its particular significance.

In many contexts, words can be relatively neutral; that is, they may lack positive or negative connotations. For you, *railroad crossing* may be a word without powerful connotations, meaning simply a place where a track crosses a highway. But to a neighborhood that has experienced several near-fatal accidents at a railroad crossing, the word may be charged with anger and political energy. Similarly, to a potential renter, the Watergate complex in Washington, D.C., may be no more than a cluster of buildings. But for most people, the connotations of *Watergate* overwhelm the simple meaning to conjure up remembrances of Senate hearings, break-ins, wire-taps, slush funds, and the resignation of a President.

Political connotations Political words and phrases are particularly rich in connotations that shift according to the audience reading them. To liberals, most of these phrases have favorable connotations:

> Affirmative Action
> busing to achieve racial integration
> government action
> national health plan
> the union shop
> registration of firearms

To conservatives, the same terms have such negative connotations that they have developed equivalents that express their feelings:

> reverse discrimination
> forced busing
> government intervention
> socialized medicine
> right to work
> gun control

A sensitivity to connotations may aid you in appreciating the richness of individual words. All the words below describe ways of walking, but each has connotations fitted to particular times and feelings:

to saunter
- what you do on a sunny day
- dapper, well-dressed folks
- happy, pleasant
- easy, graceful
- whistling

to shuffle
- soles scraping the ground
- hands in pockets, uneasy
- baggy pants
- slowly
- gray day

to trudge
- heavy feet, shoes
- sad, tired, perhaps weak
- heavy, burdened
- dismal, cold

Many more examples could be offered to demonstrate the importance of connotations. Your task as a writer is to keep track of and exploit the connotations of words you are using *for a given audience*. An allusion to "mystery meat" may, for example, win a chuckle from all the dormitory residents across the country who have on occasion dined on an amorphous clump of animal matter, but the same phrase would go down less well with a convention of restaurateurs.

Well-employed, connotations act like extra ideas added to a text, without labor or composition. Mention an apple in the proper way, and you conjure up Adam, Eve, and the whole subsequent history of mankind. Mention the cold war and your parents will recall Hungary, bomb shelters, and Sputnik. Allude to gusto, and your readers are all blowing foam off the top of beer mugs.

1. Below are pairs of words with similar denotations but different connotations. Discuss these differences and decide in what contexts each word might be used:

For Discussion

chief executive/head honcho
GOP/Republican Party
tavern/bar
downpour/deluge
automobile/wheels
Negro/Black
violin/fiddle
home/domicile
janitor/custodian

learning facilitator/teacher
prevarication/lie
period of recession/period of negative growth
library/learning resources center
athlete/jock

2. Some words, phrases, and names come quickly into fashion. For a time, everyone uses them, knows what they mean, associates them with interesting events, fads, or concepts. At the time this exercise is being penned, some of the "current" words and phrases are:

Khomeini
"10"
J. R. Ewing
recession
boycott
embargo
bail out
free agent

What words and phrases are in vogue as you read this? What do you associate with those words?

Exercises

3. Many writers keep a thesaurus handy to help them find the word they are looking for. But not all the synonyms a thesaurus lists for any given term can be treated as equivalent. Under *prosperity,* for example, *Roget's International Thesaurus* (3rd ed.) lists:

prosperousness
thriving condition
success
welfare
well-being
comfort
ease

These are plausible but not exact alternatives to the notion of prosperity. Also listed are some rather colorful synonyms:

the life of Riley
bed of roses
Easy Street
fat of the land
fleshpots of Egypt
purple and fine linen

Nouns, Verbs, and the Thesis Statement

These terms have their proper contexts—often in colloquial speech. We can imagine a senator enjoying the "life of Riley," but declaiming on national prosperity on the Senate floor.

As an exercise, browse through a thesaurus until you find an entry that intrigues you. Then write a short paragraph using as many of the listed synonyms as possible, giving each word an appropriate context. Your paragraph may take the form of an extended definition. An example:

Prosperity

On the corner of E. 9th and Euclid, the radical stood on her soap box to rail against the nation's false *prosperity.* While half the world starves, Americans rest in the *lap of luxury,* like the *fleshpots of Egypt.* This *life of ease,* this *bed of roses,* the wild-eyed woman charged, is sustained only by oppressed working classes all around the globe denied the *comfort,* the *ease,* the *purple and fine linen,* the *well-being* that their exploiters take for granted. *Easy Street,* she said, in this *land of milk and honey,* has been paved by denying millions their right to *high standards of living.*

Be sure to note that many synonyms listed in a thesaurus are likely to be archaic, inappropriate to most situations, or clichéd *(the life of Riley, the fat of the land).* Enjoy investigating and using such expressions in this exercise, but be sure to exercise judgment whenever you use a thesaurus for informative or persuasive writing.

4. Most schools or places of employment have words and phrases unique to them. These are words with strong, local connotations. At the University of Texas at Austin, the *Drag,* the *Tower,* and the *Longhorn* are terms with explicit and colorful local meanings. At Ohio State, everyone knows what *Buckeyes* are and where the *Oval* is.

Make a list of words with connotations unique to your school or place of employment. Define several of the words in a paragraph or two. Be sure to convey the connotations of the words.

8

The Sentence

Julius Caesar reported his victory over King Pharnaces in 47 B.C. with arrogant economy: "I came, I saw, I conquered." An American naval commander during the War of 1812, Oliver Hazard Perry, reported his defeat of the British forces on Lake Erie with similar directness: "We have met the enemy, and they are ours." And during World War II, another American, Anthony McAuliffe, leading the beleaguered 101st Airborne Division during the Battle of the Bulge (December 1944), answered a German ultimatum for surrender with a single, memorable word: "Nuts!" The missives of these three military commanders endure because of their power, directness, and simplicity; they are calculated, dramatic responses to the situations of war, dispatches that speak clearly over distance, time, and the roar of cannon.

But, allowing ourselves some license with history, we can imagine what the dilemma of the officials receiving these messages might have been had they been given no additional information: the Roman senators scurrying to discover where exactly Caesar was and what he was up to; the American military commander, William Henry Harrison, pleased by his admiral's success, but wondering exactly how many British vessels were sunk; and the befuddled German official wondering what pecans, almonds, and pistachios had to do with his demand for surrender. Was the American using a strange code?

Examined outside of their historical contexts, the messages seem inadequate. A second lieutenant, fresh from ROTC, who reported on a field action with Caesar's brevity would need Caesar's prestige and courage the next time he met his superior officer. Similarly, McAuliffe's pointed reply might be admired for its guts, but it is not likely to be taught at West Point as the model of military communications. In contexts other than the one in which it was delivered, the statement would need amplification, clarification, and development.

In its context, however, "Nuts!" is a splendid sentence. Why? Because a sentence is appropriately developed when the arrangement of its words meets the needs of the writer and his audience. McAuliffe might reply "Nuts!" to the enemy and "I will not surrender because I still have adequate supplies, armament, and morale" to his superiors and do an adequate job in each case. An adequately developed sentence can be viewed as a cluster of words meaningful in a given situation.

Adequately developed sentences

A paragraph, similarly, is a cluster of sentences bound by some significant meaning. And larger units of discourse—essays, reports, editorials, textbooks, novels—are significant clusters of paragraphs, the separate paragraphs (like the sentences within them) amplifying, developing, elucidating, and enlivening a major idea or ideas.

This model puts the various major components of an essay in relationship to each other, like boxes within boxes:

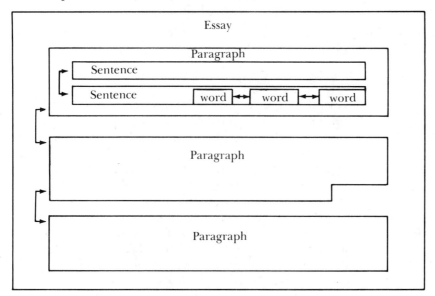

But writing is far too complex to be wholly contained or explained by any such diagram. What the model suggests is that an essay is a lively creation, a network of words, sentences, and paragraphs vibrating with thoughts and ideas. To explore an idea through written language is to fully exploit the capacities of the sentence to express, to summarize, to inform, to analyze, to comment, and to persuade.

In the previous chapter, we emphasized the importance of direct statement, of finding subjects, verbs, and simple modifiers that clarified an issue or stated a condition in a bold way: "I came; I saw; I conquered." In this chapter, we will explore some of the principles of amplification and development that enable writers to convey to readers the facts, specifications, details, arguments, contradictions, and qualifications that surround their basic ideas, that make what they say entertaining, persuasive, informative, or revealing.

Exercise

Using a dictionary of quotations like *Bartlett's Familiar Quotations* or *The Home Book of Quotations,* an encyclopedia, and other appropriate sources, investigate several of the famous short sentences that follow. Write a paragraph explaining who made the statement, when, under what circumstances, and why:

Words, words, words.
Frankly Scarlett, I don't give a damn!
I want to be alone.
Nice guys finish last.
Et tu, Bruté?
Rose is a rose is a rose is a rose.
Damn the torpedoes—full speed ahead!
L'État c'est moi.

Developing the Sentence

At times, sentences seem to have wills of their own, stubbornly fixed against their author's intentions. They want to end exactly where a writer needs an additional explanatory clause. They wear evening dress when the situation calls for jeans. Or they marshall their nouns into a conspiracy not to agree with their verbs. Perhaps sentences seem tough because they are really so vulnerable to change. A swift erasure, a timely jot of punctuation, a clause moved up front, or any of a hundred other alterations, and the sentence becomes a new creature conveying a different message in a new costume. Able writers respect sentences, but refuse to be bullied by them because they know that sentences must be brought into line if a message is going to connect, to reach its audience.

English prose

How complex or how fully developed a sentence is going to be depends, as ever, on the purpose and the audience a writer has in mind. In general, English prose has grown simpler since approximately the sixteenth century. Absolute sentence length has decreased, clauses have grown shorter and fewer, and relationships between words and modifiers are less ambiguous and more direct. Consequently, twentieth century prose is probably more readable than its predecessors, though it may be less subtle and complex. Though simpler than its ancestors, the modern sentence is by no means limited in what it can do. It remains a supple instrument by which a writer can shape that moment of contact between a reader and ideas, and choose the order and rhythm of communication.

The opening sentence

Choice is the key word. As you write sentence after sentence in composing an essay, you may not always be aware that you are making choices about their shape and design. Some sentences, especially those midway through an essay, seem to write themselves, but others give more trouble. The most difficult, time-consuming, and worrisome sentence of a paper is likely to be your first one because, at the start of an essay, you have many choices to make. The first sentence of any longer effort must grapple with the new subject and establish the organization, point of view, relationship with the audience, and more. Once these matters are resolved, the number of choices diminishes and (barring other complications) subsequent sentences may roll out with less labor. But every sentence offers potential alternatives to you in structure, length, and style.

All this is by way of explaining why it pays to learn various ways of developing sentences when many people seem to write without consciously crafting their work. Learning how and when to employ certain sentence structures gives you the option of using them when a situation demands a particular technique. Even more important, the sentence patterns you practice consciously may later become part of your semiconscious roster of options. You find the phrase you need at the tip of your pen, never realizing that at some earlier time you learned how to assemble words that way.

Typical sentence order

The typical English sentence follows an order that moves from the doer of the action (subject) to what is done (verb) and sometimes to what it is done to (object) or how it is doing (complement):

S	V
The baby	cried.

S	V	O
Lon	stubbed	his toe.

S	V	C
The weather	is	fine.

As we noted in the previous chapter, this basic arrangement and the basic sentence parts (subject, verb, object, complement) carry the brunt of a sentence's meaning. But a *simple* sentence can be modified, developed, and amplified at every point in its structure, and its structure can also be manipulated in a variety of ways.

Let's begin with two simple sentences that describe an action which are in need of development and amplification:

> A DC–10 crashed and burned.
> All aboard were killed.

Here is one possible version of the combined sentences, developed and amplified, that might serve as the opening of a news report:

> All 274 passengers and crew were killed
>   today
> when an American Airlines DC–10,
>   heading for Los Angeles,
> crashed and burned
>   on takeoff from Chicago's O'Hare Airport.

In good journalistic form, the sentence provides information without delay; the basic fact is reported—all passengers were killed—and the modifiers trail informatively after.

If we move the more dramatic facts to the end of the sentence and open with the information conveyed by the first of our two short sentences ("A DC–10 crashed and burned"), the result is a slightly more suspenseful sentence:

> An American Airlines DC–10,
>   carrying 274 passengers and crew,
> crashed and burned
>   on takeoff
>   today
>   from Chicago's O'Hare Airport,
> killing all aboard.

This version would still be acceptable in a newspaper, despite the tinge of drama. But seeing what happens when we move modifiers forward to delay the main verb suggests that the strategy might be consciously used to build tension:

> Loaded with 274 passengers and crew,
>   bound for Los Angeles,
> an American Airlines DC–10
>   lost an engine on takeoff
>   from Chicago's O'Hare Airport,
>   fell to the earth,
>   and
>   exploded in a ball of flames,
> killing all aboard.

The sentence has become a short narrative, the fate of the passengers withheld from the reader for more than thirty words, while the crash itself is broken up into three stages:

1. losing an engine,
2. falling to earth, and
3. exploding in flames.

This sentence might now be too dramatic for the daily paper, but for a writer intending to intrigue readers with a description of the disaster, the chosen structure might be just right. Notice that the climax of the sentence occurs not in the series of verbs *(lost, fell, exploded),* but in a final modifying clause *(killing all abroad)* that stands noticeably alone, adding impact.

All three versions of the two original sentences convey the same basic information (the last version adds some details), but they do it in ways fitted to different circumstances. Where quick information is needed, the first version works well; where the aim is suspense, the last might be preferred. The middle version is a compromise.

In many sentences, then, what determines how a reader reacts to information is where the modifiers are placed and how the sentence is structured. Modifiers can be placed before, in the middle, and after the subject/verb/object group, which we'll call the *base clause.* Additionally, a base clause can have several subjects, verbs, objects, and modifiers. Sentences can be developed by coordination and subordination. Modifiers themselves can be modified. A sentence can branch out, like a bolt of lightning, beginning with a general idea and unfolding in greater detail:

Modifiers and sentence structures

Base clause
   ├─ *modifier*
   ├─ *modifier*
   └─ *modifier*

Scientists are wedded to reason,
   ├─ *to the meticulous working out of consequences from*
   │ *assumptions,*
   └─ *to the careful organization of experiments designed to check those*
     consequences.
                        —Isaac Asimov, "The Eureka Phenomenon"

Or a sentence can be constructed in elaborate and significant balance:

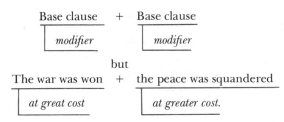

Base clause   +   Base clause
    modifier   *modifier*

               but
The war was won   +   the peace was squandered
    at great cost   *at greater cost.*

In the remaining parts of this chapter, we will examine a variety of ways to develop sentences.

Exercise   Combine the short sentences below into longer sentences in at least two different versions. Add facts and details whenever appropriate. Evaluate the effects your different versions might have on readers:

1. The fuel gauge registered empty.
   The tiny plane flew on.

2. The bases were loaded.
   Two Yankees were out.
   The score was tied.
   It was the bottom of the ninth.
   A storm was approaching.

3. The President accused the Senator of corruption.
   The Senator charged the President with cowardice.
   Both men were furious.
   Both men held news conferences.

4. The office was paralyzed.
   The computer was down.
   Lines grew.
   Customers got ugly.

5. Casca stabbed Caesar.
   Cassius stabbed Caesar.
   Diecus stabbed Caesar.
   Metellus stabbed Caesar.
   Cinna stabbed Caesar.
   Brutus stabbed Caesar.
   Great Caesar fell.
   Caesar muttered, "Et tu, Brute?"

6. The telephone rang.
   The doctor sighed.
   The news was good.

7. The report found fault with the corporation's management.
   The product line was outdated.
   The factories were antiquated.
   Too much money was spent on advertising.

8. Xerxes invaded Greece.
   His armies were repulsed.

9. The duckbill is well adapted.
   It lives an aquatic life.
   Its fur is dense.
   Its tail is flat.
   Its feet are webbed.

   > —adapted from Isaac Asimov, "What Do You Call a Platypus?"

10. We know how a yeti [abominable snowman] track can be made.
    It can be made by the sun.
    The sun melts the tracks of a small creature.
    The small creature can be a fox or wild dog.

    > —adapted from Sir Edmund Hilary, "Epitaph to the Elusive Abominable Snowman"

11. The village was tiny.
    It was called Lentshin.
    It was a sandy marketplace.
    Peasants met there once a week.
    They were of the area.

    > —adapted from Isaac Bashevis Singer, "The Son from America"

12. Good writing begins with a respect for words.
    That respect is profound.
    That respect is for their precise denotations.
    That respect is for their connotations.
    That respect is for their weight.
    That respect is for their music.

    > —adapted from John Trimble, *Writing with Style: Conversations on the Art of Writing*

13. Forces have operated to change the urban environment.
    There are three basic forces.
    The change has been for the worse.
    The first force is population concentration.
    The second force is rising affluence.
    The third force is technological change.

    > —adapted from Neil H. Jacoby, "The Environmental Crisis"

14. The success of man as a species is the result of development.
    That success is amazing.
    The development is of his brain.
    That development has led to tool-using.

That development has led to tool making.

It has led to the ability to solve problems by logical reasoning.

It has led to thoughtful cooperation.

It has led to language.

—adapted from Jane Van Lawick-Goodall, "In the Shadow of Man"

Initial Modifiers

Most writers are adept at placing modification before a single noun:

a *brown* house

a *delicate* and *costly* experiment

Modification before a base clause is only a bit more complicated:

In the beginning,
darkness covered the earth.

Packing his canary,
McTeague fled to Death Valley.

Alone at last,
the lovers sat on the couch.

Convinced of his innocence,
the jury freed Moriarity.

When the clock struck midnight,
the doors swung shut.

Although she felt uneasy,
Gina pithed the wiggling frog.

Parallel modifiers

More than one modifier or modifying clause can precede a base clause. In fact, you can often construct an effective and economical sentence by linking related modifiers through a parallel structure. A parallel structure is a series of words or phrases that share a grammatical structure. Parallel phrases differ in what they say, but are almost identical in how they say it:

Convinced of his innocence,
saddened by his story,
intimidated by his glance,
the jury acquitted Moriarity.

convinced	of	his	innocence
saddened	by	his	story
intimidated	by	his	glance

> *Although she felt uneasy,*
> *cruel,*
> *and a little silly,*
> > Gina pithed the wiggling frog.

	uneasy
	cruel
a little	silly

Initial modifiers needn't be limited to short phrases or simple parallelisms. They can grow as large as you deem necessary to serve your audience:

> *Burdened by an energy crisis growing deeper every year,*
> *governed by officials more cordial than competent,*
> *unsure of its policies at home or of its strength abroad,*
> *unwilling to make the sacrifices the times required,*
> *but too resilient to be counted out for good,*
> > the United States launched itself into the 1980s.

This long example demonstrates both the possibilities and the limitations of initial modifiers. Short initial modifiers ordinarily give information about a subject or verb that is nearby. When initial modifying phrases begin to multiply or grow in length, suspense develops as the reader anticipates the main clause which will explain the modifiers. But if the modifiers plod on too long or too obscurely, or if the base clause finally proves a dud, the reader may lose interest in the sentence or be disappointed with it:

> *Swirling like ribbons of molten steel,*
> *buzzing, whirling, humming,*
> *flashing out gleams of light,*
> > the beaters on the mixer mashed the potatoes.

Initial modifiers slow a reader down somewhat. When they are multiplied, particularly in a parallel sequence, they can sound formal, even stiff. They can be used to create drama and suspense. Properly handled, they can convey a sense of order, reason, and inevitability:

> *Because a man of his height, build, gait, and complexion was seen leaving the*
> > *apartment,*
> *because his fingerprints were found in and around the victim's room,*
> *because he had the opportunity,*
> > *the ability, and*
> > *the motive to perform this criminal act,*
> you must find the accused guilty as charged.

A. Try adding an initial modifying phrase or two to each of the following base clauses.

Example:

⌐ *The bald cypress thrives in the southeastern states.*

L▸ Valued for its rot-resistant timber, the bald cypress thrives in the southeastern states.

1. The space shuttle finally paid off.

2. The rate of inflation topped 17 percent.

3. Three nuclear dumps were closed.

4. The tax levy failed a second time.

5. She criticized his performance in the ballet.

B. Try adding two or more initial modifying phrases to each of the following base clauses.

Example:

To . . .
⌐ . . . *NATO was formed in 1949.*

L▸ To counter threats of Soviet aggression and to encourage political, economic, and cultural cooperation between Europe and North America, NATO was formed in 1949.

1. Despite . . .
   . . . the Steelers won the Superbowl again.

2. Because . . .
   . . . the jury found the dentist guilty of malpractice.

3. While . . .
   . . . the youth collapsed on the turf.

4. . . . wagon trains found their way in increasing numbers to California, the new promised land.

5. . . . the college administration decided to combat grade inflation.

6. By . . .
   . . . the company expected to increase its profits substantially.

7. Because of . . .
   . . . *Consumer Reports* rated the hairdryer unacceptable.

8. To discover . . .
. . . the agency decided to fund the research project.

9. Even though . . .
. . . the book was removed from the high school library.

10. Despite . . .
. . . Jimmy Carter was elected President in 1976.

11. In order to . . .
. . . Einstein urged Roosevelt to build the A-bomb.

12. By . . .
. . . you can cut your gasoline consumption up to 30 percent.

Modifiers in the Middle

A sentence may also be developed and amplified by the insertion of modifying words or phrases within the basic subject-verb-object structure:

> The mandrake was used as a medicine. *It is a poisonous plant of the nightshade family.*
>
> The mandrake, *a poisonous plant of the nightshade family,* was used as a medicine.

> The boy accepted the tiny trophy. *He masked his disappointment behind a brave smile.*
>
> The boy, *masking his disappointment behind a brave smile,* accepted the tiny trophy.

In both examples, the modifying phrase could be moved ahead of the base clause without altering it much. The choice is up to the writer.

Commas surrounding these modifiers indicate their mobility: they are *nonrestrictive*. A nonrestrictive modifier is one that can be eliminated without significantly changing the meaning of the word it modifies. While both modifiers in the examples do increase what you know about the subjects,

> the mandrake ⟶ a poisonous plant
> the boy ⟶ masking disappointment,

neither is essential to identifying or separating the particular subjects from the other mandrakes or boys. When a subject is followed by a modifying clause that cannot be removed without changing the subject, then the modifier is called *restrictive:*

> The boy who was weakly smiling accepted the tiny trophy.

This sentence tells the reader that the subject is the *one* boy at the assembly smiling weakly and no other. More examples:

> The townhouse *that collapsed* was mine.
> The lie *that hurts most* is the one *a friend believes.*
> The contestant *who laughs first* loses.

Restrictive modifiers are not surrounded by commas. With some phrases, commas would simply intrude:

> The townhouse, that collapsed, was mine.

But in other cases, commas subtly alter the meaning of the sentence:

> The boy, who was weakly smiling, accepted the tiny trophy.

In this version, the sentence informs the reader that the boy was smiling weakly, but he is not identified by that detail. Other boys present might be smiling weakly too.

The placement of a modifying phrase after a noun, ahead of the verb, is both an efficient and elegant technique of sentence development. Note the subtle difference in rhythm between these two similarly modified sentences:

> Lady Macbeth's lily-white and bloodstained hands needed cleansing.
> Lady Macbeth's hands, lily-white and bloodstained, needed cleansing.

The first version is correct and businesslike. The second moves more slowly, focusing first on the hands unmodified, then pausing briefly to emphasize the interesting contrast: lily-white and bloodstained. Of course, modifiers (adjectives in this case) can be placed simultaneously before and after the noun. Most readers find long strings of adjectives preceding a noun dull:

> Lady Macbeth's trembling, tiny, lily-white, and bloodstained hands needed cleansing.

But perhaps you really need to include all four adjectives: trembling, tiny, lily-white, and bloodstained. In that case, the set can be broken up, with two adjectives placed before the noun and two after:

Lady Macbeth's *trembling, tiny* hands, *lily-white* and *bloodstained,* needed cleansing.

Some strategy might even be employed in the groupings, the modifiers preceding the noun emphasizing the beauty of her hands, the two following implicating her in a bloody business. An element of time might also be introduced. **Strategy in placing adjectives**

Lady Macbeth's tiny, lily-white hands, *now* trembling and bloodstained, needed cleansing.

Like initial modifying phrases, modifiers within a base clause can be made parallel in order to organize large amounts of information and detail: **Parallel modifiers in the middle**

The internal combustion engine,
> *the single greatest contributor to air pollution,*
> *the insatiable devourer of precious fossil fuels,*
> *the mainstay of the world auto industry,*
> *the most highly developed of power plants,*
is doomed.

But modifiers that follow a noun, pronoun, or subject need not necessarily be parallel. Modifiers, for example, sometimes attach themselves to fellow modifiers:

Fort Necessity, *a timid, circular rampart built of logs hewn from the Appalachian woods near present-day Uniontown, Pennsylvania,* was the site of George Washington's surrender to the French on July 4, 1754.

Here, the modifiers trail away from Fort Necessity until the verb finally appears:

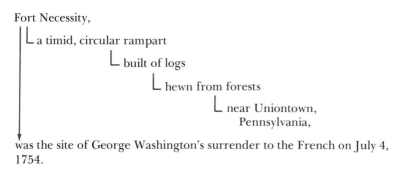

Fort Necessity,
 └ a timid, circular rampart
  └ built of logs
   └ hewn from forests
    └ near Uniontown,
      Pennsylvania,
was the site of George Washington's surrender to the French on July 4, 1754.

Modification within a sentence can bud in places other than after the initial noun. Any nouns or pronouns may need amplification or specification. Modifiers themselves may need clarification. And verbs will support additions too:

> The time came, *at last,* for the show to begin.
>
> Her angry voice rose quickly, *like a waterspout out of the sea,* and then disappeared.

Dashes and parentheses

Abrupt modifications or interruptions within a sentence are sometimes contained within dashes or parentheses. These special sets of punctuation can enliven a dull sentence or highlight an important addition, but they shouldn't be used so often that a reader begins to anticipate them in your style. Dashes within sentences usually enclose a phrase or a series of words that expand and explain the phrase preceding them:

> The most controversial presidents of this century—Wilson, Roosevelt, Truman, Johnson, and Nixon—may also have been its ablest.
>
> Death—like paregoric—can dull the senses something fierce.

Parentheses frequently enclose phrases which, if delivered on stage, might be called asides—whispered remarks slightly off the topic or outside the grammar (though not always):

> I told her (she never listens) not to swing at pitches low and inside.

Of course, they have other uses too:

> A well-chosen verb (see the previous chapter) serves its subject well.
>
> Attach the completed assembly (hinges and door) to the endpost and tighten all bolts.

Using middle modification

These and other modifiers that appear in the middle of sentences are tailored to no single writing aim. Long or paralleled phrases tend to slow up a sentence and may be more difficult to read than a phrase modified ahead of the base clause. But writers who need to convey many details or who want readers to dwell on certain ideas may find the slower rhythms of middle modification to their liking.

One warning. Too lengthy a modifying interruption between a subject and its verb can cause problems. Readers may forget what the subject is by the time they reach the verb or, if the modification is tangled enough, they may lose track of the entire sentence:

> Elizabeth I, probably England's greatest monarch and the daughter of Ann Boleyn, the woman Henry VIII wooed at the cost of a split with the Roman Church and then beheaded because she gave him only a daughter, liked drama.

A. Combine the following sentences, placing the italicized modifying phrases in an appropriate position "inside" the base sentence. *Exercises*

Example:

Paradise Lost was published in 1667. *It is Milton's great epic poem.*

Paradise Lost, Milton's great epic poem, was published in 1667.

1. Lyndon Johnson declined to run in the 1968 election. *He was the only Texan to serve as President.*

2. In the last act of Puccini's tragic opera, Pinckerton arrives too late to prevent Madame Butterfly's suicide. *He is an American naval officer.*

3. The Edsel arrived on the automobile market just as Americans were turning to VWs and Renaults. *It was an enormous, powerful gas guzzler.*

4. Beethoven was a child of the tremendous upheaval which had been fermenting all through the 18th century and had burst forth in the French Revolution. *In this, he was like Napoleon and Goethe.*

—adapted from Donald Jay Grout, *A History of Western Music*

5. The ordeal of the twentieth century is far from over. *It is the bloodiest, most turbulent era of the Christian age.*

—adapted from Adlai E. Stevenson, Acceptance Speech, Democratic Nomination for the Presidency, 1952

6. Every short story is a little act of discovery. *At least for me.*

—adapted from Mary McCarthy, "Settling the Colonel's Hash"

7. I examined four magazines to study the number and content of their ads. *The magazines were* Time, Cosmopolitan, Car and Driver, *and* Life.

8. Mark moaned piteously. *He was now our leader. His back split the air as our toboggan rushed toward the brink.*

9. La Fontaine had invented a novel form of entertainment in his poetic fables. *He was the son of a forestry official.*

—adapted from Maurice Ashley, *Louis XIV and the Greatness of France*

10. King Edward VII enjoyed pomp and display. *He was a polished and brilliant man of the world by the time he came to the throne at the age of fifty-nine.*

—adapted from David Thomson, *England in the Nineteenth Century*

B. Indicate whether the italicized modifying phrase is restrictive or nonrestrictive. Add punctuation where necessary.

1. The cat *a tawny one with dark paws* shredded the drapes.

2. The woman *who knows her mind* knows no limits.

3. We laughed at the salesclerk *whose vacuum cleaner failed.*

4. The students *who passed the test* received *A*s for the course.

5. The instructor *who packed the chute* was questioned about its failure.

6. The miners *who seemed uncomfortable* continued the public demonstration downtown.

C. In the sentences that follow, arrange the italicized adjectives in a more strategic way.

1. The *chilly, rainy, stormy,* and *dull* afternoon captured our mood exactly.

2. The *sullen, balding, irritable,* and *puffy-cheeked* owner of the club found his player's demand outrageous.

3. She is a *tiresome, plodding, predictable,* and *inarticulate* speaker. But she is an *engaging, careful,* and *kind* instructor.

4. Find a *tall, brown-haired, blue-eyed, white* male. He's the one!

D. Consider some of the ways you can use dashes and parentheses by suggesting words or phrases to fill the gaps in these sentences:

1. Flying saucers—like_____—are more talked about than seen.

2. The major oil companies—_____—reported significant increases in sales despite a soft economy.

3. The alternatives to pollution controls (_____) could leave us gasping.

4. If they had asked my help (_____), the problem could have been solved by now.

Modification at the End

A different sentence rhythm results when modification trails after a base clause. We have already examined one sentence in which details branch out from a main clause:

> All 274 passengers and crew were killed
> today
> *when an American Airlines DC–10,*

> *heading for Los Angeles,*
> crashed and burned
>> *on takeoff from Chicago's O'Hare Airport.*

Because the basic facts are stated first, readers do not have to hold clauses in their minds in anticipation of the conclusion of the sentence. Modifying clauses at the end of a sentence add limitations and specifications to something already stated:

> Jennifer fed the dog, *a scruffy mongrel shy one ear.*

> We refused to work *because conditions in the plant endangered our health.*

> It was a country road,
>> *narrow and winding,*
>> *almost a path,*
>> *overgrown in places by grass,*
>>> *briers, and*
>>> *dandelions.*

> We urged her to visit us occasionally,
>> *preferably when we weren't home.*

> Dr. Kalinowski recommended racquetball to
>> *ease her patient's nerves,*
>> *quicken his reflexes, and*
>> *tone his muscles*
>>> *grown flaccid from years of easy living.*

The differences between modifying *fore* and *aft* are most apparent when the modifiers are subordinate clauses:

Modification "fore" and "aft"

> He failed his driving test *because he struck a pedestrian.*
>
> *Because he struck a pedestrian,* he failed his driving test.

> She trod toward the invalid's room *when the clock struck one and the mansion was silent.*
>
> *When the clock struck one and the mansion was silent,* she trod toward the invalid's room.

In both cases, the first version of the sentence, in which modification follows the main clause, sounds slightly more factual and businesslike than the more intense second. The actual context of the sentence would determine which version best fits a writer's needs.

End modification is a structural habit worth cultivating, especially—though not exclusively—for descriptive prose. As a sentence

End modification and description

branches out from an initial observation (the base clause), each subsequent phrase requires the writer to carefully observe the object or idea being described:

> The plumage of the tiny sparrow amazed me, *the way the feathered overlays on his wings and throat traced intricate patterns in auburns and browns more subtly shaded and delicate than seemed fit on a creature so common.*

But end modification need not be elaborate or prolonged to be effective. A single phrase may be enough:

> He was my friend, *faithful and just to me.*
>
> The door slammed, *like the future closing to us.*

Exercises

A. Combine the following sentences, adding the information in the italicized sentence(s) to the end of the main clause.

Example:

> Gilbert Stuart (1755–1828) was an American portrait painter. *He did three portraits of Washington. One is the portrait that appears on every dollar bill.*
>
> Gilbert Stuart (1755–1828) was an American portrait painter famous for his three paintings of George Washington, one of which appears on the dollar bill.

1. The reviewer felt the book was a disappointment. *It did not summarize the current state of knowledge. It did not advance research in the field.*

2. The Constitution provides for a legislative body. *It is designed to be coequal with the executive and judicial branches of government.*

3. Squids move by jet propulsion. *They pump seawater through their bodies. They expel it forcefully.*

4. Winnetka is a suburb of Chicago. *It is famous for its tree-lined streets. It is known for its wealthy residents.*

5. Someday we will all own electronic typewriters. *These typewriters will indicate spelling errors. They will suggest where to place punctuation. They will permit us to make corrections on a text. The text will be visible on a television screen.*

6. Titicaca is a lake on the border of Peru and Bolivia. *It is South America's largest freshwater lake. It is the highest major lake in the world.*

7. Explorer I was launched on January 31, 1958. *It was the first*

American satellite. It trailed the Soviet Union's Sputnik I by four months. It discovered radiation belts around the earth. They are called Van Allen belts.

8. Prohibition was repealed in 1933. *It had caused smuggling and bootlegging. It encouraged the development of organized crime.*

9. Pagodas are pyramidal structures. *They are usually octagonal, hexagonal, or square. They may have many stories. Each story has a tile roof. The tile roofs turn upward.*

10. Nijinsky (1890–1950) was a dancer and choreographer. *He was born in Russia. He was considered the greatest dancer of his time. He is the subject of much interest today.*

11. Jim Crow laws held blacks in bondage. *They were enacted in states that practised segregation. They denied blacks access to public accommodations. They hindered the education of blacks. They encouraged segregation in jobs.*

B. Amplify the following sentences with several appropriate facts, details, and descriptions:

1. A typical television advertisement includes . . .

2. I got out of bed this morning feeling . . .

3. Nothing pleases me more than to watch . . .

4. Economically, the current stock market suffers from . . .

5. I have three reasons for taking this course, the first . . .

6. The Los Angeles portrayed in movies is a city of . . .

7. In the eighties, the sixties' generation now seems like . . .

8. A student going away to college needs three bits of advice . . .

C. Combine the short sentences in these paragraphs into longer sentences, varying the placement of the modifiers. Place some before a base clause, some within it, and some after. Compare your final versions with those of a classmate.

1.
The National Air and Space Museum

The National Air and Space Museum is in Washington, D.C. It is located on the Mall near the Hirshhorn Museum and Sculpture Garden. The space museum is one of the capital's most exciting attractions. It contains the artifacts of aviation history. In it is a replica of the Wright Brothers' first plane. Also in it is a full-scale lunar landing module. Lindbergh's plane hangs from the ceiling. It looks small and fragile. The plane carried him across the Atlantic in 1927. It was a solo flight. A full-size Skylab fills another corner of the museum. Spectators can walk through it. They examine its complicated hardware. Many comment on its cramped and sterile quarters. Every manner of flying machine is represented in the museum. There are dirigibles and zeppelins. There are fighter planes and space capsules. There are helicopters and balloons. These air and space vehicles are supplemented by various other exhibits. There is a remarkable movie projected onto a screen. The screen towers six stories. There is a puppet show.

2.
Daniel Defoe

Daniel Defoe (1660–1731) was born in London. He was the son of a butcher. By trade, he was a merchant. Late in his life he began writing novels. He is most famous for these novels. He wrote *Robinson Crusoe*. It is based on the true story of Alexander Selkirk. Selkirk spent more than four years marooned on an island. The island was Mās a Tierra. He was there 1704–1709. Defoe also wrote *Moll Flanders*. Moll is a pickpocket and a thief. She ends up being "transported" to America. She ends up in Virginia. Defoe also wrote *A Journal of the Plague Year*. It is an account of the Great London Plague (1665). It is a terrifying account. It is so vivid that many readers forget that it is fiction.

Balance and Coordination

So far, we've been examining what happens when modifiers are attached at different points along a main clause. Sentences can also be developed by multiplying base clauses, placing them in strategic relationships of comparison and contrast and then amplifying them further:

It was the best of times; it was the worst of times.

Coordinate relationships

In this famous sentence from Dickens' *A Tale of Two Cities*, two simple sentences, differing by only a single word, are joined by a semicolon to emphasize a paradox: that conditions at the time before the French Revolution were both good and bad, depending upon one's social class. The arrangement of the sentence makes it impossible for a reader to ignore that contrast. Not all base clauses joined by some coordinating word or device (<u>and,</u> <u>but,</u> <u>so,</u> <u>for,</u> <u>;</u> , <u>:</u>) fall into a pattern as dramatic as Dickens'. But whenever independent clauses (that is, groups of words that could stand on their own as sentences) are joined together, the relationship between them should be important. Clauses linked for no particular reason produce weak sentences:

> It was an exciting day, <u>and</u> I did my homework.
>
> The evidence against the defendant was formidable <u>and</u> he was acquitted.

When joining separate sentences together, you should choose the linking (or *coordinating*) element that best explains the relationship between the sentences:

> It was an exciting day, <u>but</u> I did my homework.
>
> The evidence against the defendant was formidable, <u>yet</u> he was acquitted.

Semicolons often join sentences which, taken together, form a complete picture or emphasize opposites:

Semicolons

> On the right stand the winners<u>; o</u>n the left you can see the losers.

A semicolon may also be used with a coordinating word to take the place of a comma when the sentences being linked are lengthy:

> The air currents around the 500-mile diameter of a hurricane spiral inward and up, creating enormous drops in air pressure and violent winds<u>; but</u> the weather is calm, almost peaceful, in the hurricane's eye.

Only occasionally is a colon used to join full sentences. Colons ordinarily act as pointers. Sometimes, however, one full sentence does point out or introduce another full sentence:

Colons

> One thing was certa<u>in:</u> we were lost!

The relationship between two sentences can be highlighted by parallelism and repetition:

> The Democrats won the endorsements, <u>but</u> the Republicans won the election.
>
> Bach thrills the mind, <u>but</u> Beethoven thrills the soul.

By using parallelism and repetition, you can express complicated ideas within single sentences that carefully balance clause against clause, modifier against modifier, and idea against idea. Like parallel phrases, balanced clauses share similar structures. Unlike parallel phrases, balanced clauses do not follow each other in sequence. Other parts of the sentence intervene. In the following examples, each phrase in the first half of the sentence has a partner balancing it in the second:

Balanced clauses

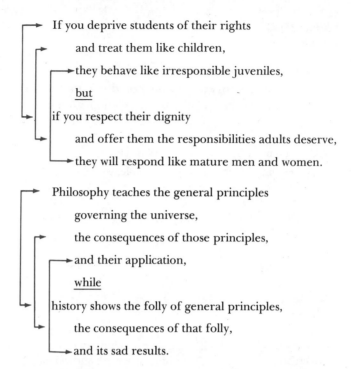

If you deprive students of their rights

    and treat them like children,

    they behave like irresponsible juveniles,

    <u>but</u>

if you respect their dignity

    and offer them the responsibilities adults deserve,

    they will respond like mature men and women.

Philosophy teaches the general principles

    governing the universe,

    the consequences of those principles,

    and their application,

    <u>while</u>

history shows the folly of general principles,

    the consequences of that folly,

    and its sad results.

Sentences like these are *architectonic;* that is, they stand like ingeniously designed buildings in elaborate harmony. In general, contemporary prose shies away from such grandly complex expressions, but they remain effective ways of making important statements of relationship or consequence. And the principle of balance they demonstrate holds true on a smaller scale to show the relationship between ideas, arguments, and other details.

Exercises

A. Complete these sentences in ways that make them "balanced":

1. All men may be created equal, but . . .

2. War is hell, but . . .

3. If all the world really is a stage, . . .

4. In theory, marriage seems the path to bliss; in practice, . . .

B. Place an appropriate coordinating word (<u>and</u>, <u>but</u>, <u>yet</u>, <u>and then</u>, <u>so</u>, etc.) or mark (<u>;</u> , <u>:</u>) between the following pairs of sentences. Try several different coordinators for each sentence. Which work best?

1. The sky was clear _____ we packed our umbrella.

2. Most people groan at bad jokes _____ they listen to them eagerly.

3. Marigolds are hardy annuals _____ zinnias are equally robust.

4. This is the problem _____ producing oil from shale could harm the environment in the western states.

5. Our hopes were riding on the investment _____ our cash was too.

6. The sunsets were spectacular _____ the sunrises were more impressive.

7. Our computations seemed to be accurate _____ the experiment failed.

8. She watched the car for more than a block _____ she called the police.

C. Try to construct an elaborate architectonic sentence. You might want to hang it on one of these skeletons:

1. If you _____,
    and _____,
  then don't expect to _____;
  but if you _____,
    or _____,
  then you may _____.

2. While it is true that _____,
  and _____,
  still we need not assume that _____,
  nor that _____.

Accuracy in Modification

Modifying words and phrases need to be chosen as carefully as the subjects and verbs they modify. As you grow more adept at commanding sentences to move as you direct them, you may have to resist the inclination to fill every space a sentence offers with a modifier. You may find parallel constructions especially tempting. Once begun, they can go on almost forever. Limit your modifiers to those that state accurately what you need to say—and no more.

In an accurately developed sentence, modifiers usually stand close to what they amplify, describe, or specify:

It was an aging bridge, *rusty and swaying.*

The laser, *a beam of amplified light,* reads the signals on the video disk.

We testified *willingly* against the hit-skip driver.

Misplaced modifiers

Few errors elude revision so easily as modifiers misplaced in some way. They end up modifying something they weren't supposed to:

Entering the store, the cowbell above the door tinkled.

Kicking and braying, grandma tugged at the mule.

My grandfather, *more or less,* is dormant most of the year.

Noticing we were low on beer, action had to be taken.

She was wearing a hat and gloves *with thick horn-rimmed glasses.*

Even though readers may know what a writer really meant, they'll chuckle nonetheless as they imagine a braying grandmother or a cowbell entering a store. Correcting a misplaced modifier usually takes some reconsideration and rearrangement. In some cases, a subject must be supplied that can do the action the modifier implies:

Entering the store, I heard a cowbell tinkle over the door.

Grandma tugged at the *kicking and braying* mule.

My grandfather is dormant, *more or less,* for most of the year.

Noticing we were low on beer, we knew action had to be taken.

Sometimes modification is not so much misplaced as carelessly strung out and in need of tighter connections to what's being explained:

The students were picked randomly, *consisting of fifteen men and women, and all of whom were freshmen at the University of Washington.*

The students, fifteen men and women, all freshmen at the University of Washington, were picked randomly.

Sometimes a modifier is plopped into a seat that swings in two directions; the word or phrase seems to modify both what precedes it and what follows:

> The scouts rowing the canoe *enthusiastically* cheered.

This sentence could mean:

> The scouts *enthusiastically rowing* the canoe cheered.

or:

> The scouts rowing the canoe *cheered enthusiastically.*

If the modifying phrase is nonrestrictive, commas alone would eliminate the question:

> The scouts, *rowing the canoe enthusiastically,* cheered.

or:

> The scouts, rowing the canoe, *enthusiastically cheered.*

Whole phrases can modify ambiguously, especially if they are used incorrectly to link two independent sentences:

> People shy away from bad news, *whether reading it or hearing it,* they don't know how to deal with it.

It is not clear whether the italicized modifying phrase explains the sentence that precedes it or the one that follows it. Moreover, the phrase itself cannot act as a coordinator. Two revisions are possible:

> People shy away from bad news, *whether reading it or hearing it.* They don't know how to deal with it.

or:

> People shy away from bad news. *Whether reading it or hearing it,* they don't know how to deal with it.

Some words are very sensitive to placement. *Only,* for example, is frequently placed in front of a verb when it belongs somewhere after:

> Jodie *only* spoke to her mother.

In this sentence, the child is doing nothing else but speaking to her mother. She is not facing her or smiling at her. But if you say "Jodie spoke *only* to her mother," or "Jodie spoke to her mother *only*," then Jodie is speaking to her mother and to no one else.

Almost is another word sensitive to placement. When accurately limiting a verb, *almost* indicates an action not quite done:

I *almost* ruined the transmission.
(But the transmission is not yet shredded metal.)

I *almost* kicked the habit.
(But I'm still smoking like a furnace.)

I *almost* failed algebra.
(But I passed!)

But, in the following examples, the verb should not be so qualified:

I *almost* knew everyone at the party.
(But you didn't quite know them? More likely: I knew almost everyone at the party.)

I *almost* guessed half the answers.
(But you didn't guess any of them? More likely: I guessed *almost* half the answers.)

Is worrying about where a modifier should stand worth this kind of effort when most readers understand what a writer really means? Yes, because if you abandon a concern for accuracy here, you lose the opportunity to express real differences. And sometimes those differences hurt:

Parachuting, Chris *almost* broke every bone in his body. (But thanks to his reserve chute, he landed unhurt.)

Parachuting, Chris broke *almost* every bone in his body. (This time the chute didn't open.)

Accurate parallel structures

Accuracy is also a concern when you are setting up a parallel sequence. Once you've initiated a parallel series in a sentence, your readers will follow it through, expecting a consistent run of elements. For example, when a parallel sequence begins after a verb, the words that immediately follow it will shape the sequence:

Almost

We searched in the basement,
            under the car, and
            upon the roof.

Racquetball requires quickness of wrist and
            acuity of eye.

Grammatically, either sequence could march on for as long as you can find reasonably matched parts:

on the ceiling,   fluidity of motion,
below the porch,   tautness of muscle,
between the rafters . . .   solidity of grip . . .

A sequence that feeds the reader an incorrect signal will be misread; the reader will find a parallel where none may have been intended:

The study attempted to discover which students
missed waking up in *that familiar bed,*
            mother's homecooked meals, and
            the family atmosphere
more—the men or the women.

In this example, the grouping of pleasant memories of home seems to signal a parallel series controlled by the preposition *in.* The students are waking up *in* that familiar bed, *in* mother's meals, *in* the family atmosphere. To save the students a strange rousing in mom's lasagna, the parallel sequence ought to begin with *waking up*:

The study attempted to discover which students
missed *waking up in that familiar bed,*
            enjoying mother's homecooked meals, and
            relaxing in a family atmosphere
more—the men or the women.

In this version, *missed* controls the parallel sequence. The students miss waking up, miss enjoying meals, and miss relaxing. The sequence gives no wrong signals.

Most lists need parallelism. The items in a list, whether simple or complicated, should share verbal structures to indicate that they are related:

Lists

A politician under pressure will act in one of three ways:
1. she will ignore the pressure and do what she thinks is right;
2. she will bow to the pressure and do what others think is right; or
3. she will smile and smile and do nothing at all.

To assemble this authentic replica of the Stanley Steamer, you will need:

1. a hammer,
2. a Phillips screwdriver,
3. the enclosed nuts and bolts,
4. a quart of high gloss paint, and
5. a plumber.

Exercise   Revise these sentences (if necessary) to improve the modification. Correct any faults in parallelism.

1. Even when secured tightly around me, few people would come close enough to touch the boa.

2. I almost broke half the eggs in the carton.

3. In his Chappaquiddick statement, Senator Kennedy was quick to attack the rumors of immoral conduct, ugly speculation, and not driving under the influence of liquor.

4. Lighting a fire, the old cabin exuded charm and warmth.

5. Although he was our leader, on this occasion, he failed.

6. Antony wins over his audience by pretending to be an inept speaker, by weeping, and with reluctance to show the mutilated body of dead Caesar.

7. Although Hitler's armies commanded the continent, Churchill urged the British nation to fight on, in the streets, on the hilltops, on the beaches, to never surrender.

8. Once considered a parlor game, hypnosis is now considered an effective tool in the battle against pain through documented field and clinical research.

9. I can only go on Monday.

10. I almost laughed out loud when he began condemning long speeches fifty minutes into his own.

11. The fund-raiser was a success with everyone who attended, artistically and financially.

12. To know what problems the student is having, to recommend solutions to those problems acceptable to student and administration, and seeing that the solution is implemented are the tasks of the ombudsman.

Some Considerations of Style

When a sentence is very short, your choice of subject and verb will determine how eloquently it speaks. In a given context, even the simplest sentence can have rhythm, power, and beauty:

> There is a special providence in the fall of a sparrow.
>
> —William Shakespeare, *Hamlet*

Longer sentences, laden with more detail, conveying complex ideas or actions, offer yet greater opportunities for honing and crafting, for fitting the parts together well. Yet making a sentence sound good—even beautiful—remains a challenge because the results aren't predictable. To begin with, well-crafted does not mean the same thing for all sentences. A fine concluding line in a lab report states the results clearly and accurately—no metaphors need apply. Additionally, successful sentences don't always follow rules or patterns that can be set down in a book. Writing remains—in part—a mystery.

We can, however, describe the characteristics and qualities that fine sentences usually possess, whatever their context. These guidelines may be too general to guarantee you a splendid sentence with every outing of your pen. But they may help you identify the problem when a phrase sounds peculiar, or when a sentence plods and plods and plods.

Contemporary sentences are economical; they say as much as possible in the fewest words. Tastes change, and some day readers may again tolerate—even enjoy—skillful twists of *thats* and *whichs*, and phrases chock full of syllables:

Economical sentences

> In that part of the Western division of this kingdom which is commonly called Somersetshire, there lately lived and perhaps lives still, a gentleman whose name was Allworthy, and who might well be called the favourite of both Nature and Fortune; for both of these seem to have contended which should bless and enrich him most.
>
> —Henry Fielding, *Tom Jones* (1749)

More likely, readers will continue to demand a taut language, free of complications and unnecessary decoration.

This ideal might be easy to achieve if we paid for words with nickels in a vending machine. But we don't. We can be as prodigal with words as we used to be with gasoline, piling high-falutin' terms on top of high-roller phrases—and it doesn't cost a cent. Just paper.

In general, economical sentences are both readable and well-crafted. Unburdened by pretentious diction or do-nothing clauses, they focus on subjects and verbs; they place modifiers right up against what they modify. They don't repeat themselves. They don't tolerate dullness.

Sentence economy, however, has almost nothing to do with length. A five-word statement needlessly employing a passive verb can be wordy:

> Dogs are disliked by Paula.
>
> Paula dislikes dogs.

On the other hand, a sentence half a page long can be a model of efficiency if it is organized carefully:

> The whole charm of the dog lies in the depth of the friendship and the strength of the spiritual ties with which he has bound himself to man, but the appeal of the cat lies in the very fact that she has formed no close bond with him, that she has the uncompromising independence of a tiger or a leopard while she is hunting in his stables and barns, that she still remains mysterious and remote when she is rubbing herself gently against the legs of her mistress or purring contentedly in front of the fire.
>
> —Konrad Z. Lorenz, "Man's Best Friends"

When you encounter a sentence that sounds clumsy check first to see if you can make some simple transformations:

Eliminating wordiness —Passive to active

> Americans were being lied to by the media.
>
> The media lied to the American people.

—Expletive phrase (*there are, it was,* etc.) to stronger subject and verb

> There was an explosion that blew the beaker apart.
>
> An explosion blew the beaker apart.

—*That, which,* or *who* clause to more direct modification

> the song which I loved
>
> the song I loved
>
> the chair which was wooden
>
> the wooden chair

> ┌─ a memory that lingered
> └→ a lingering memory

—Redundant phrase to more direct ones

> ┌─ the final end
> └→ the end

> ┌─ equally as famous
> └→ equally famous, or as famous

> ┌─ collaborate together
> └→ collaborate

Then polish the nouns and verbs, giving attention to subjects, and cut out any words that don't do their job.

Here's a checklist to help you skim the wordiness off your sentences:

1. Use strong verbs and adverbs.
2. Use precise nouns and adjectives.
3. Use parallelism often.
4. Put modifiers close to what they modify.
5. Avoid the passive voice.
6. Avoid *that, which,* and *who* whenever possible.
7. Avoid expletives whenever possible.
8. Avoid repetition and redundancy where inappropriate.
9. Avoid clichés and jargon where inappropriate.

A checklist

To state all these guidelines as one: cut out any part of a sentence you don't need.

Eliminating dead weight can be a challenge to a writer, almost a game. The payoff comes in sentences that sound sharp, stark, and professional. Let's examine a bloated sentence:

> I caught a glimpse of a small crowd of people who were obviously being entertained by someone or something.

This tedious sentence conveys a little information in many words. The subject—*I*—is fine. But the verb and object deserve scrutiny because they're a cliché (guideline 8): *caught a glimpse.* If a cliché fits a situation exactly, it is defensible. If not, we can choose stronger expressions:

glimpsed at, spied, encountered. Next we should examine *a small crowd of people.* Does the context require the specification here *of people* (guideline 9)? If not, *small crowd* might suffice since crowds are usually made up of people. The slimmed version now reads:

> I spied a small crowd.

Who were is immediately expendable (guideline 3); deleting the words brings the modifier *being entertained* closer to the crowd it describes. Lastly, we might question *someone or something.* In context, the pairing might be justified, but since a *someone* could be included within the larger class of *something,* we can employ the latter:

> I spied a small crowd being entertained by something.

Hardly a medal-winner, but better than it used to be. It delivers its gram of information faster.

Specialized vocabularies

Sometimes wordiness results from a writer's attempt to embellish an idea by employing the vocabulary and customary language (idioms) of a particular profession. When addressing a specialized audience—a group sharing a particular expertise—a writer may use whatever terms that group is trained to recognize. Doctors, for example, speak a language intimidating to the layman, but easy and efficient to them, full of acronyms and abbreviations: *EKG*s, *BP*s, *IV*s. Specialists in the psychology of learning describe a familiar concept like *memory* in terms they have invented: long-term retention, elaborative rehearsal, levels of processes, and so on. Sports too chatter with jargon incomprehensible to the uninitiated:

> The first baseman, connecting on a breaking pitch from the southpaw, bounced into a double play.
>
> The blitz failed when the quarterback escaped the rush and scooted around end for a quick TD.

In their proper settings, specialized vocabularies and idioms save time and mental energy by conveying information quickly.

Jargon

But specialized vocabularies can cause problems when a writer misjudges her audience and assumes that most of her readers recognize the technical terms she is using. An honest misperception of an audience's ability differs, however, from the use of technical language to confuse or intimidate readers, to make them believe that an idea is too complex for them to understand. Writing like this is jargon-mongering:

> It was the conclusion of the committee that selective minimization of vehicular circulation in the downtown sector of the urban complex could impact upon the environment with the effect being the realization

of a positive commercial benefit on the part of retail merchandisers in that sector.

The committee concluded that cutting traffic downtown might increase shopping.

After laboring for months to document the truth of the second statement, a committee might feel uneasy saying something so simple. So it resorts to the first as language equal to its efforts. But the public would be better served by the unadorned truth. Language used to elevate the simple to the complex, to banish the clear in preference of the obscure, to hide the unpleasant truth for the pleasant falsehood is ugly. Don't tolerate it in your own writing, or anyone else's. Whenever you find yourself slipping into obscure prose, step back for a moment and ask yourself one question: what am I really trying to say? Then say it.

Repetition

In some ways, repetition is like wordiness. A significant word or phrase may appear dozens of times within an essay without troubling anyone. But let the same word show up twice within the same sentence without some sign that the writer intended it so, and the reader is frowning unkindly. One misplaced word, one syllable too many, one phrase repeated, and attention begins to wander:

> The *team*'s manager was certain he'd *remain* with the *team* for the *remain*der of the season.

This dislike of repetition is, however, highly selective. Certain words—articles, conjunctions, prepositions—can appear again and again without irritating readers because they draw so little attention to themselves. Their job is to guide an audience toward an appreciation of the nouns and verbs and their relationships. Yet even prepositions can grow tedious if strung out in sequence: "in the house, under the bed, inside a box."

When a major part of a sentence is repeated, readers expect the repetition to be significant, to have some purpose of amplification or emphasis:

> *Down, down* I come.
>
> Marion *ate* and *ate* and *ate*.
>
> *Destroy* the free press and you *destroy* democracy.

Parallel constructions, of course, are devices of deliberate repetition:

> This government of the people,
>   by the people, and
>   for the people
> shall not perish from the earth.

And there are others. Repetitions that seem accidental will weaken a sentence; repetitions strategically employed can give a sentence drama and rhythm.

Sound and Rhythm

Rhythm is the pace of a sentence, the way it moves from word to word, phrase to phrase, clause to clause. The harmonies of the sentence are difficult to describe, but important in their impact on readers. As we've seen, doubling clauses or modifying phrases gives a feeling of balance or contrast:

> The Yankees finished last; the Tigers finished first.
>
> He was a gentleman and a scholar.

Tripling clauses conveys a sense of completeness. Three examples, three bits of evidence, three descriptive phrases are often enough to make a case. The number is almost magical:

> . . . of the people, by the people, and for the people. . . .
>
> You failed the exam because you misunderstood the question, didn't reply with facts, and concluded poorly.

Multiplying the elements of a sentence beyond three adds weightiness to evidence, thoroughness to persuasion, fullness to description:

> You are born and no reasons given, a man or a woman, an Arab or an Andaman islander, an African pygmy or an Egyptian Pharaoh, a Chinese coolie or an English gentleman, a St. Thomas or an Ivan the Terrible.
>
> —W. Macneile Dixon, "Human Nature and the Human Situation"

Words and sounds

Sentence rhythms are also bound inseparably to the sounds of words and the ways they fit together. Short words pound out a harsh beat:

> A cold steel rod broke the ground.

Longer words move more slowly:

> The enterprise of imagination is a voyage of discovery through the labyrinths of the intellect.

The blending of consonant and vowel sounds can produce startling effects. Poets provide the most vivid examples of language fitted precisely to meaning. In these lines, for example, Milton orders his words to hiss at Satan returned to hell:

> . . . he hear<u>s</u>
> On all <u>s</u>ide<u>s</u>, from innumerable tongue<u>s</u>
> A di<u>s</u>mal univer<u>s</u>al hi<u>ss</u>, the <u>s</u>ound
> Of publi<u>c</u> <u>s</u>corn.

> —*Paradise Lost*

And Alfred Tennyson would have us hear, as well as imagine, doves and bees as he describes:

> The moan of doves in immemorial elms,
> And the murmuring of innumerable bees.

> —*The Princess*

These lines are cited not as models but as reminders of what words can do. Whether you intend that they should or should not, words will mesh their consonants and vowels, will march their clauses to a particular pace. Writers who at least occasionally exploit the sound of words to emphasize their ideas add one more entry to their composition résumé. But a caution: developing a sentence requires a commitment to an idea. Devices of sound and rhythm should not so intrigue you that you change a meaning to fit into a balanced pair of clauses or add a word to complete an alliterative pattern. In *A Midsummer Night's Dream,* Shakespeare gently mocks authors who overdo alliteration when he has a character describe the pathetic death of Pyramus, a famous lover:

> Whereat, with **b**lade, with **b**loody **b**lameful **b**lade
> He **b**ravely **b**roach'd his **b**oiling **b**loody **b**reast.

A writer mindful of these cautions can use sound and rhythm advantageously. A vigorous point can be driven home by short words, a minimum of modifiers, tough consonants, and emphatic punctuation:

> The time has come for tough action—now!

Another thought may require equal emphasis but a different tone and a different pace of exposition:

> Charity is patient,
>   is kind;
> charity does not envy,
>   is not pretentious,
>   is not puffed up,
>   is not ambitious,

```
               is not self-seeking,
               is not provoked;
               thinks no evil,
               does not rejoice over wickedness,
     but       rejoices with the truth;
               bears with all things,
               believes all things,
               hopes all things,
               endures all things.
```

—I Corinthians 13:4–7

Notice how, in the latter example, variations in the lengthy parallel structure head off the danger of monotony. Notice too how the final matched set of four clauses brings the sentence to a satisfying close.

Summary

We have emphasized in this chapter some of the techniques writers employ to give thoughts comfortable habitation within sentences. Watching how these devices operate in the prose of others, experimenting with these techniques on your own—structuring important sentences strategically, shifting modification to speed or slow a thought, multiplying clauses fore and aft, excising wordiness, exploring alliteration—will encourage you to discover other properties of language. We observed earlier that sentences seem to have a will of their own. You can be just as tough, developing the instincts and the knowledge you need to herd clusters of words into those significant and mature arrangements that allow a writer finally to lean back, review his work, and smile. Well done.

Exercises

A. Take a familiar expression, quotation, or maxim, and "update" it by inflating the language egregiously. Compare your updated saying with those of your classmates. Are you able to recognize the original expressions?

For example:

> To be, or not to be: that is the question.
>
> —William Shakespeare, *Hamlet*
>
> The question we must consider is whether or not we should continue our existence.
>
> The proposition that must be considered by this committee assembled here today at this point in time is whether we should continue being in existence or whether we should terminate our participation in the existential program impacting on us.

B. Pare down these sentences:

1. All these miscellaneous ideas have been assimilated and have sifted themselves down into some reasonably coherent synthesis.

2. Being left without an appropriate farewell can have a detrimental effect on the average person.

3. I realized that if I were ever to reach law school, I would have to increase my competitiveness in the skill of symbolic communication.

4. "Family," to me, is a family-type show.

5. Everyone has his or her different ideas about marriage, and everyone is entitled to his or her own opinion.

6. Since a lot of students attending college are away from their parents for the first time while attending college, they can be adults and drink.

7. Many factors compose an excellent cheerleader, and one of the most important factors, if not the most important factor, is a lively personality.

8. I am not alone in expressing my opinion about breakfast and its importance.

9. The Texas Longhorns were not favored to win because of unfavorable factors.

10. I've often wondered if everyone's taste in toothpaste is the same and which brand is most widely used of those most often advertised.

C. Translate these sentences into English:

1. The services you render no longer fit the current or foreseeable needs of this firm. Consequently, at this time it is necessary for the management to implement the termination of your employment.

2. Our records indicate that the discourse unit charged to you by this facility on January 3 is in a condition of overextended use and must immediately be returned to the learning resources center to avoid further accumulation of the designated financial penalties.

3. The committee on vehicular transportation recommends immediate cessation of all vehicular circulation and use on or around the bridge structure and its approaches until current efforts to upgrade and resurfacize the lane surface areas are terminally completed.

4. It has been discovered by numerous learning facilitators that students who fail to complete their assigned learning-reinforcement exercises are ordinarily the same students who do not demonstrate a high level of performance on their end of the term performance indicators.

9

The Paragraph

Paragraphing

Paragraph length

Just as sentences are significant clusters of words, paragraphs are meaningful clusters of sentences. It would be convenient if paragraphs always expressed a single idea, fully developed and explained. But in practice, the shape of a paragraph depends upon what it does and where it does it. Paragraphs in newspapers frequently run no more than a sentence or two; those in news magazines are usually longer; paragraphs in books may cover half a page or more. In fact, a single article appearing under these different formats might be indented at different places and still reflect consistent principles of division. The following report, for example, might form a single long paragraph in a book, three shorter ones in a news magazine, or five still shorter ones in a newspaper:

The influx of small foreign cars into the American market in the late 1950s produced panic among the major American manufacturers. In the fall of 1959, the companies responded with three new American compact cars: the Falcon, Valiant, and Corvair.

The Falcon, Ford's first small car, was dull as the news in Peoria, a placid sedan with a drooping hood and pie pan taillights. It sold well to Americans eager to save gas.

Chrysler's entry, the Valiant, was the biggest, fastest, and sportiest of the new cars. Bristling with pushbuttons and adorned by a fake spare on its fastback deck, the Valiant proudly claimed to be "nobody's kid brother."

Finally, there was the Corvair, Chevrolet's compact and the most radical American design in a decade. Air-cooled, rear-engined, tiny and spartan, the Corvair captured the hearts of many drivers with its discrete suggestion of the exotic and the oddball. But more Americans preferred the plain jane Falcon.

None of these American sedans could match the fuel economy of the foreigners, the Fiats and Renaults and Volkswagens. They weren't supposed to. Detroit designed the Falcon, Valiant, and Corvair to be a little bigger, a little smoother, a trifle more comfortable, and just a few dollars more expensive than the competition from across the sea. Detroit expected these little fellows to grow up.

What paragraphs do

A paragraph is a flexible device. It may dutifully develop a topic sentence. It may indicate a shift in ideas. Or it may give a reader a moment of rest or recapitulation. Some paragraphs introduce an essay or concept, some explain, others defend, still others prove or draw conclusions. And an important class of paragraphs does nothing but bridge the gap between two parts of an essay. Each of these paragraphs will have its "proper" length determined by the aim, audience, and subject matter of the essay it finds itself in.

Whatever the length or function of a paragraph, the short indentation that precedes it functions as a signal. Your job is to make that signal a division in the essay that helps organize information. Your reader should understand the purpose served by the pause and feel some larger meaning in the cluster of sentences. When its sentences are arranged and grouped to serve a writer's aim and audience, then a paragraph is appropriately developed.

Exercise

Divide the following passages into paragraphs. Compare your versions with those of a classmate. What prompted you to start new paragraphs? Would your paragraphing be different if you expected the passage to appear in a newspaper? A magazine? A book?

1. What is modern art? A skeptical public has been asking that question for more than a century now as it evaluated a parade of artistic

movements and artists awesome in its vitality and innovations. Perhaps no extended artistic period has encouraged so much genius (and junk) as the movement loosely described as "modern art." The movement began in the middle of the nineteenth century when impressionism taught artists and the public alike new modes of representation, new ways perceiving the world and the place of the artist in it. Impressionism led to postimpressionism, and then to fauvism, orphism, expressionism, cubism, surrealism, constructivism, minimalism, and dozens of other sects and schools, each expanding the definition of art. To each new "ism," the public reacted with outrage, horror, and, gradually, approbation. The roster of artists generating and supporting these movements is equally long and impressive. Modern art has given the public the opportunity first to revile and then to embrace such names as Monet, Renoir, Gaugin, Van Gogh, Modigliani, Mondrian, Picasso, Cézanne, Dali, Klee, Pollock, and de Kooning. Over the decades, these artists formed an international community, spreading their techniques and innovations from France and the continent to all parts of the western world, even into the Soviet Bloc, where the official line has preferred social realism to the decadent, nonrepresentational works of the modernists. Yet even after more than a century of revolutions and experiments, modern art remains an enigma. Praised in the schools, bartered at fantastic prices, the works of modern artists still provoke comment and curiosity. Is it art—really? Aren't Uncle Walter's sunflowers more appealing than Van Gogh's? Have any women ever looked like the ones Picasso painted? It may well be that such questions are an essential component of art in a century as strange and troubling as the twentieth.

2. The bus driver dropped the two women off at a street corner, then continued down the highway. Within moments we had left Jennings and were confronting broad fields and grazing cattle again. The passengers, mostly older blacks and young whites, stared blankly at the flat land around them. One white girl, her drooping eyelids fighting off sleep, read *The Great Republic,* a history book. Little conversation could be heard; from the front of the bus came some talk, but in hushed voices. The trip dragged on endlessly; time, not distance, had become the barrier between places. Four minutes out of Jennings, the bus entered Ledbetter, stopping at the E. Stuermer Gen'l Store, a wooden one-story building. A hand-painted sign on the store's front porch advertised B-B Ice Cream, "It's Always Good." Only about ten buildings lay within sight—a few houses, old, poor, and weathered; one or two shops; a couple of gray, rusted sheet metal structures, the kind seen only in small Texas towns. One paved road intersected the highway at Ledbetter only to disappear into the trees and dust. A small black woman got off there. She looked sixty years old but, having no gray hair, she could have been fifty. Maybe years of work had worn on her. The woman wore a plain blue and green plaid dress and carried her possessions in a grocery sack that she used as a suitcase. As she stepped

off the bus, she expressed her appreciation to the bus driver. The trip resumed, the endless stream of cows and pastures, the passengers gazing out the windows in silence. Myself among them. The two women who got off the bus in Jennings would have to walk home from the street corner; the woman in Ledbetter, from the general store. I could imagine what awaited them: run-down houses, old furniture in need of reupholstering or repair, worn draperies on the windows—meager treasures which represented half a century of hard work. How had these women spent their years? Laboring for meager wages; raising large families, hoping each child would have a better life than they did; rearing their children religiously and themselves living in a God-fearing manner; witnessing the rise of the black man in the South; surviving in a harsh world. All were possibilities; maybe all were realities.

—Greg Smith

Topic Sentences at the Beginning

Many—but not all—paragraphs arrange themselves around a topic sentence. The topic sentence (which functions like the thesis sentence in an essay) makes the statement that the remainder of the paragraph will explain, asks the question that the rest will answer, makes the assertion that subsequent phrases must document, presents the object that will eventually be described. This simple paragraph design is satisfying and logical, moving as it does from:

Statement and proof

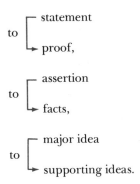

A topic sentence that appears at the beginning of a paragraph is roughly equivalent in structure to a sentence in which modifiers follow the base clause. That is, almost all of the development, amplification, and specification occurs after the statement of a main idea. For paragraphs that develop from initial topic sentences, there are two basic models.

Parallel Development

In the first model, each sentence developing the topic idea functions like an element in a parallel series:

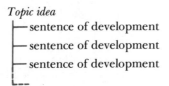

Topic idea
— sentence of development
— sentence of development
— sentence of development

The parallel sentences may be similar in shape and content, yet each is tied more closely to the topic sentence than to its neighbors. Here's a simple example of such a paragraph:

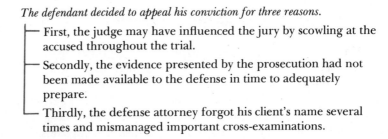

The defendant decided to appeal his conviction for three reasons.
— First, the judge may have influenced the jury by scowling at the accused throughout the trial.
— Secondly, the evidence presented by the prosecution had not been made available to the defense in time to adequately prepare.
— Thirdly, the defense attorney forgot his client's name several times and mismanaged important cross-examinations.

Each supporting sentence presents one reason to explain why the defendant intends to appeal. These reasons are connected by the topic sentence, not by their relationships to each other. Paragraphs that follow this design are like the sentences we described as architectonic: they give the impression of careful planning and precise documentation, particularly when the supporting sentences are either numbered or paralleled. Paragraphs of this type work particularly well when a writer is classifying or evaluating:

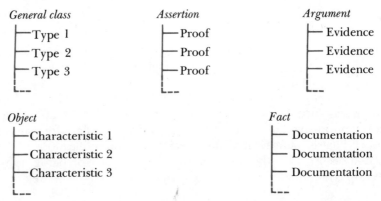

General class
— Type 1
— Type 2
— Type 3

Assertion
— Proof
— Proof
— Proof

Argument
— Evidence
— Evidence
— Evidence

Object
— Characteristic 1
— Characteristic 2
— Characteristic 3

Fact
— Documentation
— Documentation
— Documentation

As each separate bit of proof, evidence, and documentation is added to the paragraph, the argument seems to grow stronger and more difficult to refute, particularly if the evidence is strategically arranged.

To this model, a concluding sentence may be added to restate the original assertion in a way that capitalizes on the newly-presented evidence:

Argument (topic idea)
— Evidence (strong)
— Evidence (stronger)
— Evidence (strongest)
Conclusion

> *"Yes, Watson. It was Moriarity who kidnapped Lord Chillingsworth.* His wallet contained a detailed map of Lord Chillingsworth's apartment, tracing the exact path of entry and escape the kidnapper took. He has a record of holding wealthy nobles for ransom. And his footprints exactly match those found outside the victim's window. *So what choice had I but to arrest him for a crime he so certainly committed?"*

Paragraphs with this structure can be even more tightly organized if the topic sentence states explicitly what the subsequent sentences will demonstrate and in what order:

> The President blamed *the oil companies, the Congress,* and *the American people* for the energy problem. The *oil companies,* he said, were too interested in profits and corporate expansion to increase their exploration for new energy sources. *The Congress,* in its turn, failed to adopt an energy policy that fit the nation's needs. And *Americans,* he charged, were using too much oil to run air conditioners, cars, and boats. There was plenty of blame, he concluded, for all.

Exercises

1. Write *short,* basic paragraphs based upon the structural models on page 240. You may write a single paragraph for each model or several versions of two or three of the patterns. Underline the topic sentences in your paragraphs.

For example:

General class
— Type 1
— Type 2
└ - - -

→ *There are two major classes of whales, the toothed and the toothless.* Toothed whales are predators; they use their teeth to capture and hold fish and other sea creatures, which they devour whole. Toothless whales are filter feeders; they pump huge volumes of water through their mouths to trap floating plankton.

2. Develop a paragraph from exercise 1 at greater length, filling in details which your original, basic paragraph may have omitted:

> *There are two major classes of whales, the toothed and the toothless.* Toothed whales are predators; they use their teeth to capture and hold fish and other sea creatures. Toothed whales have a single blowhole. Among the best-known and largest of the toothed varieties is the sperm whale. They grow as large as 70 feet and live 80 to 100 years. Toothless whales are filter feeders; they pump huge amounts of water through their mouths to trap floating plankton. Toothless whales have a double blowhole. The blue whale is the largest of the filter feeders. In fact, the blue whale is the largest creature ever to exist on earth, some specimens exceeding 100 feet in length and weighing as much as 120 tons.

3. Write a paragraph based upon this model:

> *Argument* (topic sentence)
> ├── Evidence (strong)
> ├── Evidence (stronger)
> └── Evidence (strongest)
> *Conclusion*

4. Write three or four topic sentences that state explicitly what the subsequent sentences in the paragraph will discuss. Develop one of the sentences into a full paragraph.

5. Outline the organizing pattern of the following paragraph. Should it have a concluding sentence?

> If you wanted a small car in 1968, there wasn't much choice. The Beetle from Germany was the prime example and the most popular minicar. Buick sold a few Opels just marginally more exciting than refrigerators. And for $1,795 Plymouth would import a Simca for you sure to warm the cockles of every mechanic's wallet. No one took Japanese cars seriously then. To most Americans, a Subaru was still something you did in the privacy of your bedroom.

Write a paragraph modeled after the example above.

6. What does the following initial paragraph tell you about the essay it introduces? Would you want this paragraph to be longer? Why or why not?

After more than five centuries, Chaucer's "Miller's Tale" continues to shock and amuse. Readers are either delighted by the ribald tale, or they are outraged, or they are uncertain whether they are really reading what they think they are reading.

Branching Development

The second basic paragraph model is less structured than the first and probably more common. It follows the pattern of "aft" modified sentences:

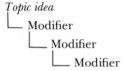

Topic idea
  └─ Modifier
      └─ Modifier
         └─ Modifier

In this type of paragraph, each sentence is linked to the one preceding it, the specifications and modifications branching away from the topic idea in an indirect but coherent pattern:

Topic idea: The car refused to start.
    A small leak opened in the rubber hose connecting the fuel filter to the fuel line.
        Gradually the crack widened, leaking fuel over the engine block.
            The spilled fuel combined with engine heat to speed the deterioration of the fuel line.
                Finally the line collapsed cutting off gas to the engine and stalling the vehicle.

In this paragraph, each element depends upon the one before it. Removing a sentence in the development would undermine the organization of the whole. Paragraphs of this kind employ connective words and transitional phrases frequently to cement the links between sentences.

The resulting structures are still quite flexible, capable of expansion or contraction at any point on their branching course. They are particularly effective in "containing" description and narration because they can link together a wealth of detail and specification:

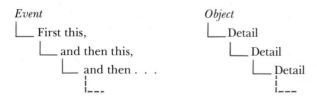

Event   *Object*
  └─ First this,   └─ Detail
     └─ and then this,   └─ Detail
        └─ and then . . .   └─ Detail
          ┆___   ┆___

Branching paragraphs often lack concluding sentences and sometimes do without a topic idea, especially in narrative situations.

Here's a version of a previous paragraph now developed according to this second basic structure.

> "Yes, Watson, it was Moriarity who kidnapped Lord Chillingsworth.
>
> The only way out of Lord Chillingsworth's room was through the window.
>
> └─That window looked out over his rose garden, muddy from the afternoon's downpour.
>
> └─Escaping through that window, the kidnapper had to step in Lord Chillingsworth's garden.
>
>   └─Lord Chillingsworth is the only gardner in England to fertilize his roses with a peculiar mixture of oyster shells and manure.
>
>   └─Moriarity's boots were encrusted with oyster shells and manure.
>
>   └─So what choice had I but to arrest him?"

Each sentence is tied to the one before it by the logic of the detective's argument.

Narrative sequences may be tied together by transitional words or phrases that emphasize the passage of time or the direction of action: *first, then, next, meanwhile.* Descriptions may use physical directions to link the elements in the paragraph to each other:

> The tomato worm, a repulsive creature, clings to the underside of soon-to-be-devoured stems. Its head, unseparated from the thick and ever-growing body, is distinguished only as the insect's eating end. Its body is an accordion of legged segments, bright green and plump as marshmallows. Its tail is marked by a single delicate fin, a tiny wavering rudder to direct him to yet more tender morsels of your pampered tomato stalks.

Here the topic sentence presents the entire object first: the tomato worm, a repulsive insect. Then the description moves down the object from head to tail—an order a reader follows without difficulty.

The models: advantages

What are the advantages of these conventional paragraph models?

Topic idea

Topic idea

The Paragraph

Order and predictability. Many readers will be familiar with such models. Paragraphs that begin with what seem to be topic sentences will—they expect—include documentation and conclusions, in that order. Readers will judge conventional paragraphs according to how ably the material in the bodies of the paragraphs documents, amplifies, and develops their main ideas.

These conventional designs have advantages for a writer too. The statement of a topic forces a writer to come to terms with an issue or idea. An intriguing main idea may require much subsequent documentation of high quality, but with a topic claimed at the outset, you know what must be done. Moreover, the models help to organize thinking. To be satisfactory, a paragraph following a model will have to include and connect all the parts in that model.

A. Beginning with the following topic sentences, write paragraphs that follow a branching design: *Exercises*

1. The eruption of Mt. St. Helens in 1980 caused widespread destruction in America's Northwest.

2. The ___X___ refused to work.

3. The bombing of Pearl Harbor led to World War II.

4. The ___X___ building is a local architectural masterpiece (or disaster).

5. There are ___X___ steps to building a ___X___.

6. Doing library research requires order and method.

7. There's a proper method to reading a book.

B. Examine a dozen or more paragraphs in an essay from a college anthology. Can you determine whether the paragraphs use parallel or branching structures? Are these structures ever combined in a single paragraph?

Essay Exams

You may find special advantage in using one of the formal paragraph models when you are confronted by an essay examination. Essay questions often employ the structures in posing their problems:

Define ___X___ and give examples.
Who did ___X___ and why?
Name ___X___ and describe his/her policies.
Explain ___X___ and discuss.

Good answers reply efficiently. The topic sentence will be the core of the answer, with subsequent sentences providing the requested details and amplifications in appropriate form:

Essay question and sample answer

Essay question:
Define socialism and describe its major features.

Answer:
Socialism is a social and economic system in which the means of production are controlled and operated by the government for the good of the people.

First specification   In a socialist system, all major industries (steel, auto, rubber), all utilities (oil, gas, electric, phone), and all major services (medical, social, environmental) are owned, coordinated, and run by government boards and agencies. Profits derived from industries are either minimized or diverted to support nonprofit operations or institutions.

Second specification   What citizens lose in relinquishing all economic control to the government is compensated by a full-scale commitment to social welfare. From the cradle to the grave, the citizen is cared for with a guarantee of shelter, food, health care, and livelihood.

Third specification   But political freedom is retained within the socialist system. Rulers are responsible to the electorate, and the system itself is not beyond recall.

Notice that each detail in this essay/paragraph could be much more fully developed.

Topic Sentences Elsewhere

Shaping paragraphs

The essay exam is a special writing situation which encourages deliberate handling of structure and organization. But you may find in much of the writing you do that paragraphs, like sentences, are not something devised strategically. You begin shaping your thoughts and phrases so that sentences within a group connect with the ones before and after them. At a point when you *feel* you have made some major or complete point, you end one paragraph and begin another. And so the essay develops.

Will such paragraphs have topic sentences clearly stated at the beginning? Some will; some won't. And those that don't may be as clear, well-argued, and entertaining as the others. Paragraphs can vary in structure as much as sentences, provided that their structures serve both the writer and the reader.

Transitional paragraphs

Those structures may be defined by the position of the main idea. A transitional paragraph, for example, might have its focus in the middle, its first few sentences summarizing the previous paragraphs, the sentences following introducing the matter of the next paragraph. The paragraph core acts like a hinge for the paragraph and the essay:

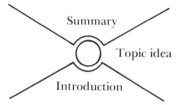

We have now examined the liberal side of the busing issue, the compelling need to take drastic action, to alleviate the lingering effects of racism. *But conservatives regard the medicine as worse than the disease.* As we shall see, they attack busing as costly, repressive, and hurtful to education.

Or a main idea might occur at the very end of a paragraph. Such a structure might be appropriate to generating suspense, the full sentences acting exactly like the parallel initial modifying clauses we examined in the previous chapter. The topic sentence clarifies and explains preceding sentences of detail. It serves as both main idea and conclusion:

Topic sentence at the end

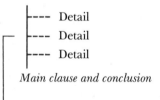

Rolling thunderheads gathered in a clear sky. The air thickened, stifling even the hint of a breeze. The birds and insects fell into an ominous silence. *A great storm was imminent.*

Such a paragraph structure can appropriately end an essay by lining up observations drawn from the essay as a whole and then linking them to a final observation:

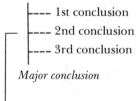

So this study shows that as income rises, so do prices. As prices rise, strong economic and social pressures lead to additional income

gains. But once a wage-price spiral begins, prices generally can increase faster and more often than wages. *Therefore, the wage-earner will tend to lose economic clout in an inflationary situation.*

Two topic sentences

Some paragraphs, like binary stars, may have double centers, particularly when a writer wants to compare or contrast ideas and objects:

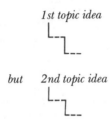

Such a structure breaks easily and naturally into two separate paragraphs. But when you see an advantage in housing the contrast within a single paragraph, it can be done if the transitional links are clear and distinct:

> *Most people like watermelon plain and ungarnished.* The cold, juicy fruit provides mouthfuls of succulent taste and texture. *<u>But</u> others insist on embellishing the melon.* They douse it with salt or cream, or cut it into fluted wedges or tiny balls that inevitably scurry off your plate, across the linoleum, and under the dog's paw.

Like sentences, paragraphs can take almost any shape. How deliberately you construct your paragraphs will depend upon the kind of writing you are doing, how much time you have to do it, and what your readers' expectations are. Very often, paragraphs will take their shape from the subject you are working with. Don't mistrust them because they didn't grow out of some approved textbook sequence. But don't rely entirely on intuition to discover an appropriate paragraph design when you are puzzled and unable to start. Invent a thesis. Maneuver details around it. Consider whether your thoughts lead to a particular conclusion. Or perhaps your thought is a conclusion in need of evidence. Topic sentence first? Topic sentence last? In the middle? Not at all? Find the design most appropriate to what you have to say and use it.

Exercises

1. Does every paragraph array itself around a topic sentence or idea? Can you always identify a plan of development in a paragraph? Perform an experiment to find out. Examine several short essays paragraph by paragraph. Examine a short story. Examine a newspaper article. Examine an editorial. How often can you identify clear topic

sentences or clear patterns of development in these pieces? In which types of writing do paragraphs seem carefully structured? When do the paragraphs seem more casual? If you have the time, quantify your results (perhaps using a table) and write a paragraph explaining your conclusions.

2. Examine the paragraph structures and the placement of topic sentences in one or two essays you have already written. Do you typically use a parallel or a branching design? Can a reader determine the topic sentence in your paragraphs?

3. Write a paragraph with the topic sentence in the middle. What problems do you have coming up with such a paragraph outside the context of a full essay? What might the function of such a paragraph be in an essay?

4. Write a paragraph with a topic sentence that also serves as the conclusion.

5. Write a paragraph with two topic sentences.

6. The following paragraph is from a research paper on Elizabethan ghosts and *Hamlet*. Which sentence is the thesis? Is the thesis supported with evidence? Does the paragraph have a concluding sentence? Should it?

> Elizabethans placed restrictions on the ability of ghosts to talk. Clark notes that the people of the day thought a ghost would not speak unless spoken to by an educated man.[9] Prosser writes that the person addressing a ghost had to know Latin.[10] Shakespeare includes these aspects of ghost lore in *Hamlet* by having Horatio, who has been away at school in Wittenburg, address the ghost of Hamlet's father. Marcellus urges Horatio to talk to the spirit, saying, "Thou art a scholar, speak to it, Horatio" (I.i.41).
>
> [9] Cumberland Clark, *Shakespeare and the Supernatural* (London: Williams and Northgate, 1931), p. 65.
> [10] Eleanor Prosser, *Hamlet and Revenge* (Stanford: Stanford University Press, 1967), p. 100.

—Julie Richter

Developing a Topic

A paragraph ought to deliver on any promises its topic sentence makes. Accurately developed paragraphs, however, are not always neat shelves of fact and logic. An idea can be advanced and developed accurately even when the demonstration itself might be refuted factually or logically. What matters in determining accurate development in these

Accuracy

cases is the writer's aim. Here, for example, is a thesis that might be documented or refuted with weather statistics: Cleveland is the coldest city in Ohio. Even if this assertion turns out not to be factually true (Toledo or Akron might be colder on the average), the idea might still be accurately developed in a different way:

Thesis	*Cleveland is the coldest city in Ohio.* I remember going to a football game one December in the city's Municipal Stadium, a huge
Narrative mode used to explain the thesis	drafty horseshoe squat on the shores of Lake Erie. The wind roared through the stands and snow was falling. I had a thermos of hot chocolate with me; halfway through the first quarter of the contest, I poured myself a cup of the steaming brew. Suddenly, the Browns intercepted a pass and, in the excitement, I left the chocolate unattended on the seat beside me while I clapped and yelled. The Browns marched slowly down the field and finally put the ball over the goal line. The Browns scored on a short run by Frank Ryan who was quarterbacking then. I'm not sure who the Brown's quarterback is now. When I reached for my chocolate to celebrate the touchdown, crystals of ice
Strongest evidence	bumped against my lips. *In the time it had taken the Browns to score, the chocolate had begun to crust with ice!*

This paragraph does not prove that Cleveland is the coldest city in Ohio. But the incident does vividly convey the sternness of December in that town. A more carefully qualified opener might satisfy sticklers for absolute accuracy:

> Cleveland is a cold place to spend December.
>
> Cleveland is one of the coldest cities in Ohio.

But in some contexts, the original topic sentence might be defended as playful exaggeration.

Where the paragraph does veer away from accurate development is in the two sentences that talk about quarterbacks:

> . . . The Browns scored on a short run by Frank Ryan who was quarterbacking then. I'm not sure who the Brown's quarterback is now.
>
> Topic idea: Cleveland is the coldest city in Ohio.

Every other sentence in the paragraph adds a detail to the short narrative that documents the coldness or contributes to the exploit of the freezing chocolate. But the cited pair does not, especially the second sentence. Measured against the thesis and the writer's method of development, the two ought to be cut out.

Ordering the Ideas in a Paragraph

What order should the elements of a paragraph take? Paragraph structures are too varied to set down absolute rules. Generally, the parts of a "conventional" paragraph that the reader will scan most attentively are the beginning, the end, and, to a lesser extent, the opening and closing of the development section:

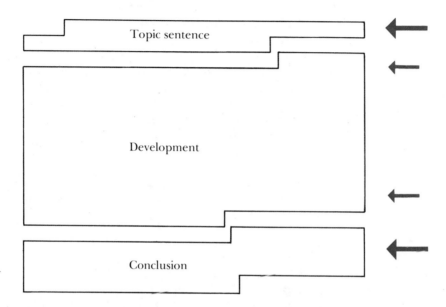

The last example, idea, or fact mentioned in a paragraph will probably be better remembered than the first.

Given this general design, you can employ one of several strategies to convey information accurately and effectively. When the elements of your development are equally important but of varying interest, the least interesting material can be shunted to the middle of the paragraph, the most interesting spotlighted at or near the end. When there is a gradation of importance in what you are discussing, the most important material should probably be presented last. The reader will remember it there.

Sometimes an element of the development may be so important that you may want to leave off a concluding sentence entirely, and leave the facts to speak for themselves. Or, employing an unconventional paragraph structure examined in a previous section, you may want to begin with the facts and conclude with the core idea, thus giving the last sentence the double emphasis of conclusion and thesis:

The great vaults soar a hundred feet or more. The unstressed walls, supported by curved buttresses fully visible on the exterior, are broken by huge expanses of stained glass depicting saints and scenes from the Bible. The statuary too delights and instructs, filling every space and nook in the structure with an emblem of faith. *The classic Gothic cathedral is a masterpiece of form and function.*

Fitting a Paragraph Together

When ideas fit together well in a paragraph, they deserve sentences complementing their harmony. Many of the devices that hone sentences to their sharpest also work well for paragraphs. Variations of sentence length and structure, rhythm, balance, and sound can smooth the texture of a cluster of sentences, making it seem all of a piece.

In many writing situations, relatively simple sentences do the job well enough; there's no need for them to do more than state the facts:

As the temperature in the container was lowered, the respiration of the turtle grew shallower. At a temperature just above freezing, breathing could not be observed. The turtle was removed from the container and examined. No respiration was apparent. The turtle was returned to the container where the temperature was raised gradually. At 35°F, breathing resumed.

Instructions, lab reports, directions, insurance claims, and many other writing jobs require a style no more adorned than this. We expect a paragraph of instructions on a box of cake mix to be short, factual, and elementary. But then we're probably beating eggs or measuring shortening as we read. Similarly, an insurance claims adjuster reading forms is looking for facts. He scans an accident report looking for them, not for an argument or amusement.

But the feature writer, editorialist, prelate, administrator, politician, or student may not have a captive audience to entertain, persuade, admonish, educate, convince, or impress. For them, the paragraph strung together from the most basic sentence types may not satisfy their aims or audiences.

Sentence variety in a paragraph

At the least, a variety of sentence lengths ought to be employed in any given paragraph. Often, no preplanning is necessary to achieve a pleasing diversity of lengths because—as we have seen—sentences are creatures elastic enough in their motions and modifications to be counted on to be different. But it makes sense for you to review a paragraph after you've written it to be sure you haven't accidentally written a cluster of sentences varied in their structures but similar in length.

Length itself is no virtue. Three sentences in a row each fifty words long may irritate a reader as much as a string of monotonously short ones—and probably more. If you've written three such whoppers, rescue the paragraph with one tough fellow barely the width of the page. Conversely, if most of your sentences have been short-winded sprinters, conclude the paragraph with a long-distance runner.

Short sentences have special virtues. Admittedly, a paragraph composed only of short sentences can be as dull as a plate full of grits. But a short sentence can be a stunning opener when it is followed by other, longer clauses:

> *The proposition is peace.* Not peace through the medium of war; not peace to be hunted through the labyrinth of endless and intricate negotiations; not peace to arise out of universal discord. . . .
>
> —Edmund Burke, "Speech on Conciliation with the Colonies"

Conclusions can be equally startling and memorable if a short sentence is highlighted by longer ones. Even loquacious Hamlet concludes his life with but four words: "The rest is silence."

Unusually long sentences can be intimidating at the beginning of a paragraph, especially when they try to convey a great deal of information all at once. A difficult opening may make readers suspect a windy paragraph. If your opening sentence is lengthy, be sure it is clearly phrased and conveys its information intriguingly. "Aft" modification might be an intelligent strategy for a paragraph opener.

Elsewhere in paragraphs, long sentences pose no unusual problems. In a persuasive essay, they can be especially effective in bringing thoughts to a conclusion:

> Finally, whether you are citizens of America or citizens of the world, ask of us here the same high standards of strength and sacrifice which we ask of you. *With a good conscience our only sure reward, with history the final judge of our deeds, let us go forth to lead the land we love, asking His blessing and His help, but knowing that here on earth God's work must truly be our own.*
>
> —John F. Kennedy, Inaugural Address

If you find that the development of your paragraph will require some long and complex sentences, consider whether you can make those sentences parallel. Parallel sequences can give a paragraph intensity and rhythm. But to prevent monotony when arranging full sentences in parallel chains, you must usually allow for more variety within their structures than you would within the matched clauses of a single sentence. A paragraph too carefully patterned can rock like a dinghy:

Near the seashore is a small timbered house. Its windows are bleak and cold, like misshapen eyes. Its porch is warped and tottering, like an aged bridge. Its roof is patched and tattered, like worn-out jeans. We spent our vacation there.

Generally, as paralleled sentences grow longer, the danger of a monotonous sentence rhythm lessens because longer clauses invite variation:

1. The neighborhood group presented the city council with three reasons for opposing the zoning action. *A tire factory* at the edge of their property, they argued, *would pollute the water,* lowering the recreational
2. value of nearby streams and lakes. *A factory would increase traffic* significantly, endangering the many children in the neighborhood
3. bussed to school. And *a factory would alter the character* of the quiet community, turning a placid suburb into an industrial park. The council agreed with this reasoning and denied the zoning change.

At the paragraph level, rhythm serves both to tie related sentences together and to move a reader through your thoughts at an appropriate pace. Parallel sequences of three or more sentences sound powerful, insistent, and sometimes eager. They are usually followed by sentences structurally quite different that slow a reader's pace to indicate indirectly that the series is concluded.

Balance in paragraphs

Parallel sequences of only two sentences can be *balanced* expressions. Within a paragraph, balanced expressions function like pillars supporting an arch; they convey stability and elegance. They effectively enhance a contrast or comparison, and can be the underpinning of elaborate structural designs:

Thesis

If this	then this
and
If this	then this

so
Conclusion

```
┌────────────────────────────────────────────┐  ┐
│  I agree                                     │  │
└────────────────────────────────────────────┘  │
┌────────────────────────────────────────────┐  │
│  I agree                                     │  ┘
└────────────────────────────────────────────┘
```

but (thesis)

```
┌────────────────────────────────────────────┐  ┐
│  I disagree                                  │  │
└────────────────────────────────────────────┘  │
┌────────────────────────────────────────────┐  │
│  I disagree                                  │  ┘
└────────────────────────────────────────────┘
```

and consequently . . . .

Paragraph structures this elaborate may seem artificial, but the resulting paragraphs may sound quite natural:

> (1) A just society cannot afford *not* to inflict the death penalty. If a society acts to prevent the suffering of the innocent, it must also act to insure the punishment of the wicked. And if a nation pretends to believe in justice, then it must admit that evil exists as a threat to justice. Consequently, in those cases in which terrible injustice is done to the innocent, society must demand the ultimate justice—the life of the wicked.

> (2) I agree that a society must act to prevent the suffering of innocent citizens. I agree too that the concept of justice implies the existence of injustice. But I do not accept the idea that the concern society demonstrates for its defenseless citizens requires it to be cruel and vindictive. Nor do I believe that justice and injustice in the law are opposites that require Newtonian reactions. If that were the case, we would sentence the robber to be robbed and the rapist to be raped. Capital punishment is not needed in a just society.

Neither of these paragraphs is casual—the kind you produce on a moment's notice. They present elaborate, even difficult, arguments; the balanced structures guide a reader through them. Such paragraphs are often the stuff initial or concluding paragraphs in long, serious essays are made of. The rhythms are stately, yet moving.

Paragraph rhythms

The rhythms of less "crucial" paragraphs in an essay can be just as fit, even though they may be the product of less deliberation or, as is usually the case, no planning at all. In such cases, after drafting a paragraph, you can work on its sounds and rhythms, joining clauses when a sentence sounds choppy, inserting a word or phrase where there seems to be a gap—all without distorting the meaning in the paragraph or inflating the diction. You can even sacrifice a bit of economy if adding a word or phrase produces a better sentence:

> He was my kind and good friend.
>
> He was my friend, kind and good to me.

Deliberate repetition   Deliberate repetition can also contribute to the movement of a paragraph, especially when the repeated word or phrase occurs at the beginning of a sentence. Conjunctions—especially *and*—can create a dignified pace when repeated deliberately, both at the beginning of sentences and within them. Some famous literary and biblical passages employ this rhythmic device:

> "... *But* my time hieth fast," said the king. "Therefore," said Arthur unto Sir Bedivere, "take thou Excalibur, my good sword, *and* go with it to yonder water side, *and* when thou comest there I charge thee throw my sword into the water, *and* come again *and* tell me what thou there seest."
>
> —Thomas Malory, *Morte D'arthur*

> In him was life; *and* the life was the light of men. *And* the light shineth in darkness; *and* the darkness comprehendeth it not.
>
> —John 1:4–5

Coordination of exactly this kind is rare in contemporary prose, but the device remains effective. In persuasion especially, a sharply repeated *and* or *but* can nail an argument, even a flimsy one, together:

> *And* who was it, my friends, who forced Congress to build that new bridge when our old one collapsed? *And* who was it found the money to improve our beloved library? *And* our schools? *And* our roads? *And* who can you count on to serve you in this district, year after year? *And* who will you reelect this November?

The example shows both repetition and coordination in an exaggerated form. A skillful writer—or speaker—can exploit the advantages of repetition without exhausting them.

Many of the paragraphs you write or read will not seem distinguished by any features of rhythm or sound. You write or read them without noticing how they do their jobs. And yet such paragraphs may be extraordinarily well-shaped, given their particular mission. Not every paragraph nor every kind of writing requires a pause of admiration. But when you do encounter that passage, linger over it long enough to examine its structure, to admire its fit.

Here, for example, is a taut little paragraph describing the night before an auto race twenty-four hours long: An analysis of paragraph rhythms

> At night, the sun settles itself beneath the rim of the high banks like melting butter, leaving the speedway in chilly darkness, the cars congealing in pools of oil, mechanics, and insufficient illumination. The mechanics tinker into the night, their mutterings and laughter muffled in the clump of infield garages. Tonight is clear. Saturday is the race. And Saturday night and all day Sunday, the same race.
>
> —Larry Griffin, "The Daytona 24-Hour"

The opening sentence is a whopper, almost half the length of the entire paragraph. But since most of the modification comes after the base clause (the sun settles), a reader moves into the sentence with little difficulty, probably enjoying the comparison of the sun to melted butter and the unusual image of pools of oil, mechanics, and light. After that long opener, you encounter a shorter sentence almost exactly like it in structure (base clause followed by lengthy modification). While not similar enough to be parallel, the sentences do echo each other. Hence, a reader feels some rhythm. Then suddenly a short, sober sentence breaks the paragraph right down the middle, a startling contrast to the first two sentences: "Tonight is clear." It too has an echo:

> Tonight is clear.
> Saturday is the race.

And now the author wants to suggest the length and monotony of a race that will last twenty-four hours. So he crafts a sentence with the same structure as the preceding two, but to avoid monotony, he shortens it. The sentence might have read:

> Tonight is clear. Saturday is the race. And Saturday night is the race, and all day Sunday is the same race.

But that's too repetitive. So he writes:

> Tonight is clear. Saturday is the race. And Saturday night and all day Sunday, the same race.

The twice-repeated *and* and *Saturday* and the twice-repeated *race* suffice to produce the rhythm. From a sprawling opening, the paragraph contracts gradually and neatly to a quiet but firm ending.

A. Revise the following paragraphs:

1. Writing a paper is a detestable chore. It is like cleaning closets or defrosting the refrigerator in that, like both these activities, writing is a job you put off until the very last possible minute in the hope that you will discover something to say that inspires you to finish the despicable task quickly and painlessly. But ordinarily no such remedy appears, and so, with the task bearing down on you, you begin writing and writing, tearing up outlines that didn't work, revising page after page, working late into the night until, at last, you are finished, and then you discover that the essay really isn't due until next week!

2. In 1952, Richard Nixon delivered the "Checkers Speech." Nixon was then a senator from California. His political future was on the line. He was charged with corruption. The New York *Post* was making the charges. In his speech, he attempted to clear himself of the charges. If his speech failed to clear him, he would have lost his place on the Republican ticket. He was running with Dwight Eisenhower. Eisenhower was the presidential candidate; Nixon was the vice-presidential candidate. Their wives were named Mamie and Pat. The Checkers Speech was a success. Its language was awkward. But despite the awkward language, Nixon won the favor of his viewers. His speech was televised. He used a strong logical appeal. He also used a strong emotional appeal.

3. The ability to express one's self is natural. A person is born with the ability. In order to be developed, self-expression must be encouraged in children. But to encourage a child is hard. The suggestions presented to him or her will either encourage or discourage a child's self-expression.

4. Ralph Bunche enjoyed a distinguished career. In 1904, he was born in Detroit. In 1928, he began teaching political science at Howard University. In 1941, he entered government service. In 1945, he became the first black to head a division of the State Department. In 1946, he joined the newly-formed United Nations, where he worked for peace in the troubled Middle East. In 1950, he was awarded the Nobel Peace Prize for his efforts. In 1971, he died.

5. Academic degrees in America are of all kinds and all types beginning with the Bachelor of Arts and Bachelor of Science degrees awarded after the completion of a set number of hours at an institution of higher learning. Next up the ladder of academic degrees awarded at American institutions are the various Master's degrees in the arts and sciences awarded after the completion of work done after the attainment of the aforementioned Bachelor of Arts or Science degrees. Finally you may seek to attain the next step up which is the last step, and that is the Doctor's degree in philosophy, medicine, divinity, law, and so forth, all degree attainments reached usually after the completion of a Master's degree, followed by years of subsequent coursework, and the preparation of a dissertation. Other degrees are also granted by institutions of higher learning. These are often honorary degrees.

B. Compare the details and the transitions in the two paragraphs that follow. Which would be more satisfactory? Under what circumstances?

The Pocket Camera

Pocket cameras are ideal for vacationers. These cameras are so small that they fit conveniently into a pocket or purse. Their light weight makes them easy to handle and no drudge to carry. With a pocket camera, the vacationer is freed from bulky cases, film cartridges, and other devices that make picture-taking on vacations a chore. Picture quality is good, the resulting snapshots being much bigger than the camera itself. Pocket photography is relatively inexpensive. Cheap models are available in all camera lines, film is readily available, and processing doesn't cost an arm and a leg. In short, the pocket camera offers the vacationer convenience and quality at a low price.

The Vacation Camera

Pocket cameras are ideal for vacationers. These tiny cameras, hardly larger than a wallet, slide conveniently into a pocket or purse. Their light weight makes them easy to tote around a beach or a crowded Disney World. A pocket frees the vacationer from the bulky cases, film packs, and other paraphernalia that can make vacation photography tedious. Just as important, picture quality from the pockets is good, and the prints are bigger than the cameras themselves. Best of all, pocket photography is relatively inexpensive. Cheap models are offered in all camera lines, and processing doesn't cost an arm and a leg. In short, the pocket camera offers vacationers convenience and quality at a low price. Who could ask for more?

10

Developing the Essay

An overview of the essay

Like sentences and paragraphs, full essays vary in length according to the aim and audience for which they are written. One type of essay, the editorial, may, for example, defend an opinion held by a newspaper's staff or owners on an issue of national importance. That statement and defense will ordinarily be brief—three to five paragraphs—and emphatic, the editors being more interested in a forceful explanation of their position than in a thorough one. More lengthy explorations of the same issue, presenting all the relevant arguments and data, might appear in serious journals of public affairs, in government white papers, or in collections of articles examining the issue.

Again as with sentences and paragraphs, the structure of an essay can range from the simple to the complex. We can outline model essays according to the now familiar patterns:

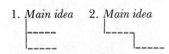

1. *Main idea*   2. *Main idea*

Onto both of these models, we can lay a still more basic design: essays have a beginning, middle, and end. The beginning introduces ideas and draws a reader into a subject. The middle, usually the longest section, gets the work done by developing the ideas. The conclusion terminates the essay, summing up, stating conclusions, suggesting alternatives, problems, or new directions.

The Multi-Paragraph Essay

When the beginning/middle/end structure is imposed upon the first essay model, the result is the classic, four-to-seven-paragraph essay design:

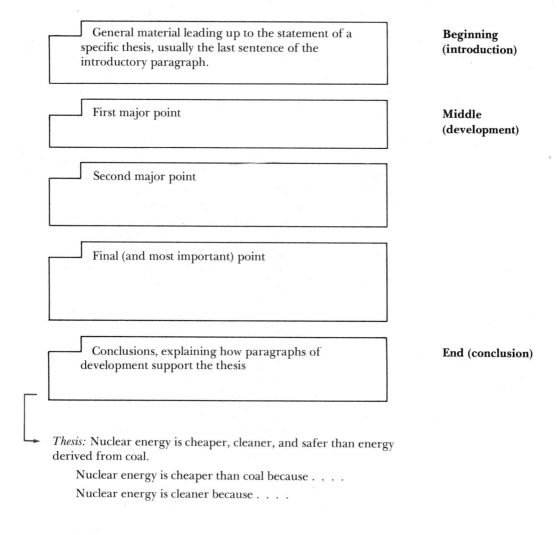

General material leading up to the statement of a specific thesis, usually the last sentence of the introductory paragraph.

Beginning (introduction)

First major point

Middle (development)

Second major point

Final (and most important) point

Conclusions, explaining how paragraphs of development support the thesis

End (conclusion)

Thesis: Nuclear energy is cheaper, cleaner, and safer than energy derived from coal.

Nuclear energy is cheaper than coal because . . . .

Nuclear energy is cleaner because . . . .

And finally, nuclear energy is actually safer than . . . .

Conclusion: Because nuclear energy is cheaper, cleaner, and safer than the energy derived from coal, we should . . . .

With the exception of school essays, few compositions, professional or otherwise, follow this rigid pattern. Why bother with it then? Because despite its rigidity, despite its yawning predictability, the four-to-seven-paragraph model organizes subject matter coherently. The thesis of the essay stands in clear relationship to the paragraphs following it:

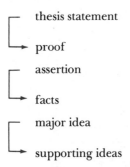

thesis statement

proof

assertion

facts

major idea

supporting ideas

When to use the four-to-seven-paragraph structure

Following the systematic presentation of supporting materials in the development section, a conclusion wheels around to restate the thesis and sometimes to advance it a bit further. The four-to-seven-paragraph essay is, thus, a dependable formula for producing clear exposition and argument. It is effective in arranging evaluations and classifications. And it is a fine device for answering essay questions since it allows a reader to grasp, at the outset, the writer's design for the entire answer.

This multi-paragraph model quickly becomes a constraint on a writer when it is taken as the only or the best shape an essay can take. As even a casual reading of professional essays will show, an introduction may run longer than a single paragraph; the development section may have two major points or twenty and state them in as many paragraphs; and the concluding paragraph may be a single sentence or several paragraphs, or be eliminated entirely. Nothing in the multi-paragraph formula represents *the* model for good writing. It is *a* model, easily remembered and visualized. When a thesis statement breaks into a small number of parts, or when you are classifying or evaluating something, comparing or contrasting, or just listing reasons, you can consider employing the four-to-seven-paragraph model. Each of these topic ideas, for example, might be appropriately mated to the model:

> Runners fall into three classes: the everyday-at-dawn fanatics, the after-work toilers, and the late evening looking-for-a-friend-because-I-really-hate-to-run plodders.

The American worker needs an inflation-proof income and more incentive to work hard.

The FAA found six reasons for ordering the grounding of the aircraft.

But under no circumstances should a topic idea be mangled or mutilated just to fit the scheme.

Essays that Branch

The second basic essay model represents essays which rely on the movement from paragraph to paragraph to convey a sense of structure and organization, not on a preconceived design for the whole:

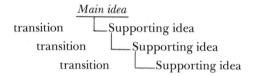

Actually, the model above is probably too orderly. To represent the twists and turns a writer might make in exploring an idea, a design like this one might be more accurate:

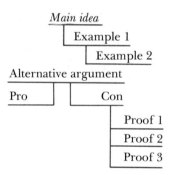

In this type of essay (which we've encountered in the section on exploratory writing), readers must understand where they are at any point and how they got there. The shape of the whole effort is not revealed to them at the beginning. Instead, each paragraph of development links up with the one before it and the one after it without any necessarily *direct* connection to a thesis statement. The article follows the motions of your thinking.

Essays of this second type rely heavily on transitions—the subject of the next chapter. Transitions tell readers where the development of an essay is heading and why. And so long as readers understand the

Transitions in essays that branch

relationship between paragraphs, a writer is free to vary the emphasis given to any one section of the development, to turn away from the main subject to explore a related point, to examine alternatives, even to contradict himself. Here's a rather long example:

Thesis: Although she was, in some ways, just a caricature of the sixties' generation, Janis Joplin had the potential to be an artist.

Piece of My Heart

The introductory paragraph (in the narrative mode) does *not* lead to an explicit thesis statement.

I remember the morning I heard Janis Joplin had died, and the uncaring way the world rolled on. I went to class that day and took notes on Kierkegaard or perhaps it was Nietzsche. I remember the gloating in my cousin's voice as she offered me her sympathies. She had long regarded my tastes in music as peculiar and my affection for Janis as downright unhealthy. And now the woman had done herself in with a needle. I recall rushing into town that afternoon to scour the five-and-dimes for the poster of Janis I had regarded as too juvenile to own before. And I remember playing her albums in the evening, enduring her clumsy accompaniments to savor that voice grinding and caressing its way through song after familiar song. How could the music suddenly be so bleak? How could she die so young?

A second narrative paragraph leads to a key question and observation.

I had noticed her voice for the first time on the radio, croaking its way through the chorus of a single called "Piece of My Heart." I bought the album that contained the song even though at the time I had no phonograph on which to play it. But a friend did, and the record grew thin from use, Janis' caterwaul streaking down the hall of the dormitory, overwhelming the flaccid sincerities of Joan Baez and the Muzak orchestrations the Beatles were using then. "Why do you listen to that stuff?" friends asked. We smiled archly because we thought we knew.

Yet the question was a fair one. I can admit it now. Her voice was untutored, her arrangements laughable, her imitation of the blues blue-eyed and half-a-quart too sweaty. But in the late sixties, you listened to music not for how it sounded, but for what it said and how it felt. And Janis sang about feelings we hadn't experienced yet, but craved.

This paragraph seems like a digression . . .

. . . but it returns eventually to the main topic.

Yet frankly, we were hypocrites. Like much of that sixties' generation, we spent many an evening complaining about the failings of our nation, its corruption, pollution, decadence, and war madness. And then we would get up in the morning at our small private school, watch the sun rise over the green Allegheny foothills, and shuffle to a spotless cafeteria where fat German nuns competed to stuff us full of sausage and hotcakes. We debated Marcuse and Sartre, mimicked outrage and passion and guilt (all of us safely deferred from the menacing draft), and then spent the afternoons belaboring a football or complaining over a milkshake about "the girls at the Hill." And feeding coins into a juke box to hear Janis moan about love. What awful, violent, dirty music it was. How could we like it, wise as we were? But we did.

For you see, Janis was a caricature of ourselves, mostly glitter and hype, singing about pains she didn't really feel to an audience of white kids who thought they understood. How different she was from the girls we dated—and how they resented her rasping appeals. Liking Janis was a silent male protest against the type of women we were told (and believed) we needed, the demure, *Cosmo* wisps we pursued, entertained and wooed for four years, and would marry come graduation. And pity the girl not born to this image, the dumpy one— ugly, stringy-haired, trench-faced. Unless she was Janis. For ironically the very sort of woman we were conditioned to scorn and ridicule with alcoholic vigor in bars at night had become our Helen, a splendid goddess to taunt our reluctant cover girls.

Still, Janis was more than just the brilliant promotion of Columbia Records. She suspected and we suspected that *the feathered boas she flaunted, the obscene gestures, and the Southern Comfort clutched in a trembling hand concealed a real artist, maybe even a singer.* Janis was our connection to a world more threatening and dangerous and violent than any we dared enter ourselves. But Janis did. She appeared with Raquel Welch on *The Dick Cavett Show* once, outrageously costumed, gaudy, sweating after a set. Poor Raquel, sitting next to this shameless parody, looked like Tupperware. She made a joke about Janis' virginity, but the audience laughed at Raquel. *Slowly Janis was discovering that she didn't have to be what she wasn't because she was remarkable enough in what she was.*

But then she died. And all of us who had liked her and praised her had to endure the tsk-tsks of righteous moralists. Had to happen, they observed. Self-destructive. Self-consumed. But Janis, snickering, had one more joke to play—an unreleased album. The day it became available we rushed out to buy it, several of us from the same dormitory floor. And then we listened separately, smitten and amazed. I walked into the hallway and there stood Vic, an affable hippie. He smiled and said just two words: *Bobby McGee.* I nodded in agreement. We had been right all along. *For that song proved Janis an artist. She could sing. And we didn't have to lie to ourselves anymore.*

	Important transition
	First statement of the thesis
	Another digression
	The thesis reformulated
	Return to theme of opening paragraph
	Thesis and conclusion

This predominantly narrative essay is tied together by a thesis statement that gradually evolves as the article develops. At the outset, there's nothing to indicate how "Piece of My Heart" will end. The analytical portion of the essay does not begin until the end of the second paragraph: "'Why do you listen to that stuff?' friends asked. We smiled archly because we thought we knew." Several times, the essay swings away from Janis Joplin to consider the attitudes and activities of the author and his friends. But finally it returns to consider the nature of Joplin's talent in relationship to the feelings of those who listened to her in the sixties. The whole essay, it turns out, fits together in a way appropriate to telling a story about both Janis Joplin and the writer recalling the day she died.

If the essay had followed the multi-paragraph model, its thesis and structure would have been more explicit:

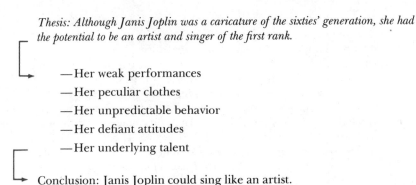

Thesis: Although Janis Joplin was a caricature of the sixties' generation, she had the potential to be an artist and singer of the first rank.

—Her weak performances

—Her peculiar clothes

—Her unpredictable behavior

—Her defiant attitudes

—Her underlying talent

Conclusion: Janis Joplin could sing like an artist.

When to use the branching structure

The four-to-seven-paragraph model would produce an essay which reveals the writer's purpose from the outset. The branching model invites the reader to join the writer in an investigation of the subject. In the first structure, the reader traces a path made familiar by the thesis; in the second, he or she explores a new route—sometimes an unpredictable one—guided by well-positioned signs and landmarks. The essay structure actually employed in "Piece of My Heart," the branching model, is particularly appropriate to narration and description, and to longer arguments and expository pieces in which a writer wants to explore an idea.

Need for a thesis

Both models assume that an essay contains a thesis, clearly stated and separable from the rest of the essay. For most writers in many formal writing situations, the assumption is practical. Readers—and writers as well—often need a thesis to guide them. If nothing else, an explicit thesis sentence may tell a reader whether an essay about to be read contains the information being sought. But some types of writing develop without a thesis—a letter, for example, or a news report. And the thesis, when one is present, need not always be simple or in the first paragraph. A political address might discuss several separate issues tied together more by the personality of the politician than by a coherent political philosophy:

> And in my talk to you today, I will explain why we must increase spending on social programs, and why we must increase defense spending, and why we must increase the pay of government employees, and why we must cut government spending.

In a short essay, your reader expects to meet a thesis or main idea early on. But when an issue is complicated, you may have to set down background information or present several points of view before stating a thesis. Thus the idea to be developed may occur several paragraphs or pages into the essay.

Fit and Finish

The shorter the essay, the more important the surface fit and finish of the paragraphs. When an essay goes on for paragraph after paragraph, page after page, your reader is apt to ignore or forget the overall design, to grow more concerned with the argument or the information than with the skill in its arrangement. (This does not mean that long essays are less organized than short ones, only that their structures are less visible.) When an essay is only five hundred to two thousand words long—the typical length of most college writing—you must be as concerned with variety, parallelism, and rhythm as if you were constructing a single paragraph.

In general, a variety of paragraph lengths is *not* needed within an essay if sentence variety is achieved within the individual paragraphs. Too many short paragraphs may irritate readers; too many long ones may bore them. But long sequences of moderately-long paragraphs (approximately five to ten sentences) will pose no problems. In fact, the paragraphing may hardly be noticed. Within an essay, an unusually short paragraph can have the same strategic effects that a short sentence has in a paragraph. In some cases, you may want to isolate your thesis in just such a short paragraph. Or a significant conclusion or transition might be housed in a paragraph a single sentence long. They will be noticed.

Paragraph length in an essay

Short paragraphs

Unusually long paragraphs have fewer strategic uses. You might want to emphasize the sheer numbers of something, such as grievances, reasons, statistics, by grouping them in a formidable paragraph. But such groupings intimidate a reader and slow down the pace of an essay.

Long paragraphs

In essays that adhere to the multi-paragraph model, the length of paragraphs in the section of development should roughly parallel the importance of the materials within those paragraphs. The most significant point should receive the amplest treatment. When an entire essay covers only two or three pages, most readers will draw inferences about the importance of various ideas from the size of the paragraphs alone. Given only the bare outlines of the two essays below, many readers would assume that the most significant information will be found in paragraphs two (I) and three (II):

Emphasis

I.

Thesis

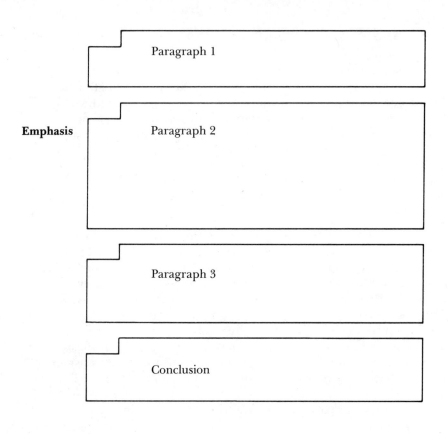

Emphasis

Paragraph 1

Paragraph 2

Paragraph 3

Conclusion

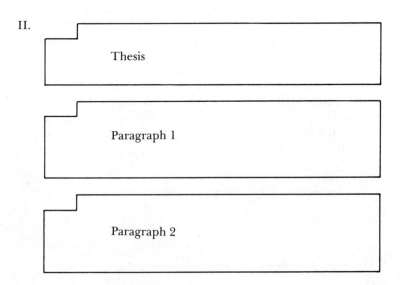

II.

Thesis

Paragraph 1

Paragraph 2

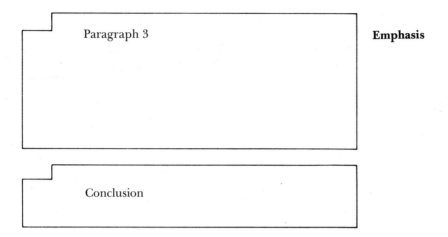

Such assumptions, of course, may be completely wrong. But the shape of the essays may lead readers to make them. When an essay runs longer than six to ten paragraphs, your reader is less able and less likely to notice and compare the lengths of paragraphs.

Parallel paragraphs

In the same way that sentences can be made parallel within paragraphs, paragraphs can be matched within essays to achieve balance, contrast, or other emphatic relationships. Beginning adjacent paragraphs with similar phrases or structures will create parallel relationships between them. Any listing device—numbers or chronological transitions—will have the same effect. Here are some matched sets of paragraph openings which would put paragraphs developed from them in close relationship:

> The first reason for the defeat of Napoleon at Waterloo . . . .
> The second reason for his defeat . . . . ·
> The third, and most significant, reason for the emperor's loss . . . .
>
> In the morning, we . . . .
> In the afternoon, we . . . .
> At night, we . . . .
>
> Even if we conserve fuel, the US will have to depend on foreign oil
> imports . . . .
> Even if we find new sources of oil, the US will still . . . .
> And even if we develop new sources of energy, Americans will have
> to . . . .

In some kinds of essays, parallelism may extend well beyond the initial sentence of the amplifying paragraphs into the structures of the individual paragraphs themselves. In such essays, every part has some partner, some related component tying it to the thesis:

Oh Boys!

The most abused school kids are not blacks trooping into segregated schools, or girls taught by custom and suggestion to be housewives and secretaries, but little boys forced to conform and compete in a situation stacked against them. Much more than girls, boys learn to hate school because their teachers turn education into a dull, passive business. *Boys do less well than girls in the elementary grades because they are forced to compete with girls, because they are expected to behave like adults, and because they are judged by middle-aged women.*

Three-part thesis statement

(1) Because they are forced to compete with girls whose rate of maturation puts them one to three years ahead of boys at the same age, little boys in the classroom feel less secure and consequently act more **(2)** outrageously than the models of virtue seated next to them. They don't learn to read as quickly, and so they come to dislike reading. They don't concentrate on their studies as hard as girls because they haven't developed habits of patience and tolerance. So time and again the teacher's finger strikes out in complaint, pointing out that the smartest student in class is a girl. And she may also be the tallest and the strongest. Adults quickly forget the difference a year can make to the **(3)** young. Yet seven- and eight- and nine-year-old boys must compete with girls whose physical and emotional development they won't match until they are approaching their teens.

(1) Because these "older" girls are relatively well behaved, teachers expect as much from the boys. But boys won't sit as quietly as girls, and **(2)** so they get hollered at and punished. They don't like to stand in lines or wait to take a turn, so they stay after school and endure the teacher's stony silence while the little ladies troop home. The greater the energy of boys is evident from the moment of birth. Male infants kick and roll and toss more than females. And the tendency never diminishes. Yet **(3)** teachers expect the seven-year-old to be a good boy when to really be a good boy he ought to be running, yelling, building, and exploring, not learning Joyce Kilmer's "Trees" by heart.

(1) Because these little boys are taught and judged primarily by women, they are rarely given the chance to develop their male intelligences and **(2)** skills. Women—especially mothers—are far less equipped than men to understand the virtues of anarchy and good-natured roughhousing that accompany boyish curiosity. They have never been little boys themselves. They don't realize that during their years of growth, boys **(3)** must be treated with rugged respect, not mawkish authority. Yet they are the ones left to reward and punish, pass or fail, encourage or humiliate generation after generation of young men.

Thesis restated and advanced

Clearly then, young boys will not be properly educated until they are segregated from girls at the elementary school level, are taught in an environment adapted to their enormous physical energies, and are exposed to more male teachers capable of understanding them. Until that time when such a program can be established, we shall have to put up with sullen, often violent youths who enter young adulthood contemptuous of education and the society that supports it.

Parallel elements between paragraphs contribute to rhythmic effects within essays. The most rhythmic essays are likely to be those designed to persuade, where parallelism, balance, and repetition emphasize important examples or concepts. These devices also serve to tie an essay together, the subject of the next chapter.

1. Examine the structures of several short stories in an anthology or magazine. Outline them to determine whether the pieces systematically develop a thesis or whether a thesis evolves as the essays progress. Can you draw any conclusions about the relationships of overall structures to the subject matters or the purposes of the essays?

2. Examine several very short pieces (6–10 paragraphs) in an anthology or magazine. This time, consider how the physical arrangement of paragraphs affects your perception of the essays or articles. Do the longer paragraphs tend to contain the more significant arguments or pieces of information? Do short paragraphs focus on important ideas or conclusions? In what other ways are you influenced by the physical appearances of the texts you are reading?

3. The piece that follows develops according to the branching model. No explicit thesis guides a reader from paragraph to paragraph. What, then, holds the essay together? Are there any points where the organization seems deliberately abrupt? What would be lost if the essay followed a more explicit plan of development? What would be gained?

After reading "Crazy Mrs. Kazaard," briefly sketch an alternative outline for the essay, as is done in the chapter for "Piece of My Heart."

Thesis: Mrs. Kazaard was the strangest woman we ever met.

Crazy Mrs. Kazaard

Mrs. Kazaard was a strange old lady. She lived in a tiny, white cottage just across the road from an open field where itinerant preachers set up tents on hot July evenings. Folks would swarm under the ragged canvas, men in limp T-shirts, women in dull plaids dragging scowling sons who'd rather be torturing lightning bugs. In the stifling heat, the good folks would clap and sing and save their souls, inspired by a preacher whose voice seemed to lift the tent flaps. Mrs. Kazaard never attended these affairs, and never complained about them, though the sounds of salvation must have kept her awake many nights. But the people passing her house would point menacingly to it and warn their children: "Don't go there."

Perhaps they feared she would treat children the way she treated her cats. Long- and short-haired felines swarmed over her cottage, posted on her mailbox, hid in the deep grasses that served as her lawn, all in search of comfortable spots to snooze away dull afternoons. It was widely rumored that Mrs. Kazaard shoved most favored cats into her refrigerator on really hot days, from which they would emerge too numb to protest, too indignant to appreciate the favor the woman thought she had done them.

One hot afternoon, my cousin, Martha, ventured to Mrs. Kazaard's when an entire afternoon of selling cookies for a church society hadn't produced a single purchase. The old lady beckoned Martha into her kitchen and offered her some milk. Martha declined, but the woman went to the refrigerator anyway. No cats crept out. The woman removed a plate of cookies laced with creamy icing. Martha ate one timidly while crazy Mrs. Kazaard smiled and sorted through her purse for the dollar my cousin's bland merchandise cost. Martha's mother later scolded the girl for entering the house. The rest of us kids, disappointed that no cats had crawled from the icebox, still hoped Martha might yet sicken from some dreadful poison in the cookie she had eaten. She didn't.

What made Mrs. Kazaard peculiar in most folk's eyes, I think, was that she was old and lived alone, tended to her own business, and, most damningly, sang to herself loudly when she strung her clothes along the line in her backyard. If she were so happy, she should not have shown it so openly. She should have gone to church, too. Then people would have known she wasn't strange.

4. For one or more of the topics listed below, or one assigned by your instructor, develop a thesis sentence appropriate to an informative, demonstrative, exploratory, or persuasive essay. Then create two full outlines, one with a four-to-seven paragraph structure, the other following a branching design. Which organization seems best suited to your projected essay? Why? If your teacher instructs, write an essay based on the more appropriate structure. Some potential topics:

the cruise missile	nontraditional medicine
college athletic scholarships	the US and Taiwan
federal budget deficits	Detroit and imported cars
gymnastics	minority and majority rights
punk rock	public transportation
chemicals in foods	censorship and the media

11

Transitions

Some of the most important action in an essay occurs in the blank spaces between sentences and paragraphs. In moving from sentence to sentence, a reader must be able to follow the path you have laid out. Arguments, ideas, thoughts, details, and facts must fit together in a pattern that conveys the meaning you intend. But your mind sometimes works faster than your pen. Ideas flare out, examples multiply, and thoughts snap like sparks across a page, producing rows of words and slapdash punctuation. You examine the page, read it, and smile to discover how well you have expressed what was on your mind. But typed up and presented to a reader, the same words raise questions and doubts—and maybe some hackles: "What does this mean?" "What's the point of this example? This phrase?" "How did you get from this assumption to this conclusion?" "I don't see the connection here." You may resent the interrogation and perhaps even cast aspersions on your reader's intelligence: "Any child would understand what I meant here. I can't spell out every detail for the sake of slow minds."

Committing thoughts to words almost always involves risks. Our ideas are full and rich and vital, fleshed out by all the imaginative powers we have. By contrast, words are stark and simple—mute scrawls on flat paper. Ideas must speak through dead ink and fiber.

And yet words will work. Ideas will flow from a writer's mind to a reader's with their substance substantially intact if the gaps are filled, the needed bridges thrown from sentence to sentence, paragraph to paragraph. The result—a thought shared through the medium of language—is a commonplace, everyday miracle. Transitions are the mortar that holds an essay together, the replies to questions a writer imagines his reader asking, the directional signals a writer expects his reader will need.

Transitional Words and Phrases

The strongest and most influential transitions are the single words or short phrases that hang out on the corners and at the entrances of sentences and paragraphs, shouting directions:

Common transitional words

and	still
also	so
in addition to	therefore
moreover	consequently
yet	in summation
after all	hence
but	and then
however	until
nevertheless	before
on the contrary	afterwards

Such words (there are dozens more) are explicit and powerful signals to a reader that what follows stands in a precise relationship to what precedes. Without a transitional word, these two sentences are puzzling, a study in contradiction:

> You are boring. I like you.

Filling the gap with a transition doesn't explain the contradiction, but acknowledges it, pointing it out as just that, a contradiction:

> You are boring. *But* I like you.

Most other transitions have a comparable ability to shape meaning.

Transitions as filler
Some relatively innocuous transitions serve as genteel pauses for

breath or subtle murmurs of concession or doubt: *indeed, of course, it seems, as a matter of fact.* Unfortunately, these expressions are often used as filler phrases dropped into an essay as much for their sound as their sense. They ought instead to emphasize some point, drawing attention to a statement that might seem like an insignificant matter of fact without the short transitional preface. But writers often get away with using them carelessly. Not so with other transitions. Placed at the beginning of a sentence or paragraph, transitional words and phrases will be noticed and will direct a reader's attention so powerfully that there is a potential for abuse. Well-laid transitions can deposit a residue of sense on pure foolishness:

The power of transitions

> The world is round. *So* we are told by legions of scientists, educators, astronauts, and globe-makers. *Admittedly,* the evidence for a circular earth is formidable. *And yet,* isn't the evidence for the alternative just as convincing? Surely it is no accident that mariners, surveyors, engineers, and pilots use flat maps to plot their courses and designs. *Similarly,* travellers crossing the entire country or going only from one end of town to the other have no use for a globe. *On the contrary,* they unfold a flat paper map to trace the flat route they are taking. *Most convincing evidence of all,* how many people have experienced the world as round? A few astronauts, a few pilots in high-flying spy planes. To the vast masses of humanity, the world seems flat when they plow their fields, pave their streets, or trudge to school. *Consequently,* the world must be flat. The testimony of billions of souls is more likely to be reliable than the abstract theories of a privileged few.

Few readers are likely to be corralled by the spurious logic in this paragraph. But if transitions can sound so reasonable arguing that the world is flat, imagine what they can do in more genuinely controversial situations. With each signal of direction, a writer coaxes her reader into a temporary agreement: if you want to follow me, you must understand that here I am conceding a point, here contradicting another, here adding an idea, here digressing, here showing similarities, here differences and here finally drawing conclusions. Certain transitions, particularly those that lead to conclusions *(so, therefore, consequently)* invite a reader to judge, to accept or reject what follows. But most others prod and cajole, providing information and assistance. They are reviewed less critically.

Because of their persuasiveness, transitional words and phrases placed at the tips of sentences and paragraphs would seem to be ideal devices for fitting an essay tightly together. But just because they are so forceful and visible, they can seem heavy-handed. A reader who encounters a transitional phrase at the beginning of every sentence will grow tired of that scheme of organization, useful as it may be. The structure of the essay begins to seem like a skeleton worn on the outside: something clumsy, even ugly. This fault hurts most in short paragraphs where the transitions may be grander than the conclusions.

Limits to transitional words

Transitional Regions

Relying primarily on transitional words at the beginning of a paragraph to guide a reader through an essay can cause another problem. In an essay, the gaps between individual paragraphs will usually be the ones in most need of filling or bridging. In an essay of four paragraphs, for example, there will be three critical junctures:

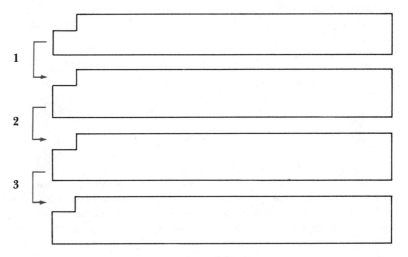

We can station a transitional word at each junction to link the essay together:

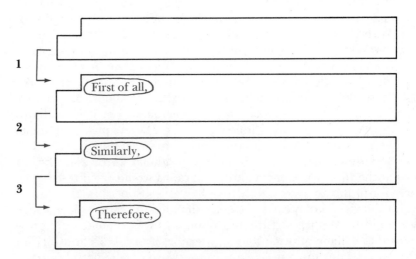

For some writing situations, these links may be solid enough. But note what a small proportion of the essay is working to fit the whole together.

The circled areas are the *transitional regions,* those parts of an essay responsible for connections. When transitions occur only at the leading edge of the initial sentences in paragraphs, the whole composition will hold together, but the linkages may be frail. One faulty transition and the structure collapses.

Any devices that will expand the region of transition and push the connections deeper into the essay itself are likely to produce more impressively fitted papers. Many such devices are available.

Enumeration, Chronology, and Parallelism

One that we have examined in a previous chapter deserves brief mention again: tying an essay together by listing its parts in the thesis statement. The enumeration may be explicit:

> In the latter part of the fifteenth century, Spain resisted war with Elizabeth I because of 1) profitable trade with England, 2) Turkish pressures on the Spanish empire, and 3) difficulties inherent in attacking the British Isles.

Or it may be more subtle:

> Although Spain had powerful reasons for resisting war with Elizabeth I, King Philip II launched his Armada to punish England for its religious heresy and its privateering.

In either case, the thesis sentence, planted somewhere in the introductory paragraph (most likely at the end) would strengthen the ties between the introduction and subsequent paragraphs of development. And, if selective repetition or parallels are maintained between statements in the thesis and the subsequent paragraphs, the transitional region can be expanded even more. For example:

> Although Spain had powerful reasons for resisting war with Elizabeth I, King Philip II launched his Armada to punish England for heresy and privateering.

> Indeed, Spain's reasons for resisting war with Elizabeth in 1587–88 were substantial . . . .

> Nevertheless, Philip launched his Armada to punish England's religious heresies, which . . . .

> Similarly, the Armada took to sea to put an end to English privateering which . . . .

> In summary, ...

Paragraphs may also be connected to a main idea numerically or chronologically, although these techniques too tend to put the transitional region at the leading edge of each separate idea:

Chronology

First of all . . .

Secondly . . .

Thirdly . . .

Lastly . . .

At daybreak . . .

Later that morning . . .

And then . . .

By evening . . .

Parallel structures Parallelism may be used with both these types of enumeration to move the transitional link from the front of a topic sentence into the sentence itself and —if entire paragraphs are structured in tandem—deeper. Here, for example, are parallel paragraphs from the development portion of an essay. Their shared structure allows the reader to contrast their separate subjects effectively while at the same time following the structure of the essay as a whole:

> A second type of note-taker is the lead-grinder, the student who fills pad after legal pad with dull, almost illegible pencil marks. This student ordinarily sits near the front of the room where he can hear the teacher's every word. The first syllable the teacher utters sets the lead-grinder's pencil in motion, sending it smoking down the page, capturing every jot of wisdom, except those that fall during the few half-seconds it takes this practiced scholar to occasionally resharpen his blunted instrument.
> The third variety of note-taker is the wishful writer, the dewy-eyed class member who buys enormous notebooks with gaudy covers, but rarely fills a page. This student inevitably sits in the back of the room near a window, where the teacher's drone won't intrude upon his meditation. Occasionally his gnawed pen wanders into contact with paper to trace a word or a tree or the name of his latest *amour*. But not so often that it ever runs out of ink.

The result is an intricate structure, with the entire paragraph furnishing linkages of theme and language. Such structures and transitions work best with classification and evaluation essays where it is your task to keep a number of objects before your reader's eyes simultaneously.

But not all types of writing invite or allow the kind of parallel structures that turns whole paragraphs into regions of transition. What else can be done to drive transitional regions deeper into an essay?

Questions

One way is to employ questions strategically. Even used unstrategically, a question invites or demands a reply. The expectation of an answer provides the connection. Stand-up comedians use the technique all the time to introduce and tie together wildly-scattered material:

> Have you been in a grocery store lately? Why prices are so high that . . . . And what about the banks? My banker told me . . . . And speaking of money, what ever happened to the two dollar bill? My uncle . . . .

You have heard this sort of patter so often you can recognize it without the jokes. But the interrogative technique works because an audience listens to a question—even one it is not expected to answer—automatically.

In an essay of any length, the thesis itself can be a question or it may reply to an unspoken one:

> Why did Philip II launch the Armada?
>
> How can student note-takers be classified?

Either of these questions might stand as a thesis from which full essays—the replies—might be drawn. Questions can also be used to direct the development of paragraphs, the subsequent sentences responding to an inquiry that opens the paragraph:

> But what was the strongest reason King Philip had for invading England in 1588?

Political speeches use the technique frequently, the speaker introducing an idea by formulating a question that might or ought to be on the minds of the listeners. The speaker does not expect—or really want—the audience to answer since the point of asking the questions (in most cases) is to furnish the correct reply. In 1952, Richard Nixon, then a candidate for the vice-presidency, used a series of questions in a famous address to the nation. "The Checkers Speech," as it was subsequently named, was an attempt to answer charges that Nixon had used campaign funds for his personal use. Here are the opening sentences of several paragraphs of that address:

Rhetorical questions

> Well, then, some of you will say, and rightly, "Well, what did you use the funds for, Senator? Why did you have to have it?"
>
> Well, then the question arises: You say, "Well, how do you pay for these and how can you do it legally?"

> Let me say, incidentally, that some of you may say, "Well, that's all right, Senator; that's your explanation, but have you got any proof?"

Nixon thus anticipates the reaction of his audience, turning the speech into a sort of dialogue with the series of questions tying the performance together.

Questions can grow tiresome if they are the only device of transition. Used appropriately, though, they can bridge gaps and tighten links, especially when they are posed at the end of paragraphs. Using King Philip and an already-familiar thesis, here's how a question can shift some of the responsibility for coherence away from transitional words to the movement of thought within an essay:

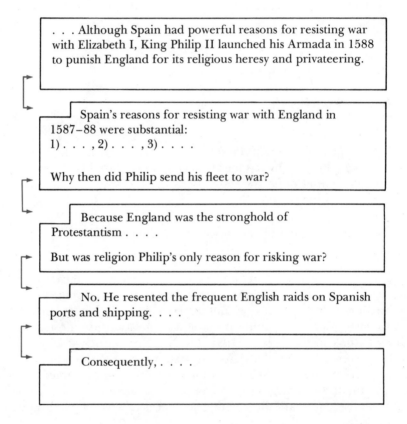

. . . Although Spain had powerful reasons for resisting war with Elizabeth I, King Philip II launched his Armada in 1588 to punish England for its religious heresy and privateering.

Spain's reasons for resisting war with England in 1587–88 were substantial:
1) . . . , 2) . . . , 3) . . . .

Why then did Philip send his fleet to war?

Because England was the stronghold of Protestantism . . . .

But was religion Philip's only reason for risking war?

No. He resented the frequent English raids on Spanish ports and shipping. . . .

Consequently, ...

In this example, the transitional region has pushed from the leading edge of each paragraph into the concluding sentence of the preceding one. To discover the answer to the question posed at the end of one paragraph, the reader moves eagerly into the next. This device, used moderately, is effective and artful.

Demonstrative Pronouns

Another useful way of binding both sentences and paragraphs together is to put to good effect a bad habit many writers have: that of allowing a demonstrative pronoun *(this* or *that)* to stand alone as the representative of a complex but unspecified and unexplained notion. When readers encounter a vague *this* or an uncertain *that,* they must pause to decipher what *this* or *that* is. But when the demonstrative pronoun is carefully specified, then whole paragraphs are made clear. Here are two examples of paragraphs that contain vague pronouns in their concluding sentences, followed by revised sentences in which the struggling demonstratives are assisted:

> . . . and the Greeks were excellent warriors, especially the Spartans, whose rigorous lives were geared to military conflict. They were well-armed and skillful hand-to-hand fighters. They lacked Xerxes' archers, however, and had only a small cavalry. *This* made them seek battle in rough and broken terrain.

> *These military capabilities and limitations* made them seek battle in rough and broken terrain where hand-to-hand combat would be more important than archery and cavalry.

> Life at the court of Versailles was expensive, and consequently, many nobles were compelled to borrow heavily from King Louis. To satisfy creditors, lesser lords were forced to sell their country estates, and with them their independence. The hectic and tiresome court rituals pitted lord against lord for petty privileges, such as holding a candle while the monarch prepared for bed. *This* led to the French Revolution.

> *This slow destruction of the nobility* eventually would lead to the French Revolution.

When you take the time to spell out what *this* is, you have, in effect, summarized an entire section or paragraph. The specified *this* or *that* explains to a reader the significance of all the preceding details, and allows the writer to capture an entire regiment of examples within a single phrase that can be referred to again and again as the need arises:

> . . . these Greek military capabilities and limitations . . . .

Every time this phrase is mentioned, your reader should recall the Spartans, hand-to-hand fighting, archers, and cavalry.

Such demonstrative phrases can serve, too, as bridges between paragraphs. In an essay on the Greek army in the fifth century B.C., we can imagine that a paragraph on their military capabilities might be followed by one on their military strategies. The transition from the first paragraph to the second might be no more complex than this:

Conclusion of
first paragraph
("capabilities")

. . . Unfortunately, the Greeks lacked skilled archers and had only a small cavalry.

Beginning of
second paragraph
("strategies")

These military capabilities and limitations made the Greeks seek battle in rough and broken terrain.

In this way, the first sentence of the new paragraph summarizes the previous one in a simple phrase, and then moves into the next, related subject. Reaching deeply into the previous paragraph, the key phrase— *military capabilities and limitations*—forms a strong transition. It is also a subtle form of repetition, yet another tie that binds.

Repetition: Nouns, Pronouns, Phrases

Synonyms

In an earlier chapter we observed that words and phrases carelessly repeated can irritate readers and lead them to question a writer's competence. But certain key words and phrases in an essay can take repetition; they even require it. In this chapter, for example, the word *transition* appears over and over again. As far as possible, it is not used more than once in any sentence, or in adjacent sentences. And since this is a rather long chapter on transitions, some variations of the term are employed. Among the words or phrases you can find in this chapter doing *transition*'s duty are:

bridges
signal of direction
gap-fillers
critical junctures
connections
linkages

Sometimes the modifications surrounding *transition* transform the word:

short transitional preface
well-laid transitions
transitional link
device of transition

A transition takes on the physical characteristics and associations of bridges, directional signals, and linkages when those things are made to stand in for it.

Simple repetition of this kind will be evident in almost any coherent essay. Here, for example, is a paragraph that uses repetition to gain coherence and rhythm. The writer is exploring the nature of the ordering power in the universe:

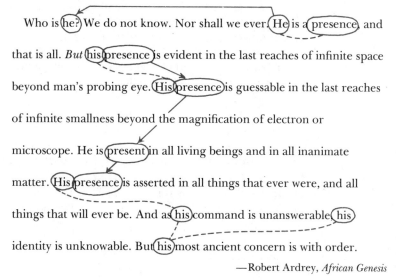

Who is *he?* We do not know. Nor shall we ever. *He* is a *presence,* and that is all. *But his presence* is evident in the last reaches of infinite space beyond man's probing eye. *His presence* is guessable in the last reaches of infinite smallness beyond the magnification of electron or microscope. He is *present* in all living beings and in all inanimate matter. *His presence* is asserted in all things that ever were, and all things that will ever be. And as *his* command is unanswerable *his* identity is unknowable. But *his* most ancient concern is with order.

—Robert Ardrey, *African Genesis*

Sometimes you may have to take care to focus your reader's attention on key words or phrases in an essay. This task is ordinarily done early on, in the introduction or shortly thereafter. In this first example, notice how the *this* in the second sentence works to identify what will probably be a key phrase throughout the essay:

> A major cause of inflation throughout the 1970s was the automatic increase in federal taxation that occurred as income grew, jumping taxpayers from tax bracket to tax bracket. *This escalating federal taxation* . . . .

The first sentence identifies the key idea; the second sentence names it.

Sometimes the key terms can be very different, but their shared meanings make the connection:

> The *Saturn V* rumbled on the launch pad, great rolls of flame and smoke belching from its tail. Then the *gargantuan missile* rose slowly and . . . .

In these sentences, *Saturn V* and *gargantuan missile* are equivalent phrases that imperceptibly do the work of a transition. Such equivalent phrases are a useful form of repetition, especially when a writer wants to avoid belaboring any one word. But occasionally a writer ventures too far in discovering synonyms for a key word, the result being a paragraph or essay more concerned with variation than content:

> *Cats* are intriguing creatures. These puzzling *felines* dwell at man's doorstep or in his house, take his offerings, and share the warmth of his fireplace. But rarely will *tabby* share affection with his benefactor, preferring to remain unmoved by the blandishments that send mere dogs fawning after master's slipper. No, *grimalkin* prefers dark alleys and hidden crawls to the comfort of a lap. *Old Tom* is independent from birth to the grave, tolerant of man but little more.

Two or three variations are certainly welcome. But there's no need to find a new word for cat with every sentence. *Grimalkin* and *Old Tom* scrape the bottom of the thesaurus.

Pronouns and referents

An occasional pronoun might have helped. *He, she, it, they,* and all their kin function as links between sentences, so long as the pronoun has a clear and accurate word from which it derives its particular meaning. These *referent words* will ordinarily be the nearest plausible noun preceding the pronoun that shares its number (singular or plural):

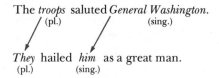

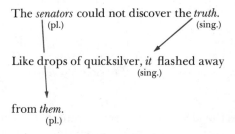

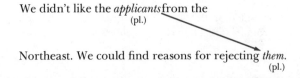

Repeated phrases

Another linking device is the repetition of phrases or entire sentences. Probably the most famous example of strategic repetition occurs in Mark Antony's oration over the corpse of Caesar in Shakespeare's *Julius Caesar*. Anthony begins by describing the character of Caesar's assassins:

> Brutus is an honorable man, So are they all, all honorable men.

Then, as he recounts the good deeds of Caesar and the facts of the brutal murder, Antony repeats and varies his references to *honor* eight more times until he has turned the meaning of the word on its head:

> I fear I wrong the honorable men
> Whose daggers have stabb'd Caesar.

The recurrence of the word is the one constant in Antony's long and impassioned address to the citizens of Rome. *Honorable men* sticks in the craw and memory, a fighting phrase that ties the speech together.

A shorter speech than Antony's and one perhaps as famous employs repetition consciously as a transitional device: Abraham Lincoln's "Gettysburg Address." Its 267 words are bound by transitional words, and devices of enumeration, chronology, parallelism, and repetition. It is almost too tightly joined:

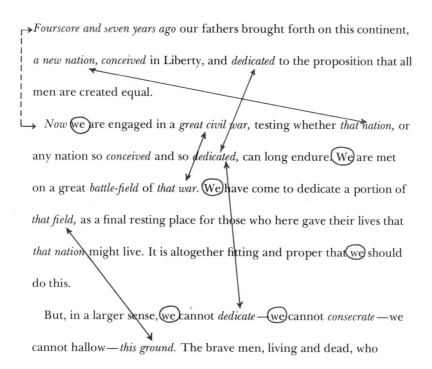

Fourscore and seven years ago our fathers brought forth on this continent,

a new nation, conceived in Liberty, and *dedicated* to the proposition that all

men are created equal.

Now we are engaged in a *great civil war,* testing whether *that nation,* or

any nation so *conceived* and so *dedicated,* can long endure. We are met

on a great *battle-field* of *that war.* We have come to dedicate a portion of

that field, as a final resting place for those who here gave their lives that

that nation might live. It is altogether fitting and proper that we should

do this.

But, in a larger sense, we cannot *dedicate* —we cannot *consecrate* —we

cannot hallow— *this ground.* The brave men, living and dead, who struggled *here,* have *consecrated* it, far above our poor power to add or

detract. The world will little note, nor long remember what we say *here,*

but it can never forget what they did *here.* It is for us the living, rather, to

be *dedicated here* to the unfinished work which they who fought *here* have

thus far so nobly advanced. It is rather for us to be *here dedicated* to the

great task remaining before us—that from these honored dead we take

increased *devotion* to that cause for which they gave the last full measure

of *devotion*—that we here highly resolve *that these dead* shall not have

died in vain—*that this nation,* under God, shall have a new birth of

freedom—and *that government of the people, by the people, for the people,*

shall not perish from the earth.

Sequences

Certain sequences within paragraphs and essays can have a connective function. Like several other connective devices we have examined, they operate on the shoe-not-dropped principle. In Lincoln's
speech above, the line "But, in a larger sense," tells the reader to expect
a paragraph that differs from the preceding one in substance though
not in structure. If you encounter a question in an essay, you expect it to
be followed by an answer. When you meet a *first of all,* you anticipate a
secondly, thirdly, and *lastly.* Likewise:

> *if* can imply a subsequent *then;*
>
> *despite this* can imply a subsequent *this is the case;*
>
> *although this* can imply a subsequent *this happened;*
>
> *whenever this* can imply a subsequent *then this;* and
>
> *because of this* can imply a subsequent *this happened.*

At first it may seem that these connectives (there are many others) work
best within sentences to establish the relationship between individual
base clauses:

> If Victorian England heartily endorsed serious learning and
> scholarship, it also supported the most bizarre exhibits, shows, and
> entertainments under the guise of entertainment.

Despite NASA's best efforts to prevent it, the Skylab space station tumbled to earth in 1979, its pieces scattering across Australia.

But full essays can also be held together by similar principles of expectation. Either of the simple sentences above could be turned into complete articles linked, in part, by the sequence implied by:

> if *this* . . . *this;*
> despite *this* . . . *this*.

The first part of the first essay (which could run one paragraph or several) might discuss Victorian efforts to establish museums, learned societies, and schools. But all the while that readers were absorbing this material, they would be anticipating the promised part of the essay depicting the freak shows, exotic exhibits, and hoaxes. The second essay might open with a detailed account of NASA's attempts to keep the Skylab in orbit. But all the opening paragraphs would operate under the shadow of the initial *despite* until the essay finally turned to the subject of the spacecraft's fiery descent. If either of these essays failed to present the promised material, the readers would feel that the essay was incomplete.

Introductions and Conclusions

Patterns implied by such constructions as *if* . . . *then,* and *because of this* . . . *this* are ordinarily established in the introductory paragraph of an essay. They are frequently part of the thesis statement. But even those parts of an introductory paragraph that do not form the thesis can be used to tie an essay together. Both introductory and concluding paragraphs have the power to shape all the material in between, giving it coherence and unity.

How much work an introduction must do depends upon the type of essay it is introducing. Some introductions must only set down facts while others bear the responsibility of winning a reader's approval or interest. An essay may begin with a quotation, a question, a paradox, a contradiction, a bold statement, a threat, a jest. It is up to the writer to fit an appropriate introduction to any given piece of prose. But whatever the opening strategy chosen, a writer ought to exploit the natural relationships between the opening and closing paragraphs. If, for example, an essay begins with a quotation,

> "Patriotism," the English man of letters, *Samuel Johnson,* once observed, "is the last refuge of a scoundrel,"

that quotation might serve as matter for comment in the concluding par-

agraph—even if neither the quote nor its author finds mention elsewhere in the body of the essay:

> And so that is the condition of this country's foreign policy and the
> character of its foreign policy makers. *Samuel Johnson,* if he were alive,
> might find the State Department full of patriots.

A connection of this kind (which works especially well in a short essay)
puts a hoop around the whole composition, and tells the reader that you
are in control of the subject. The essay seems tight because a conclusion
that recalls an introduction suggests that you had the ending in mind
from the outset. The essay has design:

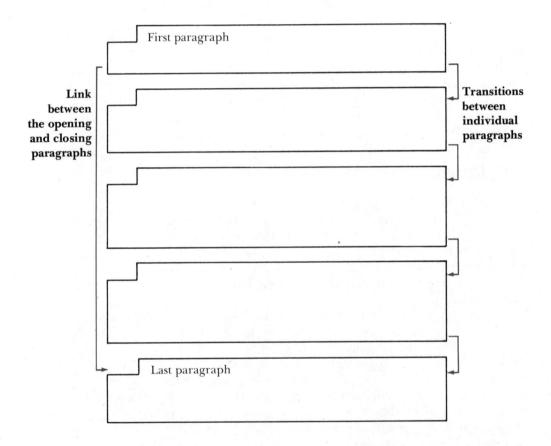

**Link
between
the opening
and closing
paragraphs**

First paragraph

Last paragraph

**Transitions
between
individual
paragraphs**

**Recalling the
introduction**

The technique is not limited to opening paragraphs employing
quotations. A character or circumstance mentioned in the first paragraph, a notable phrase, a frightening statistic, a frank assertion—all
these invite some sort of recall in the concluding paragraph:

Opening   My grandfather, a coal miner in the back-breaking days before machines and safety rules, appreciated the changes labor unions brought to the pits. But in more recent times, laborers show less concern for . . . .

Closing   That is the state of American coal fields in the 1980s. Your grandfather and mine would not recognize much of the sophisticated equipment today's miners enjoy. Even less recognizable to them would be the attitudes of their sons and grandsons . . . .

Opening   One out of every eight Americans is functionally illiterate despite compulsory education and billions of dollars for schools. One out of eight. Why has education failed so dismally in reaching that fraction of the population?

Closing   The means to improve education are there. Not until we employ them can we begin to reduce that awful proportion—one in eight—of Americans who cannot use language for their own best interest.

If an idea used in the opening and closing of an essay also appears in the development section, in the body, that essay can be said to have a motif. An essay on poverty, for example, might open with a vivid description of the conditions endured by a particular household. This family might then appear in subsequent paragraphs as the particulars of poverty are described. Then the effects of poverty might be summarized in a final paragraph where the poor folks are spotlighted one last time. This repeated element or motif increases the number of connections in the essay. The device of using a single example—a single family—to represent a much larger group is a favorite technique of the news media. A story on tornado damage will focus on one household that lost everything; an account of medical care costs will trace the costs of a particular patient. It is a technique open to abuse, to simplification and emotionalism. But it can give coherence to persuasive essays.

Motifs in a long composition need not be formal or even consistent. Any repetition of a relatively complex idea will establish a motif in a work. In this text, for example, you may have noticed that many of the sample essays, paragraphs, and sentences deal with politics, baseball, Shakespeare, automobiles, and history. These topics are not thematically connected either to each other or the subject matter of the text, but because the subjects appear over and over again, they become part of the character of the book.

Here's what an essay with a single motif might look like in outline:

Poor Folk

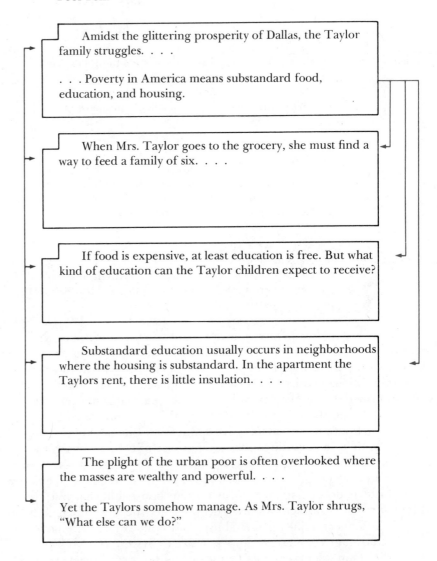

Amidst the glittering prosperity of Dallas, the Taylor family struggles. . . .

. . . Poverty in America means substandard food, education, and housing.

When Mrs. Taylor goes to the grocery, she must find a way to feed a family of six. . . .

If food is expensive, at least education is free. But what kind of education can the Taylor children expect to receive?

Substandard education usually occurs in neighborhoods where the housing is substandard. In the apartment the Taylors rent, there is little insulation. . . .

The plight of the urban poor is often overlooked where the masses are wealthy and powerful. . . .

Yet the Taylors somehow manage. As Mrs. Taylor shrugs, "What else can we do?"

Exercises

1. How regularly do professional writers rely on transitional words at the tips of sentences and paragraphs to bridge gaps in their prose? Survey a newspaper, a news magazine, a specialty magazine, several editorials, and several argumentative pieces to find out. In what type of writing do you tend to find the greatest number of explicit transitions per 500 or 1,000 words? Tabulate your results, and write a short essay reporting your findings to your colleagues.

2. Fiction is often arranged chronologically. Examine the transitional devices used in several short stories to indicate the passage of time. Report your findings to your colleagues in a short essay.

3. Examine the way parallelism is used as a connective device in the short essay "Oh Boys!" in the previous chapter. Do you think it is effective to have all three middle paragraphs begin with the same word? How do the conjunctions *but, yet,* and *so* function as connectors within the paragraphs?

4. Some writers frown on the use of questions to focus or connect essays and paragraphs. Too artificial or flashy, they say. But the technique is ancient and honorable. Platonic dialogues, for example, are strings of questions that lead gradually to the revelation of a truth. In the paragraph that follows, from a fifth century work on rhetoric, observe how the two initial questions state the thesis of the passage and define the kind of evidence that the rest of the paragraph must develop. Then write a paragraph modeled after the passage, opening it with one or more questions that state the thesis.

> Therefore, since infants are not taught to speak except by learning the expressions of speakers, why can men not be made eloquent, not by teaching them the rules of eloquence, but by having them read and hear the expressions of the eloquent and imitate them in so far as they are able to follow them? Have we not seen examples of this being done? For we know many men ignorant of the rules of eloquence who are more eloquent than many who have learned them; but we know of no one who is eloquent without having read or heard the disputations and sayings of the eloquent. For boys do not need the art of grammar which teaches correct speech if they have the opportunity to grow up and live among men who speak correctly. Without knowing any of the names of the errors, they criticize and avoid anything erroneous they hear spoken on the basis of their own habits of speech, just as city dwellers, even if they are illiterate, criticize the speech of rustics.
>
> —Augustine, *On Christian Doctrine,* trans. D. W. Robertson, Jr.

5. For each of these short passages, find a phrase that makes the italicized, unspecified *this* clear.

Example:

> Martha lashed out at Tammy angrily. The punchbowl crashed to the floor. A neighbor came to the door to complain about too much noise. A baby screamed in a backroom. *This* made Kate decide to leave.

This *tumult and confusion*

A. The air grew heavy and moisture-laden. The sky loomed dark overhead, faintly luminous at the horizon. The wind dropped, and all the birds grew silent. *This* made us expect a tornado.

B. "*This* is just disgusting! First, the fan belt flies off. Then the transmission starts leaking. And now I need a valve job. The car has only 13,000 miles. Can't your mechanics do something?"

C. The mayor refused to release the funds, arguing that they were reserved for urban development, not for salaries. The safety forces would not lower their initial demands for more money and increased benefits. *This* meant that a strike could not be avoided.

D. Casey, the manager, winced as his rookie shortstop overthrew first base, allowing the winning run to score on what should have been the last out. The home crowd roared, mocking the player who had given their team victory. The youth trudged sheepishly toward the dugout where Casey glared, spat out his chaw, and cursed. But then his anger was gone, and Casey put out a hand to comfort the shaken rookie. Both men smiled. *That* is what makes Casey a great manager.

6. Copy a short essay, speech, or editorial, and give it the kind of detailed analysis applied to the Gettysburg Address in this chapter. Does your subject exhibit the same degree of coherence? Why or why not? Why does Lincoln use so much repetition?

12

Revision

Revision can begin with the first words you write. It can continue through the writing process. In fact, revising may be inseparable from composing since both acts involve choices, changes, reconsiderations, emendations, evolutions, and revolutions of thought and language. Revision is the *writer's* process of exploration and change. It differs from editing or proofreading which is a relatively mechanical act that occurs after the writing and revising are completed. Editing is the tidying up that makes a text presentable, the correction of spelling errors, grammar, usage, and typographical slips. Occasionally, editing can be entrusted to a secretary or editor. Revision belongs solely to the writer.

Revision, editing, proofreading

These distinctions help give revision its rightful place in the act of writing. Many of us have a difficult time composing. The words come slowly, the ideas don't fit together, the sentences sound artificial or clumsy. We fill up a page, scratch out half of what we wrote, crumble up the sheet, and start over again. An afternoon's work may produce nothing more than an overstuffed wastebasket. And we conclude that we are inept writers, incapable of easy, clear, and rapid exposition. But we err in assuming that good writing comes easily and that capable writers compose without much labor.

What slows most writers down is making the decisions, wrestling with the choices that constitute revision, coming to terms with the inescapable evaluating and reconsidering of words, sentences, paragraphs, and whole essays. There is no reason to expect that the first words and phrases that come to mind represent the best choices in a given writing situation. They are simply a starting point, a temporary commitment to which you are not bound in any way. The moment you find a better word, a sounder structure, a more specific example, then the old word, structure, or example goes out the window. Precisely because writing is revising, and because the process of composing does not move in a straight line but lurches and digresses all across a page, you can expect that writing will be slow, time-consuming, and often frustrating. That's normal. Crumpled paper is normal. Additions, rearrangements, crossouts, erasures, paste and scissors, arrows and emendations are tools of the writer's trade.

Nor should you think that labored composition is the curse of literary, artistic, or professional writing only. Even an apparently simple writing job—an office memo, a letter to the editor, a letter home, a job application form—can involve formidable strategies and shrewd assessments of aim and audience. All prose is subject to change and reconsideration.

Sometimes making changes—especially deletions—is painful. You have an investment of time, energy, and thought in anything you compose. And often you will be satisfied if the language you've produced is merely adequate. You would rather not tamper with it, as long as it runs. Revision then seems like additional work—work that offers no guarantee of improving what you have already penned. At times like these, remember your readers. They are relying on you to clarify a notion. What seems like extra effort to you may in fact be necessary labor if these readers are to understand an idea. Take the time to make a change when you sense a change is needed.

Writing is revising (margin note)

Revision and How You Write

How you revise depends upon your habits of composition. Some authors write slowly, sentence by sentence, polishing each thought and phrase before moving on to the next. Others construct sentences quickly, but pause at paragraph divisions to review what they've accomplished, to check whether their new paragraph hangs together. Still others rough cut an entire essay at a single sitting. They start with an idea

Methods of composing (margin note)

they've considered and allow it to develop freely and impulsively on a page, line after line, paragraph after paragraph until they feel they've reached an end. And of course, writers regularly combine these methods of composing. They may labor over key sentences—theses, openings, closings—or tinker with critical paragraphs until they've got them right. Other parts of the same essay, however, seem to write themselves, falling out of the pen in a smooth flow of ideas and phrases. No method or combination of methods is inherently better than any other. How you write is apt to be as unique as your handwriting.

Sentence by Sentence

If you ordinarily write sentence by sentence, you probably need to pay particular attention to how useful your paragraphs and paragraph groupings are to your readers. Your concentration on sentences could distract you from considering how the larger elements of your piece, particularly paragraphs, are functioning. Then too, check to see that whatever viewpoint or argument you began with is still held at the end of your essay. In your slow and steady movement from sentence to sentence, you may be gradually modifying your thoughts without realizing it. Because of your studied attention to the shape of your sentences, chances are good that your transitions between them will be sound, and that the sentences themselves will be individually well-phrased. But be sure to review them in larger groups too where you can detect problems with repetition or rhythm more easily.

Paragraph by Paragraph

If you typically pause to review what you have done after each paragraph, critical points for you will occur at the juncture of paragraphs. Each paragraph may be a masterpiece, coherent in itself. But how do they fit together? Have you been able to sustain an argument? If, for example, your essay calls for a parallel development of three major points, are the paragraphs that develop those points reasonably similar? If not, you may want to restructure them so that they accommodate the larger design of your essay. The reader will appreciate this modification. If you revise paragraph by paragraph, be careful that the satisfaction you feel when you complete each unit does not make you reluctant to revise those finished paragraphs later if new and better ideas pop up as you move deeper into the essay. Don't be afraid to move paragraphs around or to cut out any that aren't pulling their weight. Don't let small triumphs undermine the major campaign and distract you from the major aim of your composition.

Full Draft Method

If you write full drafts rapidly, you face a formidable task of reassessment when you put down your pen. But you are probably aware that your first draft is a test-bed of ideas, an exercise in exploration. As the draft progressed, you may have discovered that one aspect of your subject came to dominate the whole essay. For example, an essay on fighter planes of World War II has become an account of the British Spitfire. You could revise the draft to include other aircraft. Or you could simply admit that it's Spitfires that you want to write about and revise your thesis accordingly. The initial draft helped you to find the real subject.

Even if the ideas in your complete draft develop consistently, review them critically as a reader might. When you write quickly, without pausing to rethink or reconsider, it is easy and natural to omit details and transitions. In later drafts you may have to add whole paragraphs or reorder those you have written. You may want to change your point of view. You may find that the first several paragraphs just spin their wheels, circling about the subject without really moving. If you compose by the full draft method, see what happens to your essay if you pluck out the first paragraph. Often, your new lead will be tough and dramatic.

Reconsider your sentences. Do they create or support the tone you want? Are they varied? When writing quickly, most writers grab the simplest formulas off the shelves. Many sentences will open with expletives: *it was; there were; it seems.* Passive voices intrude where the active would work better. Verbs lag, nouns blur. The text begs for textures, colors, details bypassed as the writer dashed toward a conclusion. But— as we noted in an earlier chapter—hasty composing can produce startling, energetic phrasing and powerful analysis. Don't purge this initial energy from your text by gutless retreats from these original achievements. If they are valuable, stick with them.

Commitments to your readers

Whatever method of composing you use, your concern in revising must be for your readers. How will they regard what you have written? The words you put on a page are commitments. For example, if you write:

The best solution to the problem is . . . ,

the word *best* places a burden of proof on your shoulders that won't come off until you have provided the facts, arguments, and examples that prove that your solution is, indeed, the best. You've given that expectation to your readers. But what happens if, as you write, you discover solutions as good as your own or better? Or what if your own reasoning convinces you that your solution won't work? You can abandon your initial scheme entirely, or modify it:

One solution to the problem is . . . . But it has these limitations.

What seems like a plausible solution, . . . , proves to be no solution at all.

In both cases here, your revision has provoked reconsideration which has, in turn, suggested more complex lines of reasoning. You have examined the word *best* in the same way that some of your readers would and found it wanting. You have anticipated objections.

Critical moments in any sentence, paragraph, or full essay occur around words or phrases that state, qualify, and link. If you are supporting a particular thesis, examine it with the eye of a skeptic who assumes there is something wrong with it. Assess carefully the implications of the qualifiers:

all	never
many	unquestionably
most	in every case
every	generally
usually	in this case
sometimes	always

Are these words accurate in the context you employ them? Have you provided your readers with the explanations of context they need, or the examples that justify the qualifiers? Can they understand the movement implied by the transitions you intend to use:

similarly	consequently
in contrast	so
moreover	then
henceforth	it is clear

Is what follows *consequently* truly the effect of the previously described clause? Is the *it* really as clear as you claim? Does your contrast really reveal significant differences?

Choices have consequences which a writer must examine if an exposition or an argument is to seem coherent. But even a logically chosen detail or example must be presented in terms an audience will agree to. For example, you may think that you have described the plight of a middle-income family pinched by inflation and income taxes in terms that evoke sympathy:

Understanding your audience

The Smiths, a family of five, have watched their buying power erode more than 25 percent in the last three years even though their combined annual income has risen from $38,000 to $42,000. Crushed by a mortgage, car payments, debt on a boat, real estate taxes, city, state, and federal income taxes, Mr. and Mrs. Smith spend their evenings trying to balance their strained budget.

An audience of middle-income Smiths would nod in appreciation of the family's dilemma. They've felt the same pressures. But if you are writing to a more general audience that might include people whose incomes (combined or otherwise) do not even approach $42,000, you'd want to modify your presentation to de-emphasize the Smiths' income and possessions:

The Smiths, a family of five, have watched helplessly as their buying power decreased by more than 25 percent in the last three years. Though they seem to enjoy the good life, both Mr. and Mrs. Smith work long hours away from home to manage the endless payments of a lifestyle they were conned into believing they could afford. Their dream has crumbled and they must now choose which of their children will go to college. The Smiths can afford to send only one.

This tear-jerker anticipates some of the reservations an audience might have to the initial version.

Revision also takes place on the level of sound and language where, once again, you must try to add vigor and details and eliminate misunderstandings and miscues. Far easier said than done. We often have a difficult time *hearing* the difficulties in our own prose when we read through it. Our minds unconsciously add details to a passage that it may not actually possess. But readers lack these details and hence may slip over what we consider to be the main point because no signal in the text tells them it is the main point. Like readers of mystery stories, they may ignore a casual clue because they don't appreciate how important it may be at the end.

Rereading your work

Many writers attempt to solve this problem by reading and re-reading what they have written before moving forward. They fit every new sentence into the context, structure, and rhythms of the sentences that precede it. The process of writing becomes rhythmic itself: two steps backward, one forward. The steps back sometimes return a writer all the way to the start of an essay or to the beginning of a major division. The new sentence or paragraph benefits from a review of the thoughts and phrases that establish its context. Try this method. If in working your way back you stumble over a phrase that doesn't fit, an example that seems imprecise, a word that now seems misplaced, pause to modify, add, or delete. Whatever makes you stumble will surely cause your reader to fall.

Cutting-and-Pasting

Cutting-and-pasting is a technique some writers use to save time when revising longer essays or rearranging shorter ones. Rather than completely rewriting a piece, they clip the parts worth saving, rearrange them if necessary, and connect them with new paragraphs and transitions. You might begin with an essay like the one that follows:

Original essay:

Checkmate

In 1952, on the occasion of the "Checkers Speech," the political future of Richard Nixon, then a senator from California, was on the line. By virtue of strong logical and emotional appeals, Nixon's Checkers Speech overcame its stylistic clumsiness to win the California senator a place on the Republican national ticket with Dwight Eisenhower. In fact, the speech probably gave a boost to the entire campaign effort, which culminated in the election of the first Republican president since Herbert Hoover in 1928.

The key to Nixon's success is documentation. Nixon reads from an audit and a legal opinion, prepared by two distinguished firms, that clear him of any wrongdoing. Then Nixon tells the public exactly what he owns and owes, and it isn't much—certainly not the holdings of a man thriving off of political graft and slush funds. The logic of Nixon's case is tight enough to acquit him of the charge of corruption.

But Nixon might have lost his case if he depended on logic and style to carry him. The speech lacks eloquence, especially in the early paragraphs. The second paragraph, for example, is convoluted and confused. Nixon's thoughts seem muddled. He recovers thereafter, but time and again he interrupts his argument with irritating asides: "And let me say," "Now, just let me say," "I should say this." Even more disruptive and bothersome are the questions that Nixon uses as transitions through much of the speech: "Well, what did you use the fund for, Senator?" "What did we do with this money?" "What do we owe?" Many listeners or readers are apt to find this technique too obvious or immature.

Fortunately, Senator Nixon does not rely on style. Instead he turns to the politician's most faithful device for turning public opinion, the emotional appeal. The cornerstone of his emotional argument is an allusion to one particular political gift, a puppy named Checkers. Nixon knows that not even the staunchest legalist would expect him to rip a floppy-eared pup out of the arms of six-year-old Tricia just to please some steely-eyed Democrats. Near the end of the speech he caps his emotional appeal by reading a letter from the young wife of a serviceman who offers her last ten dollars to support the cause of "great Americans like [Nixon] and General Eisenhower." This effective strategy makes Nixon appear like a fighter for just causes against powerful, possibly communist-inspired enemies eager to destroy him by blackening his name.

If the Checkers Speech had failed to clear him of charges of corruption made by the New York *Post,* Nixon would have lost his place as the Republican vice-presidential candidate and probably disappeared into the hinterlands of California politics. But the speech was a brilliant success. Despite an awkward style of language, Nixon won the favor of his television audience through powerful logical and emotional appeals.

Rearranging the essay
"Checkmate" is reasonably well-phrased. But perhaps you want your analysis of Richard Nixon's speech to have a more systematic organization, one that lists the order of topics in the first paragraph rather than in the conclusion. You may also see an advantage in rearranging the topics, grouping the strengths of the speech together. And you may want to give some background about the Checkers Speech in the introductory paragraph.

You could rewrite the entire essay. But if you liked substantial parts of it in this original state and were pressed for time, you could experiment with scissors and paste to see what you come up with. As it turns out, the essay can be revised and rearranged rather easily with the best parts of the old text linked together by some new sentences and phrases.

Cut and pasted revision:

Checkmate

Same opening
In 1952, on the occasion of the "Checkers Speech," the political future of Richard Nixon, then a senator from California, was on the line.

Thesis borrowed from conclusion
If the Checkers Speech had failed to clear him of charges of corruption made by the New York *Post,* Nixon would have lost his place as the Republican vice-presidential candidate and probably disappeared into the hinterlands of California politics. But the speech was a brilliant success. Despite an awkward style of language, Nixon won the favor of his television audience through powerful logical and emotional appeals.

Line typed in
The speech lacks eloquence, especially in the early

Borrowed from third paragraph
paragraphs. The second paragraph, for example, is convoluted and confused. Nixon's thoughts seem muddled. He recovers thereafter, but time and again he interrupts his argument with irritating asides: "And let me say," "Now, just let me say," "I should say this." Even more disruptive and bothersome are the questions that Nixon uses as transitions through much of the speech: "Well, what did you use the fund for, Senator?" "What did we do with this money?" "What do we owe?" Many listeners or readers are apt to find this technique too obvious or immature.

New transition	But if the style of the Checkers Speech is weak, the logic it uses to prove Nixon's innocence is not. First Nixon reads from an
Borrowed from second paragraph	audit and a legal opinion, prepared by two distinguished firms, that clear him of any wrongdoing. Then Nixon tells the public exactly what he owns and owes, and it isn't much—certainly not the holdings of a man thriving off of political graft and slush funds. The logic of Nixon's case is tight enough to acquit him of the charge of corruption.
New transition	But technical acquittal is not enough for a man who would be vice-president. Nixon needs the support, endorsement, and trust of his fellow citizens. So he turns to an emotional appeal. The centerpiece of his emotional argument is an
Borrowed from fourth paragraph	allusion to one particular political gift, a puppy named Checkers. Nixon knows that not even the staunchest legalist would expect him to rip a floppy-eared pup out of the arms of six-year-old Tricia just to please some steely-eyed Democrats. Near the end of the speech he caps his emotional appeal by reading a letter from the young wife of a serviceman who offers her last ten dollars to support the cause of "great Americans like [Nixon] and General Eisenhower." This effective strategy makes Nixon appear like a fighter for just causes against powerful, possibly communist-inspired enemies eager to destroy him by blackening his name.
Line typed in	By virtue of strong logical and emotional appeals, Nixon's Checkers
Conclusion borrowed from opening	Speech overcame its stylistic clumsiness to win the California senator a place on the Republican national ticket with Dwight Eisenhower. In fact, the speech probably gave a boost to the entire campaign effort, which culminated in the election of the first Republican president since Herbert Hoover in 1928.

Naturally, you would not hand in a cut-and-paste essay to a teacher or employer. But such a text can be given to a typist who would then produce the final, clean copy. Or, if both the original and revised sentences and paragraphs were produced on the same typewriter and you cut and pasted with care, then the cut-and-pasted version could be duplicated. The reproduced text will be almost as clean as a newly typed version. (Many teachers, however, will not ordinarily accept research papers or reports that are copied. They demand an original. Consult with them before handing in even a clean cut-and-paste job.)

Evaluating What You Write

Revising is a process of constant evaluation. But judging prose—especially your own—is far from easy. Perhaps you don't find much difference in the way things are written. You may have browsed through books a teacher assured you were "masterpieces" only to discover that they seemed no better phrased to you than a sports column or the IRS tax forms. Writing is writing.

It is easy to treat much of what gets into print casually, as part of the endless, seamless production of a mysterious "they." It rarely occurs to us that one morning's newspaper editorial might be better phrased or argued than the next's. Or that much of what we read is written by anyone at all. Who cares who writes the daily TV listings or the blurbs in a catalogue of merchandise:

10:30 **1/2

OEDIPUS THE KING (1968) Christopher Plummer, Orson Welles. A young man realizes, to his horror, that he has married his mother and killed his father.

9:00 **1/2

THE BLISS OF MRS. BLOSSOM (1968) Shirley MacLaine, Richard Attenborough. The bored wife of a brassiere manufacturer hides a lover in the attic, where he lives for years.

(C) *Men's trimmer belt* helps control your paunch as it gives your back the support you want. Elasticized fabric with plenty of muscle to hold you in; flannel lining at back for warmth and extra comfort. Comfortable enough for all-day wear at work. White. *State waist size:* 33,34,36,38,40,42,44.

(10) *Precision-machined grinder/sausage maker* has 5 edges to chop, grind or mince. Sausage stuffer attachment. Cast aluminum.

Many people prosper in this world without ever knowing exactly how a prose passage from E. B. White differs from a description of a sausage maker in a Montgomery Wards catalogue. But unfortunately, most writers do not enjoy such immunity, because before their Bic's clicked, a teacher, an employer, or an associate is asking them to produce writing that is *good*. And that is the dilemma, the unspoken problem, faced by thousands of would-be writers every time they put pen to paper and begin to compose. How do we produce something that is good when we aren't sure what good is?

It may help to have some standards, some criteria of evaluation. Three you may find useful are *appropriateness, accuracy,* and *fit.* Appropriateness is a measure of how well you have matched your purpose in writing to your audience and language. Accuracy assesses the faithfulness of your representations of reality, and the clarity of your expressions. Fit is a measure of style.

Appropriateness

You already know that language must fit a purpose, hand in glove. Persuasive essays differ from informative articles which differ from self-expressive journals or letters. But the choice of appropriate language is not always simple or natural. Considerations of appropriateness can shape every aspect of your writing. What you aim to do and who your readers are determine what you write and how successful your effort proves to be.

Compare, for example, these two evaluations of an "econobox," the Honda Civic. The first assessment is from a consumer magazine, *Consumer Reports* (July 1978), the second from an enthusiast's periodical, *Car and Driver* (July 1978):

> Normal handling: very good. Some drivers thought the steering was too heavy on sharp turns and during parking. Power steering isn't available.
>   Accident-avoidance ability: Very good. The car leaned very sharply, but it responded crisply and safely.

> You can strap on this little box rocket and wriggle your way through the metropolis at velocities that will leave pedestrians absolutely bleary-eyed. In town, the Civic is as agile and sure-footed as O. J. Simpson running through a crowded airport.

The readers of *Consumer Reports* are generally a stern, sober lot—given to counting the tissues on a roll of Charmin and weighing the meat in chicken pot pies. They want facts clearly and cleanly presented. So *Consumer Reports* shapes its prose to its audience's expectations, dividing up the evaluation fo the Honda into categories each a paragraph long: *normal handling* and *accident-avoidance ability.* The strictness of these categories is emphasized by the colon *(:)* that follows each heading. The evaluative terms *Consumer Reports* uses are short, clear, colorless, and formal: *excellent, very good* (as in the Honda's case), *good, fair, poor.* Brief comments follow the evaluation, adding only details the editors believe will aid a purchaser in judging and comparing the vehicle. Thus even the arrangement of the magazine's prose mirrors the intended impartiality of its writers.

But not all people buy automobiles the same way they buy refrigerators. To many, the car is a source of fun and excitement. *Car and Driver* caters to that readership, an audience sufficiently versed in the nuts and bolts of vehicles to find the facts *Consumer Reports* typically offers familiar stuff. An enthusiast wants to know how a car feels, and that is exactly what *Car and Driver* delivers in its evaluation of the Honda's handling ability. Its language is more emotional than *Consumer Reports'* and technically less precise. You might infer that the Civic's road-holding must be very good to be able to wriggle through the metropolis as surefootedly as O. J. Simpson, but *Car and Driver* makes no pretense to objectivity in its language. Its writers are having too much fun. Notice too that while the evaluation from *Car and Driver* sets up no expectations of what is to come in the next paragraph, the short excerpt from *Consumer Reports* leads you to expect subsequent blocks of systematic analysis.

Which selection is better written? It depends. You probably enjoyed the second one more, but the first provides more detailed and specific information. Aims and audiences shape the way language operates and the way you perceive it. You wouldn't expect *Consumer Reports* to read like *Car and Driver,* and vice versa. It's a matter of appropriateness.

Accuracy

Good writing is accurate from the ground up, from the strategy it employs in the placement of a comma to the reliability of the statistics it quotes in defense of an argument. If appropriateness were the only standard of able composition, then good manners might make good writing. But a genteel smile and a correct demeanor may conceal inaccuracy, inexperience, laziness, and even mischief (Hamlet observes bluntly "that one may smile, and smile, and be a villain"). So good writing must not only achieve an appropriate goal, but do it factually, honestly, and competently.

Revising for accuracy will fix your gaze on the world around you and enliven the prose you produce. It will encourage you to examine statements carefully to discover just what the mayor meant when she claimed she never solicited a bribe or what the teacher implied when he called your thinking "fuzzy." You'll be suspicious of words that fall too easily into place—clichés perhaps. You will avoid jargon and buzz words because they don't represent what you want to say. You will explore what a tragedy is, and a disaster, and a crisis, and not use these terms to name every unfortunate event. You may even begin to understand yourself better once you begin to understand some of the relationships between words and the world—and the ways both can be manipulated.

Fit

Our third standard for good writing comes from a term used more often to describe mechanical objects than essays: fit. Fit, in this special sense, is defined by the *American Heritage Dictionary* as "the degree of precision with which surfaces are adjusted or adapted to each other in a machine or a collection of parts." Without straining the definition too much, the collection of parts can become the components of an essay: words, sentences, paragraphs. What we want from that assembly of parts is a fit that produces the "flowing" quality many readers expect from their reading, the seamless connection of words and phrases and ideas that makes reading a pleasure.

Writing that flows

If you check the fit of the panels on a fine automobile, you will find the seams flush, the gaps even, the creases as true as an angel's conscience. All this surface beauty and precision depends, however, on a harmony of unseen parts and on the skill of the workers who fashion the product. The fit of an essay is, similarly, no casual thing, no accident. An essay that reads effortlessly is often one that has cost its author many anxious moments of construction and revision. Hidden under the polished surface are dozens of seams and welds, trials and transitions, digressions and erasures. But finally the parts fit so well that a reader may be deceived into thinking their composition was a simple thing, a natural flowing of thoughts into words.

Flowing implies motion. Not all liquids flow at the same rate; not all writers share the same tempo of exposition. In different ways, both of the following passages flow:

Old Mrs. Donovan was a woman who really got around. No matter what was going on in Darrowby—weddings, funerals, house-sales—you'd find the dumpy little figure and walnut face among the spectators, the darting, black-button eyes taking everything in. And always on the end of its lead, her terrier dog.

—James Herriot, *All Things Bright and Beautiful*

As soon as the shooting was over and the elephant lay huge and silent in the blood-spattered wreck of his den, Cross understandably allowed his concern for his ledger books to overrule his feelings and admitted the public, at the usual charge, to view the grisly scene. While he wrestled with his next problem, how to dispose of a dead elephant in the center of London, applications, advice, and distinguished sightseers came from every direction.

—Richard D. Altick, *The Shows of London*

While the author of the first passage shows a preference for relatively short clauses moving briskly, the second writer opts for longer clauses that advance at a more stately pace.

Subject matter, too, has a bearing on how well a passage moves. Even a short plunge into waters above our depth can be humbling:

In philosophers like Aquinas, the concept of "conditions" is highly formal in nature. Kant's "transcendentalism" was the first step towards a more purely historical concept of conditions. For though Kant's conditions were highly generalized, they were distinguished from those of formal logic in being exclusively the conditions of *experience.*

—Kenneth Burke, *A Grammar of Motives*

We have all labored over a difficult book, trying to decipher language that—to us—seems frozen in stone. Sometimes the problem is with us. We just don't know enough to appreciate what the author is saying. Sometimes the difficulty is inherent in the subject matter; quite simply, it's tough—the nature of phenomena, the structure of the atom, the politics of seventeenth century France.

But does that mean that challenging ideas must be expressed in obscure and twisted ways? Surely not. You no more expect all writing to be simple than all life to be easy. The expression of some ideas requires a precise and complex language to remain faithful to the truths being expressed. But some able writers can explain even complex notions to general audiences with an ease that all but hides their accomplishments. They may use any number of devices to achieve clarity: careful definitions of key terms, precise examples, unobtrusive repetition of important ideas, helpful transitions. As a result, readers may not realize what tough terrain they've crossed while riding with an expert. Writing that's well-fitted leads readers in the right direction, taking them pleasantly and efficiently, without accident or mishap, from where their thoughts, ideas, prejudices, and beliefs are at the beginning of an essay to where you want them to be at the end.

Some Analyses

How can you apply these standards as you revise? Let's examine some short passages to find out. First, a sentence:

The congregation gave its approbation to the plans for dissemination of overpopulation information.

Reading the sentence is a little like riding a corkscrew rollercoaster: both experiences leave you reeling after their movement has ceased. If their purpose is to convey information, then the parts of this sentence just don't fit together properly. The rhythm and rhyme distract a reader so much that the message is lost. Simple changes are all that's required to outfit the sentence properly:

> The congregation approved the plans to distribute information on overpopulation.
>
> The congregation approved the plans for dissemination of materials on overpopulation.
>
> The members of the church gave their approbation to a plan for distributing information on population growth.

Each of these alternatives conveys approximately the same information as the original sentence in a more purposeful way.

Now for a more difficult example. You have written a paragraph to entertain your readers with the excitement of tobogganing:

> Frank, Mark, Jim, and Mario bought a toboggan and took to the hills one December evening after a heavy snow. There were a good number of toboggan runs on the slopes. The first one they used took them through a clump of trees. When they approached the trees, Frank would give directions, and they would try to direct the toboggan away from the obstacles. But usually when he said "Left!" half the riders would lean right, and the toboggan would go straight ahead without any change in direction. Sometimes they found themselves headed straight for a tree. To avoid a collision they would roll off the toboggan. It would continue onward sometimes for several yards, and they would too.

At first glance, the paragraph seems competent. It is free of mechanical errors, and even seems to flow thanks to an assortment of transitional words: *first, when, but, sometimes.* We can assume that the facts narrated are accurate. So we are left with considerations of appropriateness. And here the paragraph fails.

Why? Consider the subject—tobogganing. Consider your purpose—to entertain your readers. Consider the main event—dodging obstacles. And then imagine what happens as a quartet of young men on a toboggan rockets toward a tree, its leader yelling commands as the threat looms bigger and bigger. Imagine them splaying left and right while their craft slices straight ahead. The situation brims with drama, excitement, and humor, but we wouldn't know it from the limp exposition in the paragraph. Details are sparse, word choices inadequate. Look at the verbs that describe the motion of the toboggan: *to approach, to go, to continue.* They accurately indicate the general directional progress of the sledders, but they lack energy. They don't convey the feeling of hurdling down a slope, wind biting, snow spraying, noses running. Instead they are calm, almost dispassionate, like the rhythms of the passage itself: "To avoid a collision, they would roll off the toboggan." Imagine the panicked tumbling of arms, legs, snow, and slats that accompanies the rolling off and then judge the appropriateness of the original sentence.

Simply put, the subject matter of the paragraph demands better treatment. While so lifeless a narration of so animated an event might be justified in an accident report or a newspaper account, the colorless language and phrasing provide only a pauper's approximation of tobogganing if the writer's purpose is to entertain.

Try this now, another description:

> It was midnight, but the moon was out, and the dry yellow stalks held the light. In our dark clothes and stocking caps, we looked like ghosts, tramping across the furrows. The flat blades crackled where we stepped, and slapped our faces. We heard the thumps of small creatures—rabbits we hoped—running from our path, and occasionally a bird darted up with a shriek from the stalks, and flew away into the night as we invaded its haunts. We were soon at the top of a gentle hill where the rows of dead corn sloped away on each side like squads of midnight soldiers. We could see the buildings in the distance, quiet, slumbering, and still. Without a word, we began to chop the stalks.

As you might suspect, this paragraph is part of a longer narrative, but as a description of a particular action, it is self-contained. Does it flow? Not perfectly—there is, for instance, an irritating and avoidable rhyme in the first sentence *(midnight/light)*. But generally, the sentences are varied in length and structure; their pace matches the tempo of the action narrated. Notice, for example, how the *ands* in the sentence below create a calm, almost eerie rhythm and how the intrusion of a single phrase—in dashes—introduces an element of tension:

> We heard the thumps of small creatures
>   —rabbits we hoped—
>   running from our path,
> *and* occasionally a bird darted up
>   with a shriek from the stalks
> *and* flew away into the night
>   as we invaded its haunts.

We might complain (remembering the last example) that *small creatures* is undecidedly unspecific, but of course the author here can only guess what was producing the worrisome thumps because "it" is unseen: "rabbits we hoped." And *creatures,* though a general term, harbors more fearful connotations than, for example, *animals*—a word that might have been chosen. There's similar concern for accuracy in other choices, and while the language of the paragraph is simple, it is not austere:

> dry yellow stalks
> stocking caps
> furrows
> thumps
> shriek
> squads of midnight soldiers

The controlled vocabulary contributes to the sober tone of the piece. It *is* midnight and we are watching the invasion of an alien landscape. All these effects of language climax with the last line: "Without a word we began to chop the stalks." These simple, solid words convey the silence of a night broken by grim, determined reaping. The language works.

One final example. You have written the first draft of a movie review:

> *Gone With the Wind* has its flaws, but is a better film than most serious critics will admit. The glorification of the slave-holding southern aristocracy and the portrayals of blacks in the film are unfortunate. The acting is often overdone, verging on the hysterical. Clark Gable, as the dashing Rhett Butler, is playing Clark Gable. The character of Melanie is too virtuous to stomach. The film has been enduringly popular with just about everyone, except a sour group of critics. What the viewers see is the corruption of a simpler world. And a passionate story of love. *Gone With the Wind* is not an ordinary tale. It is not history. It is a romance full of oversized heroines and heroes. Rhett Butler becomes Clark Gable because Gable is a more colossal figure than Butler. Decades after his death, Gable remains the screen's most memorable figure. Melanie may be too good to meet in day-to-day life. But she is not too virtuous to dwell in the imagination of viewers. *Gone With the Wind* is an exercise in imagination, a colorful dazzling adult version of the dreams of childhood—of castles and queens and gardens and knights locked in the elemental struggles all men and women recognize and cherish.

The piece seems impressive at first. Then you begin to detect problems in the fit of the language. But the discontinuity is at least partially concealed by the appropriateness and accuracy of some of the sentences.

Moreover, the review is engaging and confident. The thesis is stated boldly in the first sentence:

Gone With the Wind

1. has its flaws,
2. but is a better film than most serious critics will admit.

You expect the paragraph to unfold according to this order, and it does. The four sentences following the thesis discuss the weaknesses in the Civil War epic, the remaining ones deal with its strengths. Details are a bit sparse though, and the conclusion has gardens and castles locked in elemental struggles, a peculiar sight. But basically, the structure and language are accurate and appropriate.

Yet the paragraph still does not flow. You realize that although you have followed the plan of organization announced in the first sentence, you haven't provided your readers with many additional organizational signals or transitions.

You revise, adding many details and transitional phrases (italicized):

> *Gone With the Wind* has its flaws, but it is a better film than most serious critics will admit. *Its faults are well known.* The glorification of the slave-holding southern aristocracy and the portrayals of blacks in the film are unfortunate. The acting is often overdone, *at times* verging on the hysterical *as when Scarlett O'Hara swears by the clay of Tara never to be hungry again.* Clark Gable, as the dashing Rhett Butler, is *undeniably* playing Clark Gable. *And* the character of Melanie is too virtuous to stomach. *Yet despite all these problems,* the film has been enduringly popular with just about everyone, except a sour group of critics. What *ordinary* viewers see *in Gone With the Wind* is a story about the destruction of *a world simpler than their own* and a story of passionate love. Ordinary viewers recognize what sophisticated reviewers do not, that *Gone With the Wind* is *not a history lesson, but* a romance, full of oversized heroines and heroes. Rhett Butler becomes Clark Gable *(and not vice versa)* because Gable is the more colossal figure. *Even now,* decades after his death, Gable remains the screen's most memorable actor—*though not its best.* Melanie may be too good to meet in day-to-day life. But she is not too virtuous to exist in the imagination. *And that is exactly the point: Gone With the Wind* is an exercise in imagination, a colorful, dazzling adult version of the dreams of childhood, of heroes and heroines locked in the elemental struggles all men and women— *except critics*—recognize.

The revised review is considerably longer than the original. Additions range from single words to complete sentences, almost all functioning as bridges between the related but unconnected ideas already present in the first version. Some of what was only implied is now explained to the reader so that someone who knows little about *Gone With the Wind* or Clark Gable still has a fair chance of understanding what the author has in mind. The new version is better fitted than the original because readers no longer have to guess what the relationships between the separate clauses and ideas are. The new version isn't perfect, but it's better. And that's the whole point in revising.

Exercises

1. Write a short analysis (400–700 words) of your composition habits as they actually are, not as you think they should be. Since grade school, you have been given schemes, models, checklists, procedures and plans designed to teach you to write well. But what do you actually do when you confront a blank sheet of paper?

You may want to use an essay you have written recently as the focus for this analysis. Why did it turn out as it did? What dictated your choices of structure, point of view, opening, closing? What did you think about as you sat down to write? As you actually wrote?

What about writing makes you apprehensive? Do you compose better in the morning or the evening? Do you follow a routine? Do you write an outline? How do you know when an essay is completed?

To do this assignment well, you must be ruthlessly honest in depicting your strategies of composition. The aim of the essay is exploratory: you want to discover something about the way you write. Your organization may turn out to be "loose" as you work your way through the description or narration of a process that may seem almost beneath the level of consciousness. But don't resort to platitudes or to writing what you think a teacher may want to hear: "I begin my essays with a topic sentence and all my paragraphs have five parts. I spend hours in the library researching my topic . . ." What do you really do?

To keep your analysis fresh and honest, imagine that the audience of this essay is a close friend who would see right through you if you tried to be less than frank. When you have finished this analysis of your writing process, compare what you do with the habits of a colleague or classmate.

2. Take a short published piece of writing with a clear purpose or aim and revise it to satisfy the demands of a different aim. For example, you might transform a newspaper editorial into a news article (or vice versa), turn an advertisement into a short report, or a short biography (from an encyclopedia) into a eulogy.

3. One goal common to revision and editing is eliminating wordiness. As you pare down sentences and paragraphs, you sometimes discover that what you are saying isn't what you mean to say. Or you discover that you have repeated or contradicted yourself.

Take an essay you have written recently and reduce it to half its present length. Try to lose as little content as possible. You may have to rearrange portions of the essay, find more efficient examples, and shorten conclusions. But don't be afraid to lop, prune, and transplant.

4. Take a short article—either your own or some published piece— and radically alter the tone or point of view. For example, you may retell a first person narrative ("I was examining a cadaver when . . .") from the third person ("He began to dissect the cadaver . . ."). Or you may experiment with enlivening the cold impersonal tone of a math or physics textbook. Be sure that your revision is consistent. When you are done, briefly list the advantages and disadvantages of your revised version.

5. Experiment with cutting-and-pasting as a technique of revision. Take a copy of a short published article, or some longer typed article you have written, and cut it up between paragraphs or major divisions. Then rearrange the paragraphs in some new order, deleting what you must, adding new sentences, words, or phrases wherever necessary. Try to salvage as much of the original as possible, pasting it into your new text whenever possible to save retyping.

This exercise is artificial, but cut-and-paste revising can save you a great deal of time when you are rethinking a large-scale effort, like a research paper, term paper, senior or master's thesis, or report.

13

Glossary:

A Guide to Grammar and Usage

Abbreviations

When in doubt about the standard form of an abbreviation, check a dictionary. When you are introducing an unfamiliar abbreviation or acronym into an essay, spell out the full title and follow with the abbreviation you will subsequently use for it in parentheses:

> He formed a local chapter of the Society for the Prevention of Cruelty to Children (SPCC). The SPCC has moved quickly . . .

Avoid using abbreviations excessively. When writing about a book or play with a long title, you may use a short title or accepted abbreviation:

> *The Tragedy of King Lear* is Shakespeare's masterpiece. In *Lear,* he explores. . .

Gone with the Wind endures as the film most Americans think of when someone says "great movie." For several decades, *GWTW* has enjoyed. . .

Do not shorten titles or character names simply to avoid writing out the full names:

Macbeth (hereafter, M) conspires with Lady Macbeth (hereafter, LM) to kill King Duncan (hereafter, D). While M is killing D, LM speaks boldly . . .

Accept/Except

Accept and *except* are frequently confused. *Accept* is a verb meaning to take or receive:

The scientist *accepted* her Nobel prize.

Except is generally a preposition that suggests an exclusion:

Everyone, *except* Joan, bought a book.

Adjectives

Adjectives are words or phrases that modify a noun or pronoun:

the *red* apple
the *surly* one
the quarterback, *aging and sore*

Adverbs

Adverbs are words that modify verbs, adjectives, or other adverbs:

He dictated *slowly.*

They raised the *carefully* balanced mobile to the ceiling.

The swimmers plowed *very* sluggishly through the debris-filled current.

Affect/Effect

Affect and *effect* are frequently confused. You will generally use *affect* as a verb and *effect* as a noun:

$$\overset{\text{V}}{\text{How will the new regulation } \mathit{affect} \text{ us?}}$$

$$\overset{\text{N}}{\text{Not much. Its } \mathit{effect} \text{ will be small.}}$$

Effect can be used as a verb, meaning to bring about or cause:

$$\overset{\text{V}}{\text{Only the Congress can } \mathit{effect} \text{ such a change.}}$$

Affect as a noun appears only as a technical term in psychology.

Agreement, Pronoun/Antecedent, or Pronoun/Referent

See PRONOUN REFERENTS.

Agreement, Subject-Verb

In most situations, the agreement of subjects and verbs comes naturally:

he goes	she smiles
they go	they smile

The matter becomes tricky with plural subjects. Two or more singular subjects joined by *and* are ordinarily treated as a plural subject:

Alex is an expert.
Laurie is an expert.

Alex and Laurie are experts.

But if the subjects are joined by *or* or *nor,* the verb is singular:

Neither Alex nor Laurie is an expert.

That is, as long as the subject closest to the verb is singular. If it is plural, so is the verb:

Neither the teacher nor his *students were* aware of the rule.

But if the plural subject comes first, then the verb is singular. In short, the verb takes the number of the closest subject:

Neither the students nor the *teacher was* aware of the rule.

When a singular subject is followed by a clause beginning with *as well as,* *accompanied by, with, along with, together with,* etc., the verb remains singular:

> This rule, *along with the others,* is a pain in the asterisk.

Aims of Writing

People write to express themselves, to inform, to persuade, and to delight or amuse others. These are the basic aims of writing. Each basic aim produces a characteristic type of writing. The desire to express oneself produces self-expression; the need to inform produces informative, demonstrative, or exploratory writing; the aim to convince or move an audience to act produces persuasive writing; literary writing results from attempts to amuse and delight. See chapter three for an introduction to the aims of writing.

All Right/Alright

Alright is a misspelling. The accepted spelling is *all right.*

A Lot/Alot

A lot is two words. *Alot* is a misspelling.

Already/All Ready

Already and *all ready* are not interchangeable. *Already* is an adverb that describes time:

> He left aiready.
> The choir is already late.

All ready describes a condition of readiness:

> The troops were all ready to board the jet.

Among/Between

Among is generally used to describe the relationships of three or more things; *between* is used with two:

> There wasn't much difference between the two.
> He is among the best doctors in Toledo.
> Between you and me, I think the committee is wasting its time.

Between is occasionally used with three or more objects when *among* sounds awkward.

Amount/Number

Amount is used to describe a quantity that exists as one thing, a single entity:

> an amount of money
> the proper amount of sugar
> the amount of water in the ocean

Number is used to describe a group of things that we see as distinct or separate. The members of these groups could be numbered:

> a number of students
> a number of species
> a number of problems

Apostrophes

Apostrophes are used

—to indicate possession:

> Alice's typewriter
> the musicians' scores

—to indicate contractions:

> It's simple.
> Where there's a will, there's a way.

Problems occur when possessive forms are confused with contracted forms. (See POSSESSIVES.)

Articles

Articles are the short adjectives *a, an,* and *the. A* and *an* are indefinite articles, pointing to unspecific nouns:

> a book
> an audience

The is the definite article, indicating specific things:

> the book
> the audience

Bad/Badly

Bad is an adjective, *badly* an adverb. The adjectival form is used with linking verbs:

> I feel bad.
>
> The puppy is bad.

Badly modifies the verb. If you write "I feel badly," you are describing the ineptness of your sense of touch.

> You don't write badly.
>
> I paint badly.

Base Clause

A base clause is the core of longer sentences: the subject, verb, and object or complement to which other modifying clauses are attached. In the following examples, the italicized words form the base clauses:

> Before the war, *he worked in the mines.*
>
> *Caravaggio,* an artist of the Italian Renaissance known for his violent temper and unconventional behavior, *painted several masterpieces of religious art,* including portraits of St. Matthew, St. Paul, and St. John the Baptist.
>
> *The bridge was weakening,* shaken by the hurricane winds and the debris hurtled against its pilings by the raging current.

Brackets

Brackets, which look like squared parentheses, [ ], are used to enclose words, phrases, or any form of comment or explanation added by a writer to material she is *quoting directly:*

> The senator recalled that "he [Eisenhower] had been consistently fair and steadfastly honest."

Most typewriters do not have brackets. Brackets must usually be drawn into a text.

Sometimes when documenting a book within your paper, it may be necessary to use brackets to avoid a parenthesis within a parenthesis:

As John Williams explains in his introduction (*English Renaissance Poetry* [New York: Norton, 1963]), Gascoigne may have been the greatest poet of the native tradition.

Can/May

The distinction between *can* and *may* is disappearing in conversation, but it still holds in academic writing. The distinction is a useful one. *Can* means to be able:

> She can walk!
>
> I can find out in the library.

May implies permission or possibility:

> You may go.
>
> You may find the task a difficult one.

Capitalization

Capitalize

—the first word of a sentence:

> Go!
>
> What is the answer?
>
> I don't know.

—all proper nouns:

Paris, France	Frederick the Great
Xerox	HEW

—the major words in the titles of books, plays, articles, essays, poems, movies, television programs, works of art, etc.:

The Norton Anthology of English Literature	"Upon Julia's Clothes"
Pygmalion	*Casablanca*
"Politics and the English Language"	*I Love Lucy*
Paradise Lost	the Pieta

Don't capitalize the seasons of the year or official titles unattached to specific names:

> winter, spring, summer, fall
>
> the admiral (but Admiral Halsey)

Clause

A clause is a group of words with a subject and a verb. An *independent clause* can stand alone as a sentence. The following example contains two independent clauses:

> *We thought we had seen the best of times,*
> —first clause—
>
> but *the future brought prosperity and good fortune.*
> —second clause—

A *dependent clause* is a phrase introduced by a subordinating conjunction (*after, before, although, while, because, unless,* etc.) that attaches the clause as a modifier to an independent clause. Dependent clauses cannot stand alone:

> *While* Eisenhower gathered the allied forces . . .
>
> *After* the experiment failed. . .
>
> *Whenever* inflation rises above 10 percent . . .

Colons

Colons are useful marks of punctuation that function like arrows, pointing out something or to something. Use colons:

—to introduce a long series:

> These ten Shakespearian plays are taught most often in high school: *Macbeth, Julius Caesar, Hamlet, The Tempest, A Midsummer Night's Dream, As You Like It, King Lear, Richard II, Henry IV, Part 1* and *The Comedy of Errors.*

Don't use a colon to introduce a short series or to separate a preposition from its objects:

> **X**   He succeeded in: school, his career, his marriage.

—to join independent clauses when the second clause is directly explained by or points back to the first:

> We had a problem: we were lost.

—to introduce quotations, especially lengthy or indented ones:

> As Crowley observes:
>
> > The greater the federal debt, the higher the interest consumers must

pay on the money they borrow. They are competing with their own government for loans.

Commas

Commas indicate pauses and separations. They are used in a variety of ways, including

—to separate elements in a series:

> They bought a table, a credenza, lamps, and an overstuffed armchair.

Some writers omit the comma before the conjunction preceding the last item in a series:

> a Ford, a Chevrolet and a Plymouth

But this omission can cause problems when the series itself contains conjunctions:

> We ordered ham and eggs, chicken and chips and a burger and fries.

A comma placed before the last item in the series makes the sentence clearer:

> We ordered ham and eggs, chicken and chips, and a burger and fries.

You can avoid this problem simply by using a comma regularly before the conjunction that brings a series to an end:

> description, narration, classification, and evaluation
> the general, the admiral, and the commander-in-chief
> the Ninth Symphony, the Pathetique Symphony, and Pomp and and Circumstances

—to separate coordinate clauses joined by *and, or, nor, yet, but, for:*

> The temperature continued to break records, and the water supply dwindled.
> The apology was moving, but I did not forgive her.

When the clauses involved are short, the comma can be omitted before *and, or,* and *nor:*

Inflation boome<u>d a</u>nd employment declined.

—to set off introductory clauses:

In the beginnin<u>g,</u> darkness covered the earth.

Afterward<u>s,</u> we examined the debris left by the storm.

To provide a better representation for minoritie<u>s,</u> the city council changed the makeup of the committee.

Although he snared the pole positio<u>n,</u> A. J. Foyt growled about the new track rules.

When an introductory clause or phrase is short, the comma can be omitted.

—to set off words or phrases within a sentence:

Austi<u>n,</u> the capital of Texa<u>s,</u> has earned its reputation for easy living, good music, and good times.

The Presiden<u>t,</u> eager to cut the federal budg<u>et,</u> vetoed one bill after another.

Too much protein in the di<u>et,</u> howev<u>er,</u> can cause problems.

Notice that commas are placed before and after the words and phrases. (See also the discussion of restrictive and nonrestrictive modifiers in chapter eight.)

—to separate modifying phrases at the end of a sentence:

He was my frien<u>d,</u> kind and good to me.

Disraeli was a formidable ma<u>n,</u> both as a politician and a novelist.

The steel industry was under atta<u>ck,</u> the left accusing it of ignoring safety and pollution standards, the right of depending on government tariffs to protect the home market against foreign competition, notably from Japan and Germany.

—to introduce some quotations:

And then she said, "I am sure it was an aardvark!"

Do not use a comma to separate a subject, even an extended one, from its verb:

X   Learning to program a computer, can be a wise investment.

Use a comma whenever you need one to prevent a possible misreading.

And use them when a reader might need a short interruption after reading a lengthy clause or phrase. But do not use so many commas that your readers are pausing after every third or fourth word:

> Filled to capacity, the amusement park ride began to move, and to rotate, gradually rising, up on its axis, like an enormous, spindly, mantis.

Comparatives and Superlatives

Adjectives have comparative and superlative forms:

Adjective	Comparative	Superlative
good	better	best
high	higher	highest
able	more able	ablest
effective	more effective	most effective

The comparative form is used with two objects or ideas; the superlative is used with three or more:

> It was a good novel.
>
> It was the better novel of the two.
>
> It was the best novel I ever read.

When you use the comparative form, be sure to make clear to your reader what the two objects being compared are:

> She is a better catcher.
>
> She is a better catcher *than I am.*

> The decrease in speed occurred on his fourth run through the course, which was substantially slower.
>
> The decrease in speed occurred on his fourth run through the course, which was substantially slower *than previous runs.*

(See also SO.)

Complement, Subject

A subject complement is an adjective or noun in a sentence linked to the subject by a verb of being or existence. The italicized words in these sentences are complements:

Napoleon was a master *strategist*.

The weather is *fine*.

The prospects are *uncertain*.

Conjunctions, Coordinating and Subordinating

Conjunctions are words that link words, phrases, or independent clauses *(and, but, however, nevertheless, although, because)*.

Coordinating conjunctions *(and, or, nor, but, yet, so)* link independent clauses:

It rained, *but* the drought continued.

Subordinating conjunctions *(although, because, before, when, while, until, unless, in order that,* etc.) make one clause dependent on another:

Although it rained, the drought continued.

Because he was the judge, we lost the case.

Clauses introduced by a subordinating conjunction ordinarily cannot stand alone. They are fragments:

Although some recreational anglers spend substantial amounts of money on fishing equipment, such as quiet trolling motors and depth finders, but cannot afford the luxuries needed to compete in tournaments.

Although some recreational anglers spend substantial amounts of money on fishing equipment, such as quiet trolling motors and depth finders, many cannot afford the luxuries needed to compete in tournaments.

(See also FRAGMENTS.)

Coordinate Relationship

When independent sentences are joined by a word or phrase that explains the relationship between them, the word expresses their coordinate relationship: how they work together.

Here's an example:

It rained. The ground was still dry.

Adding a coordinating conjunction between the sentences clarifies the coordinate relationship:

It rained, *but* the ground was still dry.

It rained, *yet* the ground was still dry.

It rained; the ground was still dry.

Other coordinating words are *and, or, nor, but, and then,* and *for.*

Dangling Modifier

A dangling modifier is a word or phrase improperly placed too far from the word it modifies. Sometimes it is not given a word to modify. Ordinarily, a modifier attaches itself to the nearest noun or pronoun:

Kicking and braying, grandma tugged at the mule.

Dark and eerie, it grew colder and colder.

Dangling modifiers can be corrected by moving the phrase closer to the word it modifies, or by supplying a word for it to explain:

Grandma tugged at the *kicking and braying* mule.

Dark and eerie, the night grew colder and colder.

Dashes

Dashes can function like commas or colons. When used in pairs, they separate words, modifiers, or clauses:

The most controversial presidents of this century—Truman, Johnson, and Nixon—may also have been its ablest.

When used singly at the end of a sentence, a dash functions like a colon, with a bit more emphasis:

In his fear and rage, King Kong climbs to the top of the Empire State Building—the very symbol of the forces out to destroy him.

Jack Benny was a clown and a wit—perhaps the best of his time.

Typed dashes are made up of two hyphens, with no space left between the words thus joined:

century--Truman

(See also the section "Modifiers in the Middle" in chapter eight.)

Dictionary

A dictionary is an essential tool for a writer. Your dictionary should be medium-sized (often termed "college edition") or larger. Pocket dictionaries are convenient for spelling problems, but they lack the wealth of information and definition (and more durable bindings) of their larger, hardbound brethren. Some useful college dictionaries are:

> *The American Heritage Dictionary*
> *Webster's New World Dictionary of the American Language*
> *The American College Dictionary* (Random House)
> *Webster's New Collegiate Dictionary*

Discourse

Discourse is used in this book as a synonym for writing. More formally, a discourse is a complete written work or text existing in a particular context and situation. A novel, an article, a joke, and a telegram can all be discourses.

Division

When you run out of space at the end of a typed or handwritten line and must divide a word, do it at a point of division between syllables: syl-la-bles; el-der-ber-ry. If you aren't sure where the syllable breaks, check a dictionary.

Due to the Fact That

Due to the fact that and *the fact that* are almost always unnecessary. Eliminate them from your sentences whenever you can:

> Due to the fact that he lied on his job application, he was fired.
>
> Because he lied on his job application, he was fired.

Ellipses

Ellipses are three spaced periods (. . .) used to indicate words or phrases left out of a direct quotation. When typing an ellipsis, a space is left before, after, and between the three periods. (See also the section on "Documentation," chapter five.)

When the words omitted from the quote fall at the end of your sentence, then the ellipsis takes an additional dot, the first one a period, typed without a space after the last word in the sentence:

Kennedy's words have, alas, become all too familiar: "Ask not what your country can do for you. . . ."

When you delete whole paragraphs or pages, or several lines of poetry, indicate such a substantial omission with a full line of spaced periods:

> Of man's first disobedience, and the fruit
> Of that forbidden tree
>
> . . . .
>
> Sing, Heavenly Muse.

—John Milton, *Paradise Lost*

Elliptical Sentence

See FRAGMENT.

Enthymeme

See SYLLOGISM.

Equally as Good as

Equally as good as is redundant. *As good as* implies *equally.* Use one expression or the other, not both:

> You are her equal as a writer.
>
> You are as good a writer as she.
>
> **X**   You are equally as good a writer as she.

Example is . . . When

When you cite an example in your text, be sure to actually cite something that is an example:

> An example of a fuel efficient car is the Plymouth Reliant, which gets better than 20 m.p.g.

In most cases, that example will be a noun or noun phrase. Do not follow *example* with an adverb:

> **X**   An example of a fuel efficient car is *when* it gets more than 20 m.p.g.
>
> **X**   An example of bravery is *where* a mother lifts a car that just ran over her baby's toe.

Exclamation Points

Exclamation points are used at the end of sentences that convey unusual emphasis or excitement:

> Oh no!
>
> After eighteen seasons of defeat, we finally won!

Exclamations should be used sparingly. The excitement should be in the sentence itself, not added by the punctuation mark. Too many exclamations make prose seem self-conscious and immature.

Exclamation points are sometimes placed between parentheses (!) within a sentence to indicate a writer's enthusiasm or surprise:

> She had failed half the quizzes and two exams (!) yet she wanted an *A* for the course and had hired a lawyer to get it.

Expletive Phrase

An expletive phrase is some combination of *there* or *it* and a verb:

> *It is* inexplicable.
>
> *It seems* simple enough.
>
> *There were* three men in the room.

When the expletive phrase can be easily eliminated, it probably should be:

> Three men were in the room.

Format

What is the appropriate format for most prose? Whatever is neat and functional. Writers sometimes underestimate the impact sloppy typing or handwriting can have on readers. Readers left to puzzle over an illegible word or read around a coffee stain may lose the rhythm of a sentence—or an argument. Or a series of inconsequential errors—reversed letters, wavering margins, inconsistent headings—can fester into real irritation.

Whenever you hand in a piece of writing to an editor, employer, or teacher, remember that the paper represents the quality of your thinking and the respect you have for your audience. If you present a crumpled essay, spattered and ugly, torn from a notebook, frayed edges dangling, you should be willing to accept the consequences of such irresponsibility.

Be sure to understand what—if any—particular expectations a teacher or employer has for the format of an essay or report. Some will express preferences in size of margins, necessity of outlines and title pages, and placement of notes. Not all will accept work done on erasable paper. Find out before it is too late.

Too late is when the work is due. And finishing your work on time is an important aspect of format and presentation.
(See also STYLE SHEET.)

Fragments

A fragment is a sentence that lacks some vital part—a subject, a verb, or both:

Nuts!	On the table.
Oh, yah?	Can't do it.
Where?	

Fragments are appropriate in casual prose and in circumstances where the missing subject or verb is clearly implied:

> He [Richard Wagner] wrote operas; and no sooner did he have the synopsis of a story, but he would invite—or rather summon—a crowd of his friends to his house and read it aloud to them. *Not for criticism. For applause.* (italics added)
>
> —Deems Taylor, "The Monster"

Professional writers use fragments in this way for deliberate reasons.

The kind of fragments you want to avoid are the accidental ones that make your control of sentence structures seem uncertain:

> The habits I learned from some long-forgotten composition course, and one of questionable value.

> All of the actors who displayed an ability to convey the feeling of what medieval Paris must have been like.

> Since it is time we all experienced what discrimination feels like.

Faced with "sentences" like these, readers will be left scratching their heads. Fragments are corrected sometimes by adding words and sometimes by deleting them:

> The habits I learned from some long-forgotten composition course *are* of questionable value.

All of the actors displayed an ability to convey the feeling of what medieval Paris must have been like. *(who* deleted before *displayed)*

It is time we all experienced what discrimination feels like. *(since* deleted)

Fused Sentences

See RUN-ONS.

Handbook

Handbooks are guides to the rules and conventions of the written language. They give advice about everything from positioning punctuation marks to writing business letters. Much of this information is too detailed to learn by rote, but needed in specific situations. Useful handbooks are clear, thoroughly indexed, and conveniently arranged. Here are some useful works:

Corbett, *The Little English Handbook*
Corder, *Handbook of Current English*
Elsbree, et al., *Heath's College Handbook of Composition*
Fear/Schiffhorst, *Short English Handbook*
Fowler, *The Little, Brown Handbook*
Good & Minnick, *Handbook*
Guth, *Concise English Handbook*
Herman, *The Portable English Handbook*
Hodges & Whitten, *Harbrace College Handbook*
Leggitt, et al., *Prentice-Hall Handbook for Writers*

Hopefully

Don't write *hopefully* when you really mean "I hope" or "we hope":

⌐ Hopefully, the weather will be fine.

└→ I hope the weather will be fine.

Use *hopefully* to describe an action done *with hope:*

We watched hopefully as the physician closed the wound.

Hyphenated Words

Compound adjectives before a noun are hyphenated when they could not stand alone in front of the noun, or when they work together to express a concept:

> the well-built athlete
> a love-hate relationship
> the blue-green water
> the dreamy-eyed student

but

> the tall, American athlete
> our old, graying cousin
> the cold, blue sea
> the dreamy, sleepy student

Invention

Invention is the process and procedure of discovering what can be said about a subject. Invention is discussed at the ends of chapters two through six.

Italics

Italics (indicated by underlining in a typed paper) are used to highlight foreign words or expressions, and to indicate the titles of books, plays, magazines, newspapers, long poems, and works of art. Italics may also be used to give emphasis to key words or expressions:

> It was his *third* offense
> The Defense Department indicated the *defensive* nature of its action.

However, underlining or italics should be used sparingly.

Lay/Lie

Lay and *lie* are troublesome verbs. *To lay* means to place or put; *to lie* means to recline. Confusion arises because the present tense of *to lay* (lay) is the same as the past tense of *to lie* (lay):

> (present: to place)   He lay the book on the shelf.

> (past: to recline)   I lay there all last night.

Here are the forms of the verb:

	Present	Past	Perfect	Progressive
(to place)	lay	laid	laid	laying
(to recline)	lie	lay	lain	lying

Modal Invention

Modal invention involves looking at a subject in terms of its descriptive, narrative, classificatory, and evaluative characteristics in order to discover those aspects of the subject you want to develop. By thinking about a given subject in terms of modes, you raise questions that direct further inquiry:

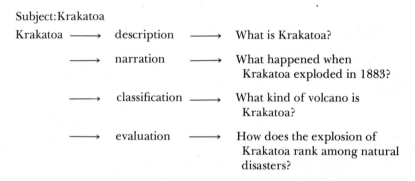

Subject: Krakatoa

Krakatoa ⟶ description ⟶ What is Krakatoa?

⟶ narration ⟶ What happened when Krakatoa exploded in 1883?

⟶ classification ⟶ What kind of volcano is Krakatoa?

⟶ evaluation ⟶ How does the explosion of Krakatoa rank among natural disasters?

See "Using the Modes to Generate Ideas" at the end of chapter two.

Modes of Writing

The four basic modes of writing are description, narration, classification, and evaluation. The modes represent ways of viewing or developing a subject. See chapter two for a complete discussion of modes.

Modifier

A modifier is a word or phrase that limits, explains, qualifies, or adds detail to another word, phrase, or base clause:

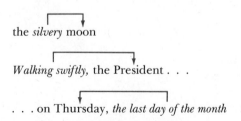

the *silvery* moon

Walking swiftly, the President . . .

. . . on Thursday, *the last day of the month*

Nouns

Nouns are words that name persons, places, things, or ideas. See chapter seven, "Nouns."

Numbers

Numbers from one to ninety-nine are usually spelled out in a text. Numbers used as adjectives are also spelled out (first, second, third; not 1st, 2nd, 3rd). Numbers above ninety-nine, fractions and decimals, dates, times, page numbers, ages, and addresses are given in Arabic numerals (101; 1/4; 3.25978; May 28, 1950, etc.).

Don't begin a sentence with an Arabic numeral.

Object

An object is a noun or noun phrase that explains what or whom the verb in a transitive structure is acting on. (A transitive verb is one that takes an object: John kicked the ball; an intransitive verb takes no object: Mary laughed.)

The italicized words in these sentences are the objects:

$$\overset{\textbf{S}\qquad\textbf{V}}{\text{Roger Maris hit sixty-one } \textit{home runs} \text{ in 1961.}}$$

$$\overset{\textbf{S}\qquad\textbf{V}}{\text{James Joyce wrote } \textit{Ulysses.}}$$

Parallelism

A parallel structure is a series of words or phrases sharing a grammatical structure:

Abandoned	by	his	party,
censured	by	his	colleagues,
indicted	by	the	grand jury,

the legislator resigned.

Parallelism can occur on the level of the sentence, the paragraph, or the essay. Check the index for more detailed treatments of parallelism.

Parentheses

Parentheses are used to insert into a text words, phrases, or whole sentences that explain, comment on, add to, or sometimes contradict what is being said. See "Modifiers in the Middle," chapter eight. Parentheses should be used sparingly.

When a parenthetical clause falls at the end of a sentence, punctuation for that sentence falls outside the parentheses:

Of course we asked (but he didn't reply)!

When a full sentence is held in parentheses, then the final punctuation occurs within the parentheses:

(Of course we asked, but he didn't reply!)

Periods

Periods are used to conclude statements:

It rained.

When a statement contains a question, the sentence still ends with a period unless the question is a direct quotation and concludes the sentence:

He asked whether he should participate.
He asked, "Should I participate?"

Periods are also used to signal abbreviations:

Dr.	et al.	U.S.A.
Ms.	Ph.D.	A.D.

With some abbreviations and acronyms, the periods are often omitted:

HUD	CBS	USA
NASA	ERA	RSVP

Possessives

Possession can be indicated in several ways:

their community
the steel mills of Pittsburgh
Lynda's Datsun 280-Z

The *'s* form is conventionally reserved for people and animate objects, though the distinction is disappearing:

> Nietzsche's philosophy
> Rover's dog house

When a singular word ends in *s*, possession is usually indicated by an apostrophe alone:

> the Ross' home
> Degas' painting

When a plural possessive is to be indicated, the apostrophe follows the addition of an *s* (when an *s* makes the word plural):

> the boy's dog (the dog belongs to a single boy)
> the boys' dog (the dog belongs to several boys)

but note:

> the goose's feathers (feathers from a single animal)
> the geese's feathers (feathers from several animals)

Possessives are sometimes confused with contracted forms of words:

Possessive	Contraction
its	it's ⟶ it is
your	you're ⟶ you are
their	they're ⟶ they are

Prepositions

Prepositions are words that indicate relationships between nouns and other parts of a sentence: *after, before, in, on, with, under, over, inside, between, among,* etc.:

You will find the answer in this *book.*

The vase was on the *mantel* in the *den.*

A sentence may end with a preposition.

A preposition at the end of a sentence is one thing up with which I will not put.

—Winston Churchill

Primary Source

When doing research, a primary source can be a work that is the subject of study, or a source that is a significant original in its field. If, for example, you are doing a paper on Edward Gibbon's *The History of the Decline and Fall of the Roman Empire,* that masterwork is your primary source. Books or articles that discuss or criticize Gibbon's work are *secondary sources.* Books like Darwin's *Origin of Species* or Aristotle's *Rhetoric* can be considered primary sources in their fields. Books that analyze these ground-breaking works, assess their impact, or extend their investigations will be secondary sources. When doing research in a given field, you will want to rely on primary sources whenever possible, and on reliable secondary sources. See the sections "Sources for Reports" and "The Research Paper," chapter five, for more information.

Pronoun

A pronoun is a word that takes the place of a noun: *I, you, he, she, it, we, they, one, this, that, these, those.*

Pronoun Referents

When you use third person or demonstrative pronouns *(he, she, it, they, this, that)* be sure a reader knows what the pronouns stand for. You need not have a referent for the pronoun in expletive constructions:

> *It* seems useless to struggle on.
> *It's* a beautiful day!
> *There's* no one here!

But in other situations, readers should not be left to decipher your intentions:

> Steve told Lester that *he* had erred in computing the figures.
>
> Steve suggested that *Lester* had erred in computing the figures.

> The automobiles were lined up bumper to bumper, row after row on the asphalt that stretched for as far as the eye could see around the

huge assembly plant in the Detroit suburb. *They* were of every style and color.

Automobiles of every style and color were lined up bumper to bumper. . . .

Pronouns must agree in number with their referents. In most cases, this is not difficult:

The *birds* picked the field clean before *they* flew away.

The *flock* picked the field clean before *it* flew away.

Some collective nouns can be either singular or plural, depending on context. In such cases, the pronoun agrees with the noun as it operates in context.

The *band* collected *their* instruments.

The *band* took *its* place on the field.

Some referents suggest that they take plural pronouns, but are in fact singular:

Each of us went *his* way.

Everyone took *her* turn.

Everybody cheered *his* loudest.

Quite often in informal writing (and more and more often in formal writing), words such as *each, everyone, everybody, either, neither,* and *anyone* are taking plural pronouns:

Everybody did *their* own thing.

Neither of them did *their* homework.

Anyone can come who has paid *their* dues.

Many readers and instructors regard these constructions as incorrect despite their widespread use.

When the words being referred to by the pronoun are joined by *and,* they are treated as plural:

Both *the Ford and the Chevrolet* will have *their* transmissions fixed.

But when they are joined by *or* or *nor,* they are treated as singular:

Neither *the Ford nor the Chevrolet* will have *its* transmission fixed.

Prose

Prose is another word for writing. It is often used in contrast to verse.

Question Marks

Question marks are placed at the end of interrogative sentences or phrases:

> Who wrote *Gertrude of Wyoming?*
>
> He asked, "How did the pump fail?"
>
> Like any journalist, she was full of questions: who? what? where? when? how? why?

Question marks are sometimes placed between parentheses (?) within a sentence to indicate a writer's uncertainty, skepticism, or doubt about the preceding material:

> The former slave, born in 1855 (?), lived to see her great grandchild graduate from Harvard.

Quotation Marks

Quotation marks are used

—to indicate direct borrowing within the body of your essay, except when the quotation is indented (See also STYLE SHEET):

> "True philosophy," John Henry Newman observes, "is the highest state to which nature can aspire."

Punctuation at the end of a quoted passage ordinarily falls within the closing quotation mark:

> I asked: "Did you go?"
>
> The committee reported that the "rocket functioned exactly as planned."

This is not the case, however, when the final punctuation is a question mark or exclamation point that is *not* part of the quoted material:

> Did the rocket function "exactly as planned"?

Quotations within quotations are indicated by using single quotation marks ('. . .') within the double marks (". . ."):

Said Senator Phoggbrane, "We must work to preserve democracy so that this government 'shall not perish from the earth.'"

—to highlight words you seek to stress or use in some special sense:

I can see that you, like Brutus, are an "honorable" man.

These self-proclaimed "defenders of the word" are sometimes less informed about the word than their congregations.

—to indicate the titles of short poems, articles, and essays, short stories, section headings, and chapter headings. Titles of books, magazines, movies, plays, and long poems are underlined or italicized.

"The Charge of the Light Brigade"
"Eliminating Wordiness"
"The Secret Sharer"
"Reasons for Writing: An Overview"
Well-Bound Words: A Rhetoric
Car and Driver
The Empire Strikes Back
Romeo and Juliet

Run-ons

Run-ons (or fused sentences) are clauses or full sentences jammed together without the aid of pauses or accurate punctuation:

My fifth grade teacher, Ms. Oleo, she wore her red hair in a tight bun that looked like a Brillo pad and she dressed in skirts that clung like cellophane to ripe fruit but she was allergic to chalk dust.

Run-ons leave readers confused and breathless because information is piled on rather than organized by the clauses. The example above might be broken into sentences at all the underlined points:

My fifth grade teacher was Ms. Oleo. She wore her red hair in a tight bun that looked like a Brillo pad. She dressed in skirts that clung like cellophane to ripe fruit. She was allergic to chalk dust.

But now the sentences are immature and choppy. A compromise is possible:

My fifth grade teacher, Ms. Oleo, wore her red hair in a tight bun that looked like a Brillo pad. She dressed in skirts that clung like cellophane to ripe fruit, and was allergic to chalk dust.

The length of a sentence has nothing to do with whether it is run-on. Even two short sentences can be improperly fused:

> I didn't find the note she left it for me.
>
> I didn't find the note she left for me.

And sentences can be very long without causing any hardship to a reader. Just recall this sentence cited earlier in the text as a model of rhythm and pacing:

> Charity is patient, is kind; charity does not envy, is not pretentious, is not puffed up, is not ambitious, is not self-seeking, is not provoked, thinks no evil, does not rejoice over wickedness, but rejoices with the truth; bears with all things, believes all things, hopes all things, endures all things.
>
> —1 Corinthians 13:4–7

When editing, pare down and repunctuate any sentences that lack pauses at those points where a breather or a piece of punctuation would serve to clarify a notion.

Secondary Source

See PRIMARY SOURCE.

Semicolons

Semicolons sometimes cause problems for writers who try to use them interchangeably with commas. But the semicolon is a stronger pause than a comma. You might choose to think of it as a fusion of comma and period. Use a semicolon

—to link closely related or contrasting independent clauses:

> The Democratic party platform promised to balance the budget, pass the ERA, and increase social welfare programs; the Republican platform urged tax cuts, opposed the ERA, and challenged the effectiveness of more government handouts.

—to join elements of a series when the series is lengthy and contains commas within it:

> Lincoln hired and fired several generals in the course of the American Civil War, among them, General McClellan, who stopped Lee at Antietam, but failed to pursue him; George Meade, who won the Battle of Gettysburg, but also failed to follow up a victory; and Ulysses S.

Grant, who finally proved to be the commander the Union needed to combat the skillful Confederate generals.

—to precede transitional words *(therefore, nevertheless, moreover, however)* used between independent clauses:

> The danger of a core meltdown passed; however, the citizens were not relieved.

> The patient shows clear symptoms of the infection; moreover, we know she was exposed to the virus.

So

So should rarely be used alone as an intensive:

> The movie was so romantic.
> The test was so hard.

Employed this way, *so* leaves a reader asking, "How romantic?" "How hard?" Complete the expression by making an explicit comparison:

> The movie was so romantic I dampened three handkerchiefs.
> The test was so hard that 60 percent of the class failed.

Spelling

Misspellings set readers on edge. Readers' reactions to errors in spelling are often out of proportion to the seriousness of the errors made. But in most formal writing situations, you can't discount such reactions. If readers will regard you as careless, inept, or illiterate if you misspell *receive, beleaguer, asphodel,* or *judgment,* then you had better spell them right.

If you are a bad speller—apt to make several errors per paragraph—you certainly ought to doublecheck any word you suspect might be wrong. But how do you detect such words?

A venerable journalism trick is to read an article backwards. The technique forces you to pay attention to individual words. A second technique is to list the words you frequently misspell and then try to classify your typical errors. If you consistently stumble over *ie/ei* words (receive, conceive, believe, relief) or words that end in *-ing* (dying, crying, tying), your list will tell you so. You can be on alert when such words come up. But don't avoid troublesome words—that's tantamount to running away from a problem.

As a last resort, you may need to rely on a second reader to catch spelling errors that slip by you. A conscientious spouse, friend, or room-mate may even be willing to help you classify your habitual mistakes or keep the list for you.

In general—whether you are a good speller or a bad one—be suspicious of words you rarely use (ague, parsimonious, mogul), of words with double consonants (really, buffet, exaggerate), of homonyms (see/sea, their/there, fair/fare), of words with puzzling vowel clusters (bouillon, bourgeoisie, ubiquitous). Examine contractions carefully, and remember that possessives ordinarily require the precise placement of an apostrophe (reader's/readers').

Many writers have trouble with the words in this list:

affect/effect
believe
its/it's
lose/loose
necessary
occurred
precede/proceed
quiet/quite
receive
there/their/they're
to/too
whose/who's
your/you're

Squinting Modifier

A squinting modifier is a word or phrase that seems to modify both what precedes it and what follows. The reader is left to puzzle over the meaning.

The girl waving *playfully* smiled.

The error is corrected by moving the modifier:

The girl *playfully* waving smiled.

or

The girl waving smiled *playfully*.

Phrase-length squinting modifiers may be responsible for run-on sentences:

One qualification for leadership is intelligence, *although it is not an essential characteristic,* it helps.

One qualification for leadership is intelligence, *although it is not essential.* But it helps.

or

One qualification for leadership is intelligence. *Although it is not an essential characteristic,* it helps.

Style Sheet

(follows *MLA Handbook for Writers of Research Papers, Theses, and Dissertations*)

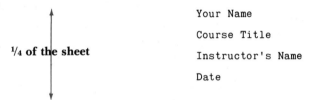

```
                                      Your Name

                                      Course Title
      ¼ of the sheet
                                      Instructor's Name

                                      Date


          Your Title, Centered, With Only the First Letters of

                     Major Words Capitalized

                                    4 spaces

              You may want to use this format for some of your

          essays.  Use 1"-1¼" margins all around.  Typed papers

          should be double-spaced.  If your composition is hand-
1"-1¼"      written, skip a space between each line of prose and          1"-1¼"

          provide margins at both ends of the paper.  Use qual-

          ity paper.  Essays ripped from notebooks look awful.

              When typing, indent five spaces at the beginning

          of paragraphs, and leave two spaces between sentences.

          Pages should be numbered at the top right-hand corner

          on all but the first page, which may be numbered at

          the bottom center or not at all.  Pages should be

          joined by paper clips or staples, never by bending the

          corners together or by using glue, tape, bubble gum,

          straight pins, or shoe laces.

                                   1
```

Whether typed or handwritten, reports and essays should be neat and clean. Proofread your final draft and make any corrections as unobtrusive as possible. Retype a text that is littered with errors and typos. Doublecheck spelling.

When using secondary sources, be sure to acknowledge them:

Triple space

> When quoting more than four typed lines of prose, indent the material ten spaces and double space. Shorter quotations may be included in the body of your text. Quotation marks are not used when the quoted matter is set off typographically. Check a handbook for all the details of citation and footnoting.[1]

Triple space

Footnote numbers, when used, are typed immediately after the quotation, slightly raised, and following all punctuation (including quotation marks), like this: "Who goes there?"[2]

Subject/Verb Agreement

See AGREEMENT, SUBJECT/VERB.

Superlatives

See COMPARATIVES AND SUPERLATIVES.

Syllabication

See DIVISION.

Syllogism

A syllogism is a formal structure of deductive reasoning. Syllogisms contain major terms, minor terms, and conclusions. The most familiar type of syllogism is the *categorical:*

> All men are mortal.   Major premise
>
> Socrates is a man.   Minor premise
>
> Socrates is mortal.   Conclusion

A second form of syllogism is the *hypothetical:*

> If the battery is dead, the engine won't start.   Major premise
>
> The battery is dead.   Minor premise
>
> The engine will not start.   Conclusion

The third form is the *alternative* syllogism:

> The answer will be either right or wrong.   Major premise
>
> The answer is not wrong.   Minor premise
>
> The answer is right.   Conclusion

In most writing situations, syllogisms are shortened into *enthymemes.* In an enthymeme, one term of the syllogism is eliminated to make a simpler, more directly persuasive argument or demonstration:

> Socrates is mortal because he is a man.
>
> The engine will not start because the battery is dead.
>
> The answer must be right because it isn't wrong.

In each case, the writer assumes that the reader will consciously or unconsciously supply the missing term:

> All men are mortal.
>
> If the battery is dead, the engine won't start.
>
> The answer will be either right or wrong.

Title

Not all types of writing require titles. When it is required, a title should adjust your readers' attitudes toward the prose to follow, should interest and inform them, and should summarize the argument in some emphatic way.

Occasionally a title will come to mind before an essay is complete; it may be among the first words written. But the test of a title is how well it fits the completed work. If, after completing an article or an assignment, you can invent no title to introduce it, you may want to reassess the entire work. If no title intelligently or engagingly summarizes your essay, then perhaps your thoughts are too general, too loosely arranged, or too dull to merit advertisement.

But not every title needs to be clever, ironic, or humorous. Indeed, the heading of an informative article or report should explain the contents accurately. A piece that explains how to boil chicken can be unabashedly entitled "How To Boil Chicken." A more clever heading might disguise what the essay is actually about.

Underlining

See ITALICS.

Unique

There are no degrees of uniqueness. An object, idea, or phenomenon cannot be *very* unique or *the most* unique. It is simply *unique*.

Verbs

Verbs are words that express action or existence: *to walk, to advocate, to be, to have.* See chapter seven, "Verbs."

Very

Very, like *really* and *so*, is an intensifier that has lost its power. Use *very* only when you mean "very!" Better yet, use a detail or stronger word to convey the impact of "very!" whenever you can.

> It was very cold.
> → It was −17° F.

> I was very angry.
> → I was enraged.

Who/Whom

Who is used as a subject, *whom* as an object. The usage is often complicated by a writer's uncertainty about what the subject of a sentence is:

> **S**
> Who came in?

> **O**   **S**
> Whom do you suspect?

> **O of Prep**   **S**
> With whom did you arrive?

Wordiness

To eliminate wordiness:

1. Use strong verbs and adverbs.
2. Use precise nouns and adjectives.
3. Use parallelism often.
4. Put modifiers close to what they modify.
5. Avoid the passive voice.
6. Avoid *that, which,* and *who* whenever possible.
7. Avoid expletives whenever possible.
8. Avoid repetition and redundancy where inappropriate.
9. Avoid clichés and jargon where inappropriate.

Exercises

A. Each of the following sentences is confused or confusing in some way. Prepare improved versions.

1. I really enjoy lifeguarding, its a great job, even though it doesn't pay well.

2. I make a practice of saying what I feel and to tackle what others doubt can be acomplished.

3. In rapid succession I came, saw, and conquered.

4. In 212 B.C., the Greek mathematician, Archimedes, used solar reflecting mirrors to set fire to Roman, enemy ships, using 4,000 bronze shields on wooden towers.

5. After research, the only means of harnessing the sun's energy practically seems to be to develop solar homes.

6. Because of crackdowns by the courts and the government, white collar crime is beginning to decrease, it must.

7. The book assists students agonizing over the pains of studying with a ten-step plan.

8. Crawling from under the porch, certain that his path was clear, the thief darted down the alley, his heels kicking up dust, his progress unabaited until, tripping over a sour, mangy cat that growled her resentment and raked his shin with a vicious paw, he panicked, lost his balance, and tumbled into a pile of tires, rags, and garbage.

9. Tact is the common term for social civility, and is a word that belongs in every civil person's vocabulary.

10. About every five minutes people cheer during the game, or when their is a touchdown.

11. A constant remark made by many visitors referred to Linus the Chimp as being like a real baby.

12. Petulia was a petite girl, her long hair tumbling over her shoulders, and with an attitude of sullen insolence.

13. There were about three of us who entered the very cavernous theater.

14. It takes alot of time, money, and people to collect data.

15. Even though I only polled 11 percent of the group, I believe my facts are accurate.

16. The athletic young person walked with a limp after the running competition, obviously in very great pain.

17. The girls tried both Pepsi and Coke and picked the container she preferred.

18. Last fall was a difficult time for my family, I left home to go to college.

19. Travellers whizzing through Masontown because with a blink of an eye one can be in and out of downtown and not even realize what they have missed.

20. Being unable to see, Mike at that time became greatly worried.

21. A list of the commercials banned by the two consumer groups are printed in the journal.

22. The biggest influence my family had on me was to love.

23. Del Rio, the quaint little town that lies on the edge of the Edwards Plateau and is exactly one hundred seventy-five miles from San Antonio, which is its only claim to fame, has only one popular music station.

24. The reports in this issue are on city, university, science, state, sports, entertainment, and general reports.

25. Man is, by nature, a prediter. But also as a rational being, he is able to determine if and when he has overkilled.

26. The livelihoods of ranchers depend on they're ability to ward off the coyotes or eagles that threaten to kill or damage their herds or crops.

27. The actions of the legislative branch and the rulings of the judicial branch have eroded the power of the executive branch of the federal government. This endangers the constitutional balance of powers essential to our system of government.

28. Knowledge is light: undirected it can only illuminate a small area surrounding it and quickly diffuses out into darkness, enlightening little, if anything at all as it travels outward.

29. According to a Sure deoderant ad, women are incapable of getting through the day without it.

30. There seems to be no escape from the unevitable heartships of life.

31. While a person is dreaming, they are in their own world.

32. The alcohol tolerance level is different for each individual, however, some quickly lose their sense of judgment after only one beer.

33. A major factor in considering a computer is whether or not the machine will save more money because of its accuracy and speed.

34. A survey of questions were given to an English class of Freshmen to determine their attitudes toward marijuana's use.

35. The rate of suicide being five-point-five per every 100,000 boys and two-point-zero for every 100,000 girls between ages 15 and nineteen.

36. An example of water pollution is when discharges of hot water from power plants are allowed to enter lakes or rivers, killing fish and plant life.

B. Edit the following paragraphs:

1.

Louis XIV

Not far from the Pallace of Versailles Louis XIV built another much smaller residence Trianon. Constructed not distant from the far end of the Grand Canal, the king and select members of his court would sail to it on summer evenings in Venetian gondolas. It was much less formal than the Pallace of Versailles and the severe etiquette did not apply. In a sense, Trianon was built by Louis to get away from it all, to relieve temporarily the pressures of court life, and enjoy a simpler life. This was very unlike his daily existence in the grand main pallace.

2.

The Armada Sails

On May 20, 1588, amid splendid trappings, the Spanish Armada set sail from Lisbon in the spirit of a crusade. Prayers were said, crosses being raised, and the fleet moved out of the harbor. It's progress was fitfully slow, the Armada was limited to the speed of its slowest ship. At Corunna, a great gail hammered it, scattering them and demoralizing the Spaniards. The English assumed that the expedition would end at Corunna, even the commander of the Armada, Medina Sidonia, asked Philip II, Spain's monarch, to delay the expedition, arguing that many men were sick, the provisions were insufficient, and that the bad weather had damaged many ships. But Philip ordered them onward, hoping for a miracle.

3.

What's In a Name

Most people dont realize how seriously the choice of a name can effect a child. But then most people aren't named Ophelia Desdemona, like me. When it comes to slapping a label to last a lifetime on a child, parents have absolute power, and, I suspect that they often give too little attention to the consequences of their choice. They are too thrilled, befudled, or upset by the screaming little bundle some nurse heaves at them to consider how it will feel when it grows older and discovers that it has been branded Orville, or Brunhilde, or Anaxagoras. Sometimes a child is named after a parent, a harmless practice when the parent is William or Randolph, Mary or Helen. But surely little Yolanda, Agrippa, and Holofernes have reason to ressent their parentage. And then their are the parents who follow shameless fads in naming their kids after celebrities or songs. A whole generation of young adults named Farrah, Elvis, Jacqueline, and Michelle. But more to be pitied are people like me who's parents allowed professional or literary interests to scar their children for life. My parents taught Shakespeare, and so I was christened Ophelia Desdemona.

4.
Science

The greatest contrast between the social and physical sciences are in the ways controlled observations are made. The two fields are inherently different in this context because the social sciences explore man and society, whereas the physical sciences investigate inantimate matter and the laws of science applying to them. Since the manner of observation must reflect that which is being observed, the methods which the social and physical sciences use to collect information must differ to a significant degree. The two diciplines are quite often labelled as the lab sciences (physical) and the non-lab sciences (social). The lab sciences, such as physics and chemistry, are unique in that they can frequently control for all the variables in an experiment accept for that which is being tested, and can therefore isolate individual causal factors through experimentation. Non-lab sciences, such as economics and sociology, must observe society in action, unable to control for all the variables.

C. One last writing assignment. Choose one quotation from the list below and—using your experiences and contemporary examples—develop it into a short essay fit for a guest columnist's spot in a popular magazine. You determine the appropriate length. Edit your final text carefully.

Patriotism is the last refuge of a scoundrel.

—Samuel Johnson

There never was a good war or a bad peace.

—Benjamin Franklin

Sir, a woman preaching is like a dog's walking on his hind legs. It is not done well; but you are surprised to find it done at all.

—Samuel Johnson

A fool and his money are soon parted.

—Anonymous

Nothing emboldens sin so much as mercy.

—Shakespeare

Our virtues are most frequently but vices disguised.

—La Rochefoucauld

Old people like to give good advice, as solace for no longer being able to provide bad examples.

—La Rouchefoucauld

The emperor has no clothes!

Of making many books there is no end; and much study is a weariness of the flesh.

—Ecclesiastes 12:12

Index

Invention
　and analogies, 17
　defined, 73–74, 331
　for informative writing, 120–28
　modal, 56–59, 332
　for persuasive writing, 174–77
　for research papers, 128–29
　for self-expression, 73–77
Investigative paper. *See* Research
　　paper
Italics, 331

J
Jargon, 69, 230–31
Journal articles
　in bibliographies, 139
　in footnotes, 137
Journalist's questions, 121–25
Journals, 68

K
Kinneavy, James L., 4–5, 110

L
Lay, lie, 331–32
Leap, inductive, 102
Librarians, 88
Library, 125–26
Lists, 225–26
Literature, 62
Liveliness, 68
Logical appeal, 156–58, 175–77
Long paragraphs, 267
Long sentences, 253

M
Magazines, 126
　in bibliographies, 139
　in footnotes, 137
Matrices of invention
　for informative writing, 123
　for persuasion, 175
Maxims, 109, 174
Metaphors, 17
Middle modifiers, 209–14

Misplaced modifiers, 222–24. *See also*
　　Dangling modifiers
Modal invention, 56–59, 332
Modes of writing, 4–5, 9–45, 332
　and the aims, 60–61, 64
　interrelationship of, 11–12
　and invention, 56–59
　and the journalist's questions,
　　123–25
　and persuasion, 175–77
　and the thesis statement, 82–86
　See also Classification; Description;
　　Evaluation; Narration
Modifiers, 188–89
　ambiguous, 223
　defined, 332
　at the end of a base clause, 214–18
　initial, 206–9
　middle, 209–14
　misplaced, 222–24
　nonrestrictive, 209, 223
　parallel, 206–7, 241
　restrictive, 209–10
　squinting, 342–43
Motifs, 170–171, 289–90
Movies
　in bibliographies, 139
　in footnotes, 137
Multi-paragraph essay, 261–63,
　　265–66

N
Name-calling, 168
Narration, 9, 10, 20–31
　and branching structures, 266
　and paragraph development,
　　243–44
　and the senses, 75
　and the thesis statement, 83–84
Neatness, 328–29
Newspaper articles, 126
　in bibliographies, 139
　in footnotes, 137
Nonrestrictive modifiers, 209, 223
Note cards, 131–34
Nouns, 183–86, 332
Number, amount, 317
Numbers, 333

Research, adequate, 135
Research paper, 128–52
    sample essay, 141–52
Restrictive modifiers, 209–10
Revision, 293–312
Rhetorical questions, 171–72, 279–80
Rhythm
    of end modification, 214–15
    and fit, 308
    and middle modification, 210
    in paragraphs, 254–57
    in parallel structures, 271
    of persuasion, 169–70
    revising for, 298
    of sentences, 232–34
Ridicule, 160
Run-ons, 339–40

S
Satire, 156
Scare tactics, 168–69
Secondary sources. *See* Sources
Self-expression, 61, 66–78, 110
Self-interest, 160–61
Semicolons, 219, 340–41
Senses, 75–76
Sentences, 198–325
    architectonic, 220
    balanced, 203
    concluding, 241, 251–52
    development of, 200–21
    economical, 227–32
    long, 227, 253
    opening, 201
    short, 227, 253
    simple, 202
    typical order of, 201
Sequences, 286–87
Settings in narratives, 25
Sexism, 168
Sexist language, 2–3
Short paragraphs, 267
Sic, 90
Similes, 17, 119
Slogans, 169
So, 341
Sound, 232–34, 298

Sources
    primary, 88, 336
    for reports, 86–88
    reputable, 162–63
    for research papers, 129
    secondary, 88, 336
Spelling, 341–42
Squinting modifiers, 342–43
Stereotypes, 109, 166
Structure of essays, 260–66
Style
    and fit, 303
    of informative writing, 117–19
    of persuasive writing, 169–74
    of sentences, 227–35
Style sheet, 343–44
Subordination, 203, 215
Summaries, 80–81, 117
Superlatives, 323
Superstitions, 166
Syllabication. *See* Division
Syllogisms, 103, 344–45
Synonyms, 282–84
System of invention, 82

T
Television programs
    in bibliographies, 139
    in footnotes, 138
That, 281–82
A Theory of Discourse, 4–5, 110
Thesis statement
    in branching essays, 265
    in demonstration, 96–98
    in exploration, 108–10
    in informative writing, 81–84
    need for, 266
    and nouns/verbs, 183
    in persuasion, 154–56
    as a question, 279
    in research papers, 128–30
    shaping of, 189–91
Thinking, 74–75
This, 281–82
Time in narratives, 21–25
Titles, 118, 339, 345–46
Tone, 118–19